ADVANCE PRAISE FOR

# GLOBALIZING
## EDUCATION

"...a superb collection of original papers about the ways in which globalization—from above, below and in-between—intersects with the urgent task of rethinking educational policies, pedagogies, and politics. In a world of increasingly coordinated capital, growing movement of people, an oppressive global regime of security, uneven distribution of new technologies, and state educational policies subservient to the logic of the market, the essays in this book seek to develop the philosophical and political resources that might address the deeply worrying trends toward mindless celebration of consumerism and the accentuation of global inequalities. In the face of this pessimism, this somewhat optimistic book is a major contribution in the re-assertion of democratic politics in education."

*Fazal Rizvi, Professor of Education, Department of Education Policy Studies, University of Illinois at Urbana-Champaign*

"This rich collection of original essays, organized around the themes of the political economy of education and the production of knowledge and identities, will be of great interest and value to anyone interested in the relationships between globalization and education. It extends and deepens discussions and appreciations of how globalization, conceived as 'complex connectivities,' pervades educational transactions of multiple kinds."

*Roger Dale, Professor of Education, University of Auckland, New Zealand, and Senior Research Fellow, University of Bristol, United Kingdom*

"This timely collection of rich and diverse studies of the complex relationship between globalization and education fills an important gap in our understanding of these processes."

*Susan Robertson, Professor of Sociology of Education, University of Bristol, United Kingdom*

# GLOBALIZING
## EDUCATION

# Studies in the
# Postmodern Theory of Education

Joe L. Kincheloe and Shirley R. Steinberg
*General Editors*

Vol. 280

PETER LANG
New York • Washington, D.C./Baltimore • Bern
Frankfurt am Main • Berlin • Brussels • Vienna • Oxford

# GLOBALIZING
# EDUCATION

## POLICIES, PEDAGOGIES, & POLITICS

EDITED BY
Michael W. Apple, Jane Kenway,
and Michael Singh

PETER LANG
New York • Washington, D.C./Baltimore • Bern
Frankfurt am Main • Berlin • Brussels • Vienna • Oxford

**Library of Congress Cataloging-in-Publication Data**

Globalizing education: policies, pedagogies, and politics /
edited by Michael W. Apple, Jane Kenway, Michael Singh.
p. cm. — (Counterpoints: studies in the postmodern theory of education; vol. 280)
Includes bibliographical references and index.
1. Critical pedagogy. 2. Education and globalization. 3. Politics and education.
I. Apple, Michael W. II. Kenway, Jane. III. Singh, Michael.
IV. Series: Counterpoints (New York, N.Y.); v. 280.
LC196.G58   370.11'5—dc22   2004026608
ISBN 0-8204-7120-8
ISSN 1058-1634


Bibliographic information published by **Die Deutsche Bibliothek**.
**Die Deutsche Bibliothek** lists this publication in the "Deutsche
Nationalbibliografie"; detailed bibliographic data is available
on the Internet at http://dnb.ddb.de/.

Cover art by Jane Burton, *The Other Side 15*. This image is part of
*The Other Side 2002* exhibition shown at Crossley & Scott Gallery, Melbourne, 2002.

Cover design by Lisa Barfield


The paper in this book meets the guidelines for permanence and durability
of the Committee on Production Guidelines for Book Longevity
of the Council of Library Resources.

© 2005 Peter Lang Publishing, Inc., New York
275 Seventh Avenue, 28th Floor, New York, NY 10001
www.peterlangusa.com

Printed in the United States of America

# Table of Contents

List of Figures ................................................................................. ix

Chapter 1
Globalizing Education: Perspectives
from Above and Below........................................................................ 1
*Michael Singh, Jane Kenway,
and Michael W. Apple*

Chapter 2
Globalizing the Young in the Age of Desire:
Some Educational Policy Issues ......................................................... 31
*Jane Kenway and Elizabeth Bullen*

Chapter 3
Cultural Pedagogies of Technology
in a Globalized Economy.................................................................... 45
*Helen Nixon*

Chapter 4
New Policies, New Possibilities?
Adult Learners in the Global Economy .............................................. 61
*Sue Shore*

Chapter 5
Globalizing the Rustbelt and Public Schools...................................... 79
*Pat Thomson*

Chapter 6
International Trade in Education Services: Governing
the Liberalization and Regulation of Private Enterprise..................... 93
*Christopher Ziguras*

Chapter 7
Responsive Education: Enabling Transformative
Engagements with Transitions in Global/National Imperatives ....... 113
*Michael Singh*

Chapter 8
Performing Pedagogy and the Re(construction)
of Global/Local Selves.................................................................... 135
*Gayle Morris*

Chapter 9
Developing Local Teachers' Skills for Addressing
Ethno-Specific Drug Issues of Global Proportions.......................... 151
*Scott K. Phillips*

Chapter 10
Virtual Spaces for Innovative Pedagogical Actions:
Education, Technology, and Globalization...................................... 171
*Lynton Brown*

Chapter 11
Living in Liminal Times: Early Childhood Education
and Young Children in the Global/Local Information Society......... 191
*Susan Grieshaber and Nicola Yelland*

Chapter 12
Are Markets in Education Democratic?
Neoliberal Globalism, Vouchers, and the Politics of Choice............ 209
*Michael W. Apple*

Chapter 13
The Marketization of Education
within the Global Capitalist Economy ............................................. 231
*Helen Raduntz*

Chapter 14
Teachers' and Public-Sector Workers' Engagement
with "Globalization from Above": Resisting Regressive
Parochialism in Queensland.............................................................. 247
*Peter Kell*

Chapter 15
Making Progressive Educational Politics
in the Current Globalization Crisis .................................................... 265
*Suzanne Franzway*

Chapter 16
Rethinking the Democratic Purposes
of Public Schooling in a Globalizing World...................................... 281
*Alan Reid*

List of Contributors........................................................................... 297

Index.................................................................................................. 303

# Figures

Figure 5.1: Views of the rustbelt................................................................ 81

Figure 5.2: Effects of the rustbelt............................................................. 87

Figure 11.1: Shapes software for exploring symmetry ......................... 199

Figure 11.2: TV man..................................................................................... 202

# Chapter 1

# Globalizing Education: Perspectives from Above and Below

Michael Singh, Jane Kenway, and Michael W. Apple

## Introduction

"Globalization," however defined has many and varied implications for the educational policies, pedagogies, and politics of nation-states. Yet, even given this, there is a relative dearth of education research identifying what these implications are and canvassing the issues invoked. Along with those few education scholars who are working in this space, researchers in this collection seek to help to fill this void. They are particularly concerned to both identify the diverse, complex, and circuitous ways in which globalization impacts on a range of aspects of education, broadly defined, and to affirm various existing and possible progressive educational responses. We begin this introductory chapter with a discussion of the widely contested notion of globalization and indicate the broad conceptual framework that informs this book. We then offer a scaffold for considering the effects on education of neoliberal and neoconservative globalisms, or "globalization from above." This provides a basis for elaborating transformative policies, pedagogies, and politics in education.

## Globalization

Educators face serious problems when trying to pin down the key features of contemporary times. However, across a range of theoretical and disciplinary orientations, most agree on the necessity of adopting a global analytic. Predictably, however, what this means is explored and contested at length in the literature, which reveals a dazzling array of descriptions, generalizations, concepts, and ideological standpoints. Indeed, there is a deluge of popular literature and scholarly research that seeks to define globalization, to explain its genesis, and to clarify the complexities of the economic, political, cultural, and social contours of globalizing processes.

Some focus on only one aspect, while others consider different aspects in combination. Indeed, there has been such a proliferation of research on globalization that it has emerged as field of study in its own right (Cohen and Kennedy, 2000). This field is increasingly multi- and inter-disciplinary, theoretically eclectic and now includes meta-analyses of the literature (Scholte, 2000) and, yes, even a reader (Benyon and Dunkerley, 2000).

It is not the task of this chapter to analyse the field of globalization studies or to try to pin down the meaning of globalization. Indeed, the authors in this volume enter the field from different angles and take up a range of readings. Our task in this chapter is twofold: to offer a sense of the field, thereby allowing readers to identify where the chapters in this collection fit within it; and also to provide a broad framework for the collection, that informs the chapters.

One way of categorizing the globalization literature is to divide it into two sets—that which focuses on "globalization from above" and that which focuses on "globalization from below" (Falk, 1999). We find this a useful but problematic categorization. It is useful because it offers some ready points of entry into what is an intricate set of ideas about a complex and contradictory set of processes. And, as will become clear, many of the chapters draw inspiration from it. It is problematic however, because it represents as layers what are inherently interwoven and dynamic processes. It thus obscures the manner in which many apparently disparate changes can be understood together.

More specifically it provides no way to portray the dense relationship that exists between the massive material and structural shifts associated with globalization and everyday life. A further difficulty is that due to the multiple and changing foci of their work, some globalization scholars do not fit easily into one set or the other. Indeed, that is the case for many of those whose scholarship from which the researchers in this volume draw. Nonetheless, for the purposes of this collection we will use it as a heuristic devise.

## Globalization from Above

Studies of "globalization from above" focus on the big picture and describe the major trends and patterns associated with globalization. They usually offer an eagle's-eye view of such globalizing tendencies as internationalization, marketization, universalization, Westernization, and deterritorialization (Scholte, 2000). But of course there are many possible ways of painting the picture of "globalization from above." The most common is a top-down perspective. The top is understood as peak multinational corporations and multi- or supra-national political organizations. Those who are at the top and those who adopt their standpoint inform and form this view of "globalization from above." Stiglitz (2002) indicates that some economists are especially prone to this tendency. Further, this view is widely proselytized by right-wing think tanks, many national governments, and much of the popular media. It is from this perspective that we hear of the so-called new and consensual economic world order. As Waters (1995: 116) explains, this is an ideological conception that seeks to obscure very real differences of interest and power. The master narrative here is neoliberal economics with its calls for state legislated and protected trade and structural adjustment in national economies. A feature of its underlying logic is deterministic; neoliberal economic globalization that accords with the neoliberal agenda is portrayed as unstoppable. A second logic is advocatory—globalize according to neoliberal prescriptions or perish. This "neoliberal globalism" Beck (2000: 9) associates with "the ideology of rule by the world market" which, he argues, "proceeds mono-causally and economistically...reducing the multidimensionality of globalization to a single, economic dimension, that is itself conceived in a linear fashion." While the state and the market are typically understood as being distinct but interdependent, neoliberal globalism liquidates any distinctions between politics and economics, creating a state/market formation.

A second broad set of ideas related to the notion of "globalization from above" is less advocatory and seeks to be more analytical and scholarly. It attempts to identify two main elements; the key historical shifts and the major material and cultural patterns associated with globalization. There is a particular interest in and debate about what can be understood as "new" and what is instead a continuation of the recent or distant past. Thus, for example, Benyon and Dunkerly (2000: 7–10) provide different viewpoints on the history of globalization. A main set of debates in sociology and anthropology revolve around whether globalization is an acceleration of modernity, capitalism, and colonialism that is happening in tandem with high modernity. Alternatively, the debate focuses on whether it is a recent and distinctive phenomenon associated with such processes as post-industrialization, postmodernization, postcolonialism and "disorganized capitalism" (Lash and Urry, 1994). In this regard, one focus is on processes of detraditionalization, particularly the loss of traditional institutional formations and anchors of identity. Another interrelated focus is the processes of retraditionalization involving new inflections of traditional social and cultural forms and identifications. And, of course, contemporary transitions in globalization may be characterized in terms of these complex and contradictory processes that are borne of contestation and uncertainty.

## Theorizing the Processes of Globalization: Three Approaches

In very general terms, there seem to be three way of theorizing these shifts and patterns. One set of accounts is structuralist. The driving force of globalization is the all-powerful relationship among global capital, markets, and digital technology and their associated colonizing imperatives. Another set of accounts adopts either a more dialectical view or a view drawing from structuration theory: the relationships among global/local, integration/fragmentation, and structure/agency are key concerns here. The codes are now widely acknowledged via the notion that "the global now helps to shape our every-day worlds and by our every-day acts we help to shape the global" (Giddens, 1999). Of course there is considerable debate about how this global/local dialectic is manifest and increasingly studies identify a range of local/global interactions and inflections. A third set of ideas draws on the notion of "complex connectivity." Let us consider this one in a little more detail.

"Globalization refers to the rapidly developing and ever-denser network of interconnections and interdependences that characterize modern social life," argues Tomlinson (1999: 2). He calls this "complex connectivity" and identifies different modalities of interconnection and interdependence involved; our term for this throughout the book is mesh-works. He argues that the tasks of globalization theory are to "understand the sources of this condition" and to "interpret its implications across the various spheres of social existence" (Tomlinson, 1999: 2). When Tomlinson (1999: 17) explores the multidimensionality of globalization he insists that it needs to be understood in terms of "simultaneous complexly related processes in the realms of the economy, politics, culture, technology, and so forth" and "involves all sorts of contradictions, resistances, and counter veiling forces." Similarly, Held, McGrew, Goldblatt, and Perraton (cited in Benyon and Dunkerley 2000: 11) claim that contemporary globalization "is not reducible to a single causal process, but involves a complex configuration of causal logics." Giddens (1999) contends that globalization is "a multi-causal, multi-stranded process full of contingency and uncertainty." Similarly, Waters (1995: 3) defines globalization as a "social process in which the constraints of geography on social and cultural arrangements recede and in which people become increasingly aware that they are receding." Scholte (2000: 3) agrees but also argues that deterritorialization (supraterritoriality and the emergence of trans-world spaces) is a key feature of globalization that gives it a "new and distinctive meaning." This represents an important contemporary historical development.

The key concepts and concerns of "globalization from above" scholars are reconfiguration, shrinking space, freedom from space (Giddens, 1994), compression or interconnectedness, networks, flow, speed and volume, virtuality, fluidity, flexibility, and the reshaping of power. There is a fascination here with disembedding, with the "fluid firm", with "flexible" management and labor, and with the governmental and other technologies that permit or encourage them to exist. Much associated attention is thus paid to deterritoriality, the porousness of borders and boundaries, and to the flow across national borders to different places all over the globe, of information, ideas, images, trade, investment, labor, commodities, and people. Global media forms such as film, television, and the Internet are instrumental in the global circulation of culture, information, and images. Hence, there is an intense curiosity amongst these globalization scholars about the fresh configurations of time and space that they permit and produce. They are interested in the space-less-ness and place-less-ness of images, screens, virtual worlds, and simulated, hyper-real, and "imagined spaces" (Soja, 1996) and "imagined worlds" (Appadurai, 1996). Equally, there is an interest in the "non-places," particularly those that have arisen alongside intensified travel and tourism, and the emergence of a hyper-mobile global cosmopolitan elite.

In general terms this research concentrates on the advanced corporate and "cultural economies" (Appadurai, 1996) of multinational organizations and multi- or supranational political institutions—their modes of operation and their effects. In other words, the focus is on what can be understood as the control centers and controllers of the global economy, politics, and culture, the means by which they spread their power and influence and the nature of this influence. Hence, they have a particular interest in global cities as well as global elites. As Waters (1995: 51) explains, "transnational corporations set up global linkages and systems of exchange so that the globe is increasingly constituted as a single market for commodities, labour and capital." Alongside this line of inquiry and analysis is the acknowledged paradox that there are now significant limits to such power and influence.

These limits to the power of the most powerful are related to the risks associated with ever-present threat of ecological disasters, global economic collapse, and the spread of war and of international health epidemics. Beck (1992) calls these "high consequence risks" and argues that they universalize and equalize regardless of location and class position. But he also considers the manner in which risks are distributed, claiming that class disadvantage can lead to risk disadvantage. Poverty and risk attract each other. Giddens (1994: 20) says that humanity is driven by its collective fear of the threats it has created and it is thus that survival values unite us all. Risk and reflexivity are companions. "Risk management" has become a major preoccupation of government and institutional policy makers. It involves "discovering, administering, acknowledging, avoiding or concealing such hazards with respect to specifically defined horizons of relevance" (Beck, 1992: 19–20). This creates a situation where as the risks increase so too do empty promises of security. Giddens (1994) points to the re-regulation that is occurring within and beyond nation-states as they respond to the "high consequence risks" of globalization.

## Criticism of "Globalization from Above"

We must now point to some pertinent criticisms of the research that considers globalization from above. These criticisms have prompted a number of the researchers in this volume to look "underneath" the big patterns of globalization. That said, we must also keep in mind the difficulties of generalization across such a diverse body of research. As several critics point out, much of the research into "globalization from above" is highly selective in the scales, spaces, flows, networks, and subjects of globalization that it chooses to analyse (Nagar, Lawson, McDowell, and Hanson, 2001). This selectivity means that it offers readers a rather skewed version of globalization (Koffman, 2000), often from the standpoint of what we call the Minority World (and what others might call the over-developed or first world). Indeed, the broad scale of much of this analysis draws attention away from the implications of globalization for other equally pertinent sites, flows, networks, and actors in "peripheral" spaces and places. Often obscured from view are the implications of globalization for the daily—and nightly—practices of households, diverse local workplaces, and organizations, face-to-face communities, and non-elite embodied and socially embedded actors. Thus the manner in which different places and people are drawn into the relations of globalization in various complicated ways is muted in analysis. Such foci also draw attention away from the manner in which the spaces and scales of globalization are multiple and intersecting.

Several other general criticisms are worth noting here. The first is that some such studies, particularly those that focus on information technology and its relationship to capital, are informed by a highly determinist logic. The second is that many studies operate at high levels of generalization and abstraction. These are as Scholte (2000: 1) observes, "empirically thin." A third criticism is that some (not all) such studies of globalization suffer from an ethical emptiness. As Harvey (2000) says, on occasions they talk of globalization, when they might more aptly talk of imperialism or colonialism. As these and other criticisms suggest, there is considerable contestation over representations of globalization among educational researchers and the wider circles with which they are linked. For, of course, it is implicitly or explicitly recognized that the mobilization of any globalization agenda finds highly charged responses and expressions in educational policies, pedagogies, and politics.

## Globalization from Below

The sorts of criticisms outlined above have provoked an assortment of research that seeks to extend and deepen understandings of globalization by focusing on what is variously called mundane, vernacular, or indiginized globalization, that is "globalization from below." This research work attends to intersecting geographic scales and to the uneven and particular aspects of globalization. As Waters (1995) notes, deterritorialization has proceeded most rapidly in the West but it is experienced differently from place to place. Research into globalization from below is sensitive to the unevenness and disjunctions in the practices and consequences of neoliberal globalism (Smith, 1997), for instance, its paradoxical integrating and fragmenting tendencies. As Held and McGrew (2002) observe, the inciting of ethnonationlism and the exploitation of its divisiveness and fragmentation are being reinforced by neoliberal globalism in response to the growing global inequalities it is causing.

Predictably studies of "globalization from below" have a "bottom up" standpoint in terms of their theoretical, methodological, and moral concerns. A strong theoretical orientation here is culturalist, but this is also accompanied by the theoretical orientations noted above, namely structuration theory, the dialectical, and that which also stresses "complex connectivity." While, again, much of this research is descriptive and analytical, it also often has a strong moral imperative. It is concerned with the power inequities associated with the current "geographies of centrality and marginality" (Sassen, 1998), with representing the particular in ways that do not diminish it, and with the local speaking back to power elites of the global economy (Escobar, 2001). Such studies also try to distinguish that which is part of "globalization from above" and that which remains apart from or opposed to it. Indeed, "globalization from below" studies tend to heed the advice of Raymond Williams (1982), who encourages one to remain alert to the historical interplay of competing tendencies. He calls these the dominant, residual, oppositional, and emergent tendencies and urges researchers not to focus too exclusively on analyzing the dominating tendencies or on them as the exclusive source of the new, innovative, or transformative.

One focus in this research is on the extent to which and manner in which globalizing processes are mediated on the ground, in the flesh, and "inside-the-head" (Robertson, 1992). Attention is paid to diverse peoples and places, and their complex and contradictory experiences of, reactions to, and engagements with various aspects of globalization as these intersect with their lives and identities over time (Luke and Tuathail, 1998; Urry 1995). Of related concern are the lives and spaces that are made poorer and "marginalized" by the trade and investment patterns of economic globalization particularly in the Majority World or so-called third world or the South (Freeman, 2000). Asymmetrical dependency, the rich/poor divide, and the causes and consequences of Majority World debt are very much a part of this agenda (Potter, 2000) A further interest is in those progressive, transformative social movements that have mobilized in opposition to "globalization from above," especially various aspects of corporate globalization.

Those with an interest in "globalization from below" are of course also interested in deterritorialization, flows, mesh-works, speed, time/space reorganization, virtuality, the fluid, the flexible, and the new. Equally they are interested in global trade, investment, speculation, and issues of cultural transfer. However, their interest is in localized inflections of these, in the extent to which and how such globalizing processes modulate material and territorial place, space, cultures, identities, and relationships—and in how these modulate more global trends.

Education is a crucial arena in which these tendencies work. Indeed, it is a central set of institutions and processes through which we can understand the relations within and among the global and the local. The authors included here take these issues seriously and place the realities of education center stage in their investigations of the dialectical connections education has with globalization.

The chapters to follow scrutinize the question of globalization from different angles. Some focus on neoliberal globalism (Raduntz); global forms of governance (Ziguras); and their particularly negative effects (Thomson, Apple), describing their broad patterns and how they impact on and operate within nation-state education systems. Others are more concerned with the global cultural economy, the associated flow of images (Kenway and Bullen, Nixon), people (Morris) and ideas (Reid), and on the ways in which these challenge conventional educational understandings and practices. Yet others seek to disrupt "globalization from above" discourses by focusing on the colonizing imperatives involved (Shore), by offering a reading of history that decenters Minority World views (Singh) and by pointing to globalization's retraditionalizing ramifications (Kell). The global/national/local mesh-works associated with information and communications technology feature in some chapters (Brown, Grieshaber and Yelland); but other forms of complicated connectivity are also elucidated—the diverse worlds of drugs (Phillips) and of trade unions (Franzway), for instance.

The chapters are united in their concern to acknowledge the "complex connectivity" associated with globalization and most seek to illuminate its vernacular expressions. They are also united in their ethical concern to both expose the more pernicious effects on education of neoliberal and corporate globalization from above. In doing so, these educational researchers identify, affirm, and elaborate innovative and transformative educational policies, pedagogies, and politics that challenge such effects. It is to these matters that we now turn.

## Globalization, the Nation-State, and Responsive Education

Education policies, pedagogies, and politics have, at least since the state-sponsored rise of mass industrial education in the minority world in the nineteenth century, involved major conflicts, contradictions, and compromises among groups with competing visions of "legitimate" knowledge, what counts as "good" teaching and learning, and what is a "just" nation-state and world order. Such contestation today is closely connected to economic, political, and cultural forces of "globalization from above." This neoliberal globalism continues to restructure and destructure the relations between nations (citizens) and states in opposition to both the resistance that has arisen from popular resentment to this ideological political project and the innovative efforts to build projects of democratic transformation through "globalization from below."

No analysis of contemporary transitions in education policies, pedagogies, and politics can be fully serious without placing at its very core sensitivity to the ongoing struggles over "globalization from above" that constantly reshape the terrain on which educators of all kinds operate. This terrain ranges across local communities through the nation-state to transnational agencies of global civil society. This calls for an analysis of the state's disciplining of education (and education workers) and the nation's population through (quasi-)economic models of governmental action and, in particular, the intensification of state regulatory mechanisms for privileging and giving effect to a market-oriented culture. This requires a consideration of innovative ways of the renovating the policies, pedagogies, and politics concerned with educating students *for* life. This means graduating students who can think critically and have a deep understanding of ideas, developing students able to produce knowledge by drawing on resources from different fields and integrating these with their own experiential knowledge so as to speak to their real life contexts. Providing all students with a supportive learning environment is integral to making productive education policies, pedagogies, and politics.

Western European imperialism, an earlier era in globalization, created considerable continuing complexities, uncertainties, and challenges for Indigenous peoples throughout the world. In this regard contemporary transitions in the practices of globalization are perhaps little different from those of the colonial past. However, the formation of "new" sets of compromises, "new" alliances, and "new" power blocs is having increasing influences in education policies, pedagogies, and politics and all things social and cultural. These power blocs combine multiple fractions of capital that are committed to neoliberal ideological projects to deal with the crises manufactured in public responses to and expressions of "globalization from above" (Falk, 1999: 161–62) and its associated economic, sociocultural, and ecological problems. This alliance also includes neoconservative intellectuals and movements who want to standardize and inculcate monoculturalism. There are the authoritarian populist religious who promote worries about secularity in order to impose their own narrow, exclusionary traditions on the nation. In addition, there are the ethnonationalists committed to inciting fears of those they designate as Others in order to contain the prospects for deepening and extending democratic citizenship. Particular fractions of the new middle class are also part of this alliance, finding work in managing the neoliberal ideological project, fabricating and applying gloss to its compliance techniques and surveillance technologies, and administering its market-oriented culture. This arguably fragile and fragmented alliance promotes contradictory aims. On the one hand, it seeks to create the conditions for increasing international profit, especially through disciplining labor, consumers, and democratic citizens, as well as cultivating an exclusionary focus on private interests. On the other hand, it aims to revivify a highly romanticized past based on exclusionary, segregated imaginings of home, family, school, community and nation (Apple, 1996, 2000, 2001).

However, the uncertainties and conflicts within this alliance need to be analyzed. There are tensions around the role of neoliberal globalism in manufacturing crises in the education of national/global publics as well as its containing of the democratic procedures sovereign citizens have for rule-making and will-formation in the interests of instrumental efficiencies. These stand in opposition to those who see private and public autonomy as necessarily interwoven and co-dependent. For instance, Habermas (1998) argues that the conditions for private autonomy needed to enable individuals to pursue their conception of the good life require the deepening and extension of the public autonomy through democratic procedures invested in the sovereignty of national/global citizens.

This "new" alliance links "conservative modernization," "neoliberal post-modernization," and instrumental technocracy with authoritarian populism. It relies on corporate managers to integrate education policies, pedagogies, and politics into a contradictory raft of ideological commitments. The objectives in education are the same as those that guide its economic, social, and cultural goals more generally. They include the dramatic expansion of that eloquent fiction, of the unfettered market, when in fact it is created and sustained by the state. Related objectives include the drastic reduction of state responsibility for the social and economic security of its citizens. This involves lowering citizens' expectations for the public underwriting of economic and social security and instead exposing them to mounting risks across their expanding life cycle. Other objectives include the use of public resources to reinforce the intensely competitive and inequitable structures of mobility both inside and outside institutionalized education, the "disciplining" of public culture and bodies, and the popularization of Social Darwinist thinking through exclusionary patriarchal ethnonationalist movements of resentment politics. The ways in which this is occurring and what might be done about it are the topics that this book addresses. In order to accomplish this, we raise a complex set of crucial questions.

- What is actually happening? To whom? With what effects? What are the risks and opportunities?
- What are the contradictory tendencies and tensions among the various movements and actors of neoliberalism and neoconservatism?
- What are the specific ideological dynamics at work here? What specific role do gender and race play in neoliberal reforms? How do these dynamics differ by region and nation?
- How have the processes of conservative modernization worked off of people's hopes, fears, and real understandings (their elements of "good sense") of their situations?
- Are there ways in which policy actors and movements can be brought under a more progressive umbrella? How might this be organized? By whom? What policies might enable this to be accomplished?
- What are the limitations of ideology critique? What other methods or tactics are available for engaging the governance of education policies, pedagogies, and politics?
- How and by whom has the "globalization crisis" and the problematics of educational governance been identified or otherwise constructed?
- In what ways might the research and teaching expertise of educators be deployed to respond to these problems?
- What "translations" can be made to reshape the conduct of other authorities and individuals? How can particular concerns be reframed so as to appeal to a majoritarian constituency?

- What are the possibilities for translating or otherwise reworking the technologies (or means or strategies or calculative) regimes (such as measurable outcomes, targets, percentages) used to address this crisis and its associated educational problems?
- What are the tensions and conflicts within the neoliberal alliance that have arisen around the "globalization crisis" and the problems of educational governance?
- In the effort to create responsive education what do we know about the changing culture, politics, and economics of work? What might be involved in educating students capable of creating work?

These are complicated questions. Taken seriously they enable us to gain a more detailed understanding of the realities of educational and cultural action today. They may even stimulate possibilities for creating transformative projects in the future. This book represents a collective attempt to chart the dynamics and effects of hegemonic and counter-hegemonic ideologies, discourses, institutions, and processes that are currently being built and contested in an educational world that is being radically transformed by globalizing forces from above and below.

Acting on the changes to which we pointed above requires the creation of new education policies, pedagogies, and politics. This is being done by educators, engaging constructively in producing different cultural knowledges, by increasing the active participation of educators from different linguistic and cultural backgrounds, and by building a cosmopolitan transnational identity among all students and educators. The substantial challenges of creating education policies, pedagogies, and politics that are responsive to the imperatives of these times or of renovating existing ones are compounded by the changing political economy of education, changes in the production of knowledge, and changing student (and teacher) identities in response to and as an expression of the contemporary transitions in globalization. These three dimensions are explored across the various chapters in this volume. Below we have highlighted selected issues in relation to each of these changes, beginning with the changing economy of education policies, pedagogies, and politics.

## The Changing Economy of Education Policies, Pedagogies, and Politics

Researchers in this collection explore the marketization of education, focusing on how the restructuring of the economy manifested in the corporatization of educational enterprises is related to the creation of new markets for capital investment and the underwriting of the mass sales of new information and communication technologies. For instance, Helen Raduntz (this volume) begins what others in this book also seek to do, namely identifying the internal contradictions and inefficiencies in crass, market-driven education, providing a focus for intervention in the globalization agenda that is grounded in education. In this context, Williamson-Fien (2000: 45) argues that the political projects of neoliberal and neoconservative globalism have co-jointly reinvented and repositioned the state within new problematics of governing. This has seen ideological critiques of the "education of national/global publics" used to breach the values and expertise valorized by educators so that their work is now opened up to reconstruction as constituents of market-driven business enterprise.

## The Technical Arts of Neoliberal Governance

The seemingly contradictory ideas of state-sponsored competition; regulation by market forces and a life supposedly made good by consumerism, on the one hand, and the equally tension-ridden notions of doing much, much more with much, much less; worker accountability; performance standardization; state testing; and nationalized curriculum have been used in odd ways to reinforce each other. Corporate managers have helped cement neoliberal and neoconservative positions on education for private gain into the daily lives of many students, teachers and parents. Chris Ziguras (this volume) explores how the instruments of economic globalization, specifically the General Agreement on Trade in Services (GATS), are impacting on the transnational trade in education. In doing so, he implicitly raises questions about the democratization of supranational organizations. In contrast to strong nation-states that invest in the education of the public as a collective socioeconomic good, states with a weak, complacent commitment to the sovereignty of their citizens are keen to disinvest in underwriting their citizens' social and economic security. This involves the establishment and deployment of calculative regimes to give effect to the political project of neoliberalism. This repertoire of cultural technologies of compliance embodies forms of expertise for fabricating measures of those short-term "outcomes" that are imagined as enhancing the power for effecting micromanagement. The development of an education that is responsive to contemporary imperatives confronting the nation-state and its citizens is of little concern. These technologies of audit have achieved high status and considerable market value in the hierarchy of power, especially in states with weak links to their citizens and strong commitments to acting as agents for the market. They are imagined to be effective means through which an increasing range of individuals and agencies can be micromanaged. Being continuously monitored and evaluated by the state to ensure widespread conformity with its agenda limits the time educators have for imagining and enacting transformative projects required to engage the risks of globalization. Their work is reduced a series of performance indicators that are used to make judgments about their productivity and to refine mechanisms to induce conformity—complacency—in conduct. In much the same way as "kill ratios" and "body counts" were used to "win" acceptance among the public for the American war against Vietnam (Singh, 1989), these technologies are used to measure the ideological submission of educators to the agenda of neoliberal globalism. Individuals and institutions are held responsible to the "truths" manufactured by these accountancy criteria.

Any claims to "truth" based on the expertise of the education profession or the communities with which they work are dismissed. Only speculative marketing data, heavily massaged financial reports, and corporate managerial techniques of image management count. This dismissal of the value of educating the public is intended to force on education policies, pedagogies, and politics the stringencies of neoliberal globalism, using state regulatory intervention by means of these technologies of compliance. Within the new network of valorized expertise, "performance administration" has become crucial to corporate micromanagement and a key site for the exercise of state regulatory power. Despite the rhetoric of "deregulation," neoliberal globalism operates through the institutionalization of the market in knowing and willful complicity with state mechanisms of centralized command and control. This dual regulatory dual framework hopes to optimize its operation through encouraging self-disciplinary technologies. Where this is not occurring, performance administrators are used to reinforce compliance. The use of these technologies creates an imaginary individual or private autonomy as much as it invites complacency. However, the reconfiguring of governance into an alliance between the state and marketplace against citizens, labor, and consumers enhances the possibility for manipulating individuals. People are made perpetually responsive to shifts in their economic circumstances. Competition across and within every level of the education "industry" is used to assure institutional compliance with the governmental objectives of neoliberal globalism.

## Struggles to Legitimize Enterprise Culture
## and to Naturalize Its Alliance with the State

Neoliberal governance has given rise to the development of an enterprise culture that valorizes the capitalizing of profits and the socializing of costs through tax concessions and corporate welfare provisions. The elaboration of competitive entrepreneurialism involves the legtimization and naturalization of the processes of marketization, commodification, and commercialization sustained by the state. The calculative regimes for assuring regulation by the state are used in conjunction with global/local market forces. Neoliberal globalism constructs active, self-actualizing individuals who optimize a narrow sense of the good life by their own decisions regarding consumption based on their capacity to secure credit for goods and services. The aim is to mobilize the population to work within neoliberal modes of government. Individuals are expected to learn to equate their interests with the creation of a globally oriented enterprise culture and a state that disinvests in the collective social and economic security needed for citizens to exercise their public and private autonomy.

The neoliberal vision is to institutionalize the extension of the state/market alliance throughout the social fabric of the nation. This means structuring a monoculture of enterprise into the whole assemblage of human life. This includes commodifying professional activities, family life, unemployment, and the environment. This state/market formation is extended in ways that induce everyone to play the enterprise game across the full spectrum of educational activities. The development of this enterprise culture involves the creation of conditions in which individuals see their own interests as being served by the ideological and political projects of neoliberal globalism. The result is that *they* themselves actively seek the opportunities associated with this culture. Working against every ounce of *good sense,* this project is creating a nonsense of the very rhythms of daily life. People's relationship with life and each other are being organized around a complacent, calculative, self-centered understanding of the world.

Crises of alienation, disaffection, and depression are manifestations of the stresses and strains manufactured by "globalization from above." This suggests that these processes of governance are not only messier than the neoliberal or neoconservative mindset suggests, but inefficient and ineffective. This is so especially given the constitutive role of errors, false appraisals, and faulty calculations along with political disenfranchisement, marginalization, and contestation manufactured by the historical, localizing, and ideological practices of neoliberal globalism. Nevertheless a multitude of small, seemingly insignificant, disparate, and diffuse changes interrupt the production and institutionalization of a coherent neoliberal and neoconservative blueprint. For instance, educators are struggling to force a shift from a calculative formation of international education, framed predominantly within an income-generating perspective, to another that emphasizes the education of transnational knowledge workers, national/global publics, and learners for life. Here Peter Kell (this volume) argues that neoliberal governance is a congenitally failing process; its achievement regularly fail to match the programmatic ambitions that inform its agenda. For instance, the neoconservative advocates of whites only politics have not accepted interruptions to taken for granted assumptions about global/national racial hierarchies. They have allied their exclusionary politics of resentment as well as regressive parochialism to the neoliberal agenda.

The contingent conceptions and shifting terrain of the neoliberal project provides an important focus for analysis. Pat Thomson (this volume) makes a case for analyzing conceptions of it that undermine its public relations' image as being a unified political ideal or a single economic doctrine. Given the crises in the "education of national/global publics" caused by neoliberal approaches to governance, it is important to examine the historical development of this project. This is in preference to accepting that it was ever constituted as a coherent comprehensive package or as necessarily destined to emerge as the preeminent political project of the twenty-first century. Such analyses show that there is no absolute necessity for things being the way they are. The crises in the "education of the public" caused by neoliberal globalism indicate that it is not a self-evident matter that this should be so. However, it is important to identify those factors that enable neoliberal globalism to be seen as inevitable or given. This will expose the mechanisms by which these issues have been placed above and beyond democratic political processes.

Alan Reid (this volume) shows that the governance of educational policies, pedagogies, and politics emerges from a complex, contingent and fragile assemblage of practices. The programmatic development of educational governance is far from predictable. It is better characterized as an irregular and incomplete process of planning and provision accomplished through vexed negotiations and adventitious settlements.

Given the legacies from the past—both the contestably "good" and the questionably "bad"—Helen Nixon (this volume) refuses to accept the demise or devaluing of the "education of the national/global public," which continues to be devalued through the rise of neoliberal policies, pedagogies, and politics. Thus, not all "old" educational concepts, modalities, and policies should disappear; nor should all legacies of the past be unquestioningly dismissed or celebrated. Contrary to the focus on "performance outcomes," the flow-on effects and consequences of neoliberal governance itself cannot easily be known in advance, thus the need to be alert to the risky opportunities involved. For example, there are considerable risks to how people think about key ideas like citizenship, democracy, and how their public and private actions in and on the world are necessarily interwoven. A focus on the technical arts of educational governance, with its contingencies and uncertainties, may be used to analyse the rise of forms of expert knowledge relating to corporate managerialism, performance administration, accounting, and auditing skills. This opens up spaces for questioning their legitimation is important.

In this regard, Jane Kenway and Elizabeth Bullen (this volume) critically examine the changing constructions of childhood and the difficulties for educational pedagogy in gaining the consent of the young in this age of manipulated desires. They explore what pedagogies might usefully help teachers to "enchant" the classroom. In the process, they analyse the contradictions in the resources for identity re-formation made available for education through neoliberal, consumer-media culture. They consider what can be learnt about pedagogy from those who develop the "corporate curriculum."

While lamentable, these changes present provide exceptional opportunities for serious critical reflection on both the neoliberal project and our own engagement in making significant transformations in education. In a time of massive economic, social and educational restructuring and destructuring, it is also important to consider the processes and effects of the contradictory elements of neoconservative modernization. There are varying ways in which they are mediated, compromised, accepted, and appropriated by different groups for their own purposes. They are struggled over in the policies, pedagogies, and politics of people's daily lives. This is presently happening through the international marketization of education as suggested by Ziguras (this volume), as well as the formation of nationalized curricula and the institutionalization of state testing. For those interested in more critical democratic educational policies, pedagogies, and politics, not to do so means that we act without understanding the shifting relations of power that are constructing and reconstructing the social field in which education operates. Equally as important, by studying closely what the neoliberal and neoconservative alliance involves and does, and by better understanding why it has been successful in undermining educators', good sense, we can begin to better understand how the policies, pedagogies, and politics of this alliance might be interrupted, contested, or otherwise translated.

## The Governmental Problematics of Neoliberal Globalism

Despite rhetoric to the contrary, there has been no reduction in or minimization of governmental activity or a retreat by the neoliberal state from governance. Instead, there has been an investment by neoliberal governments in strategies for institutionalizing enterprising management, which it promises will produce improved economic results for the privileged few. On the one hand, neoliberal globalism is a bipartisan political intervention by the parties of labor and capital that uses recognisable problems with state-generated welfare dependency to reject the massive achievements of the state in providing for the socioeconomic security of citizens in the face of economic crises throughout their lives. On the other hand, this governmental coalition multiplies the domains of human life destructured—creatively, crassly, or otherwise—by an alliance of the state and global/local market forces. Just as it is necessary to guard against any idealized, nostalgic reconstructions of the welfare functions of the state, it is important to reject the intergenerational production of a disaffected and dependent underclass that has now been produced by the neoliberal policies that began to take root in the late 1970s (Giddens, 1994).

The extension of the neoliberal state's regulatory power of market relations is intended to induce the shift of labor from paid workers onto consumers through the use of new technologies. Just as the supermarket shifted the cost of selling retail goods onto consumers, the costs of administering education are being shifted onto students. As customers they are expected to use new technologies to perform increasing amounts of work once performed by paid administration staff. Likewise, the retreat by the state from investing in the "education of the national/global public" is evident in the creation of an international market in educational products and services that seeks to reconstitute parents and students as individual consumers choosing within the constraints of their socioeconomic status to maximize their private interests in profit-making. The politics of neoliberal globalism is evident in its reinvention of democratic governance and repositioning of the state as the agent causing crises in the education of the public. This deep ideological commitment to neoliberal globalism exploits the resentment politics of alienated and disaffected citizens by directing it against marginalized Others (Aasen, 2003).

It is in this context that Allan Reid (this volume) investigates the impact of the "globalization from above" on education for democracy. The capacity of the state and its institutions for educating a national/global public to sustain and reinvent democratic life in a globalizing world, to bring forward and rework traditional democratic aspirations is being increasingly eroded by the neoliberal state's pursuit of its ideological project. For instance, responsive education policies, pedagogies, and politics are now needed to move beyond the exclusionary politics of the ethnonationalist project on which many states were founded to one that invests democratic power in the sovereignty of national/global citizens. In this context, Reid contends that the connections between "education of national/global publics" and the structures and practices of democracy are being undermined by the neoliberal project of cultural and economic "globalization from above." This is dramatically changing both the nation-state relationship and the education of the public *(res publica)*.

Despite the destructuring of the common wealth created by sovereign citizens through privatizing their collective assets, the neoliberal state has not escaped the globalization/localization of risks concerning their social, economic, and ecological security. The self-regulating power of the state over the nation's economy has been displaced within the framework of a larger neoliberal political project of global economic reductionism. This has resulted from and given expression to unstable and inequitable patterns of international trade along with foreign investment in nonmaterial assets traded on global financial markets. The neoliberal project presents strategies that are said to be required to ensure that the national economy is well positioned within the international marketplace and to enable the population to endorse and contribute to these new economic priorities. However, it is becoming increasingly clear that neoliberal governance has not been able to deliver strategies for effecting economically efficient competition that avoid many citizens becoming losers in the global marketplace. The targeting of the institutions required for effecting public private autonomy, including education, are being in terms of the availability of resources to fund public and private interests in new technology rather than prioritizing the rental of real estate, the marketing of food and advertising, and trade in education itself. These developments have undermined the capacity to value the work of educating the public in promoting social, economic, and ecological security for the emerging transnational order of capital and labor. This has included targeting the "what" of education, the knowledge (and the discourses surrounding it) that is considered legitimate or "official" (Apple, 2000).

## Globalizing Changes in Knowledge Production

The changing knowledge base of responsive education is most graphically represented by the role of new digital technologies. At their best these technologies may offer tools for the production of information and aids for knowledge creation, as well as vehicles for community building and emotional support. However, under corporate managerialism these creative and imaginative possibilities tend to be reduced to outdated, test-driven "tick-and-flick" regimes. Lynton Brown (this volume) points out the ways in which the pedagogical potential for using ever advancing digital technologies is intimately related to the process through which curricula are internationalized. He shows the ways in which potentially progressive, transformative curricula oriented to the responsive education of national/global publics are being undermined by the complacency of entrepreneurial managerialism and then, just as important, illustrates what might be done. Specifically, he demonstrates how the new digital technologies create possibilities for responsive pedagogies that enable global/local community mesh-working and knowledge production, providing teachers with additional, supplementary resources for their educational work. This is in preference to the complacent assumption that such expensive technologies can and should be used as instruments for effecting cost cutting through the use of either teacher-proof or teacherless "reusable learning objects." Likewise Susan Grieshaber and Nicola Yelland (this volume) look at the effects of new technologies on young children's lives and interrogate the ways in which schooling is becoming increasingly alienated from the real world of children. This work also alludes to the tensions evident in the use of schools for producing consumers for these new technologies.

Changes in the knowledge base of education are stimulating debates about the languages in which it is made accessible. There are mounting

concerns in Anglophone nations about the risks arising from the failure of
education institutions and policy makers to normalize egalitarian multilingualism. This hazard is associated with a political commitment to the project of globalizing English as the one-world language, a project that not
only meets resistance to such linguistic imperialism, but also continues to
generate a multiplicity of Englishes (Singh, Kell, and Pandian, 2002). Yet
this comes at a time when we recognize that, with the use of advancing
technologies for facilitating teacher-student interactions, knowledge production, and critical reflection, educators now have an opportunity to engage with culturally embedded, linguistically diverse human beings.
English-only policies, pedagogies, and politics are increasingly being
questioned. However, the demand for work-related, real-world education
and training conveniently ignores the realities, employment possibilities,
and niche market opportunities arising from the world's cultural and linguistic diversity.

The changing knowledge base of education requires new ways of imagining and imaging the relationship between the global and the local. Pat
Thomson (this volume) explores the possibilities represented by visual
research in becoming part of new, postindustrial pedagogies that confront
and attempt to understand globalized local settings and to argue for alternative agendas. As she demonstrates, visual investigations provide new
pedagogical possibilities for studying the ways in which the global and the
local come together in neighborhoods and public schools once created by
the state, and since abandoned by it. At a time when paid work, culture,
politics and economy have disappeared, institutions for the "education of
national/global publics" are being incited or forced to secure their legitimacy by renovating well-established work-related pedagogies such as
"lifelong learning" and "work-related learning." Those at the innovative
edge push ahead with learning *for* life including work-creating education
as well as education in the procedures for effecting democratic citizenship. Lynton Brown (this volume) continues these themes, reporting on
how and why educators' work-related knowledges are being transformed
into commodifable forms for management seeking new ways of controlling their work. He does this providing an account of how the technologization of work, what teachers know and how they learn their work, and
what, if anything, they think, know, and feel about neoliberal globalism.

Michael Singh (this volume) points to the ways both historical and contemporary issues are represented in the development of responsive modes
of "educating national/global publics," both those who are its beneficiaries

and those whose resentment is borne of their alienation and disaffection from it. He makes the case that in this context responsive education policies, pedagogies, and policies may benefit from engaging these complexities. This sees educators—as researchers, teachers, and policy actors— engaging with, and enabling citizens' engagement with the power present in the many faces of globalization from above.

## Changing Teacher and Student Identities

An understanding of complexity does not mean paralysis. Teachers engaged in responsive educational policies, pedagogies, and politics provide a source of hope in the struggles against the complacency of neoliberal globalism and the resentment engendered by globalization from above. Suzanne Franzway (this volume) points to the benefits of being sensitive to the work of policy actors and movements *already* are engaged in making responsive educational policies, pedagogies, and politics. The actions and interventions of these cross-sectoral, transnational movements address the interplay of patriarchal relations of power and governance. In particular, the feminist movement's engagement in the labor movement provides important pedagogical lessons for producing models of responsive education. Feminist policy actors now express more explicitly and self-consciously a sense of plurality, providing a more complex and nuanced definition of the globalization of responsive educational politics. Feminist educational politics draws upon the diversity of women's cultures and ways of organizing that offer realistic possibilities to revitalize transformative socio-political movements concerned to extend and deepen democracy at the state and global levels. It is important that the seemingly small achievements made by responsive policy actors be recognized, encouraged, and supported. Interruption to practices of neoliberal globalism occur everywhere, but linking them together remains a problem. Victories won in these local struggles are where lessons can be learned about how these "small achievements" are or might be connected to larger mobilizations and movements (Apple et al., 2003).

In this respect Peter Kell (this volume) explores the role of education workers in reshaping the local, national, and global orientation of their State government and the services it provides to underwrite the socio-economic security of its citizens, in particular its education of national/global publics. In addressing the well-established motto, "no curriculum development without teacher development," Scott Phillips (this volume) continues the exploration of these important issues. He argues that the predominantly Anglo-ethnic teaching service found in the United States, Canada, Australia, New Zealand, and Britain can find responsive ways to productively engage with their increasingly ethnically diverse students. Phillips employs the difficult public dialogues that arise around multiculturalism, drugs, and education as a thoughtful and useful example of this argument.

Further, as the chapter by Sue Shore (this volume) indicates contemporary "globalization from above" cannot be separated from the era of global Western European empires. Their colonization of much of the world cannot be separated from many of the contemporary disciplinary practices associated with Whiteness and its constructions of difference. Indeed, as she shows much of the disciplinary work associated with adult education is subtly scripted in this manner. A first step toward *rewriting* such scripts is to recognize the manner in which this occurs. "Race" is then shown to be a constitutive dynamic for any serious understanding of globalization and its influences, policies, and effects at the local, regional, and international levels of educating a national/global public.

These and similar crucial dynamics—and the possibilities arising from them—are taken further in the next chapters. Students' identity is being subjected to different forms of experiences due to the interrelated practices of globalization/localization. This means that the ways in which students are engaged needs rethinking.

Gayle Morris (this volume) demonstrates the multiple ways in which identities are dynamically constructed and contested. These constructions provide the resources through which students' subjectivities are experiences and shaped. It is not just that students' social and cultural conditions help shape their understanding of experience, but that these experiences embody *vital, life-sustaining learnings.* This knowledge may be identified, affirmed, and elaborated. For the past decade or more, the linguistic, ethnic, and Indigenous diversity of the student population has been enriched by the increasing presence of students from around the world. Morris argues that the changing demographic features of the student population in Minority World nations has increased educators' consciousness of the differential power relations associated with cultural, sexual, ethnic, class, gender, religious, and linguistic phenomenon, and the need for new skills for negotiating these changing global/local relations. That more and more students from over "there" in the Majority World are now over "here" in the Minority World has ruptured the racial, cultural, linguistic, and economic hierarchies that gave privilege and power to states that have grounded their politics in exclusionary ethnonationalism rather than inclusive democratic citizenship. These processes of population change and multicultural mobility embody counter-hegemonic possibilities of immense but largely unexplored proportions (Hardt and Negri, 2000).

## Democratizing Procedures for Reshaping Practices of Globalization

Much of what this book engages in is the critical analysis of the political and ideological project of neoliberal globalism. However, it is not limited to this. It both "bears witness" to the negativity of the ideological and institutional forms of neoliberal globalismand, at the same time, points to the innovative possibilities present in progressive transformative movements, struggles, and practices, many of which are going on right now in daily and nightly life. Both of these emphases are important—analyzing powerful negative effects and pointing to the innovative possibility of making ethically defensible and materially valuable differences to the public work of national/global citizens and their private pursuit of the good life. However, a word must be said here both about the significance of critique in a world in which we are constantly told that "there is no alternative" to neoliberal globalism and about the limits of such critique. The fatalistic claim to the inevitability of the neoliberal project is itself a politically motivated strategy to neutralize transformative projects oriented to deepening and extending democracy to the institutions of globalization. The dismissal of the generative power of critique denies the important role of public argumentation in sustaining democracy and in integrating citizens into national/global civil society. While those whose expert knowledges lie in the work of ideology critique may have been marginalized, this has not precluded their contribution to civic debates and actions over the policies, pedagogies, and politics of educating national/global publics. Even so there is a danger that they too may find themselves unavoidably implicated or involved in neoliberalism's compliance regimes and monoculture of entrpreneurialism.

Ideological critiques, which are paradoxically both immersed in and produced by neoliberal governance, have focused on constructing "identities" for neoliberal educational governance. Engaging in democratic argumentation over what manifestations of the crises manufactured in the education of the public, that is, the education of national/global democratic citizens; the problems of national/global democratic citizens; and the problems of neoliberal governance is necessary. For instance, these critiques point to the ways in which the state's system for educating national/global publics continues to be blamed for the problems of the economy. For instance, this is done by exporting the problems of unemployment into the state's institutions for educating the public. The narrowing of public policies of education to service instrumental economic goals enables the undercutting of the state's investment in the education of national/global publics in the interests of privatization. The marginalization and exclusion of the expertise of knowledge workers engaged in the education of national/global publics from democratic processes of educational governance, educations captured by narrowly market-oriented interests, and the deployment of corporate managerialism in education provide other points for critique.

Having said this, however, as part of our critical self-reflections it is important to consider whether our ideological critiques may have foreclosed fruitful debates on the technical and productive aspects of educational governance. For example, contemporary neoliberal regimes of educational governance may not be any more instrumental than those of the past. Despite claims to autonomy, educational institutions, disciplines, and expertise have consistently been breeched by governmental technologies across a range of issues, such as curriculum relevance or the insistence on graduating students with more technical skills. For instance, oriental, area, and Asian studies, as fields of specialist educational expertise, have for several centuries at least been made available to service government and business interests (Said, 1978). The irrationalities of neoliberal globalism may be represented as "new" forms of educational governance, but are actually the continuation and intensification of past forms. Critical analyses suggest that they might even not be quite so significant a departure from the past as their advocates would like to construct and have widely accepted. Evidence from the early twentieth century indicates that the *cult of economic reductionism* was foisted on the education of the public in the United States in the interests of the economic prosperity of business and the security of the state (Callahan, 1962).

Attempts to depict the institutions of industrial education as idealized sites of human cultivation now seem misplaced. As Franzway (this volume) indicates, a suggestion that industrial education should, or even might, constitute the "one best" site for the perfecting of human integration, development, and egalitarianism is misplaced. The institutions for educating the public combine, somewhat problematically, with the different needs of the state and the nation. They offer a means of ensuring the security of the state, including disciplining of the nation's morality though pastoral surveillance, in combination with efforts to cultivate productive and intelligent learners *for* sustaining life, *for* exercising the sovereignty of democratic citizenship, and *for* pursuing private autonomy through work. The institutions of education provide an assemblage of contingent and limited solutions for dealing with a grab bag of the state's moral as well as material exigencies and providing citizens the resources (cultural capital) for exercising their public and private autonomy.

Thus, in any critical examination of possibilities for change and continuity that makes advantages of the postindustrial era will not be helped by romanticizing the histories and commitments of either the state or the education of the public. Such examinations are likely to be strengthened by renewed critical reflection about our own taken-for-granted commitments and unexamined assumptions. This is something made increasingly necessary by transnational engagements. But, at the very same time, as Apple shows (this volume) such critical self-reflections must sit side by side with rigorous, detailed—and far-reaching—investigations of who the winners and losers are in the current situations so many educators are facing today. The authors in this book know that one must be critical and self-critical at the same time and recognize that all critical analyses are provisional given the continuities and transformations we are all experiencing. We offer this book in that spirit, as a contribution to the analyses of limits and possibilities of education policies, pedagogies, and politics that are so necessary to continue what Raymond Williams (1961) so wisely called "the long revolution." It is a commitment to this transformative project that drives the contributions included here.

## References

Aasen, P. "What Happened to Social Democratic Progressivism in Scandanavia?" In *The State and the Politics of Knowledge*, edited by M. W. Apple, et al. New York: Routledge, 2003.

Appadurai, A. *Modernity at Large: Cultural Dimensions of Globalisation*. Minneapolis: Minnesota Press, 1996.

Apple, M. W. *Cultural Politics and Education*. New York: Teachers College Press, 1996.

———. *Official Knowledge*. 2nd ed. New York: Routledge, 2000.

————. *Educating the "Right" Way: Markets, Standards, God and Inequality*. New York: Routledge Falmer, 2001.

————. *The State and the Politics of Knowledge*. New York: Routledge, 2003.

Apple, M., P. Aasen, M. Cho, L. Gandin, A. Oliver, Y. Sung, H. Tavares, and T.-H. Wong. *The State and the Politics of Knowledge*. New York: Routledge, 2003.

Beck, U. *Risk Society: Towards a New Modernity*. London: Sage, 1992.

————. *What Is Globalization?* Translated by P. Camiller. Cambridge, UK: Polity Press, 2000.

Beyon, J., and D. Dunkerly. *Globalization: The Reader*. London: Athlone Press, 2000.

Callahan, R. *Education and the Cult of Efficiency: A Study of the Social Forces That Have Shaped the Administration of the Public Schools*. Chicago: University of Chicago Press, 1962.

Clarke, J., and J. Newman. *The Managerial State*. London: Sage, 1997.

Cohen, R., and P. Kennedy. *Global Sociology*. Hampshire, UK: Palgrave, 2000.

Escobar, A. "Culture Sits in Places: Reflections on Globalism and Subaltern Strategies of Localization." *Political Geography* 20 (2001): 139–74.

Falk, R. *Predatory Globalization: A Critique*. Cambridge, UK: Polity Press, 1999.

Freeman, C. *High Tech and High Heels in the Global Economy: Women, Work, and Pink-Collar Identities in the Caribbean*. Durham: Duke University Press, 2000.

Giddens, A. *Beyond Left and Right: The Future of Radical Politics*. Stanford: Stanford University Press, 1994.

————. *BBC Reith Lectures: Runaway World* 1999 [cited May 2001]. Available from http://news.bbc.co.uk/.

Habermas, J. *The Inclusion of the Others: Studies in Political Theory*. Cambridge, UKL: Polity Press

Hardt, M., and A. Negri. *Empire*. Cambridge: Harvard University Press, 2000.

Harvey, D. *Spaces of Hope*. Edinburgh: Edinburgh University Press, 2000.

Held, D., and A. McGrew. *Globalization/Anti-Globalization*. Cambridge, UK: Polity Press, 2002.

Kofman, E. "Beyond a Reductionist Analysis of Female Migrants in Global European Cities: The Unskilled, Deskilled and Professional." In *Gender and Global Restructuring: Sightings, Sites and Resistances*, edited by M. Marchand and A. Runyan. London: Routledge, 2000.

Lash, S., and J. Urry. *Economies of Signs and Space*. London: Sage Publications, 1994.

Luke, T., and G. Tuathail. "Global Flowmations, Local Fundamentalisms, and Fast Geopolitics." In *Unruly World. Globalization, Governance and Geography*, edited by A. Herod, G. Tuathail, and S. Roberts. London: Routledge, 1998.

Nagar, R., V. Lawson, L. McDowell, and S. Hanson. "Locating Globalization: Feminist (Re)Readings of the Subjects and Spaces of Globalization." Paper presented at the Geographies of Global Economic Change Conference, Graduate School of Geography, Clark, University 2001.

Potter, G. *Deeper than Debt: Economic Globalisation and the Poor*. London: Latin American Bureau, 2000.

Robertson, R. *Globalisation, Social Theory and Global Culture*. London: Sage Publications, 1992.

Said, E. *Orientalism*. New York: Pantheon, 1978.

Sassen, S. *Globalization and Its Discontents*. New York: New Press, 1998.

Scholte, J. *Globalization: A Critical Introduction*. Houndmills, UK: Macmillan, 2000.

Singh, M. "Measurement of Progress: 'Kill Ratio,' 'Body Counts,' and Other Performance Indicators." *The Australian Administrator* 10, no. 5 (1989): 1–7.

Singh, M., P. Kell, and A. Pandian. *Appropriating English: Innovation the English Language Teaching Business*. New York: Peter Lang, 2002.

Smith, N. "The Satanic Geographies of Globalization: Uneven Development in the 1990s." *Public Culture* 10 (1997): 169–89.

Soja, E. *Thirdspace: Journeys to Los Angeles and Other Real and Imagined Places*. Oxford: Blackwell Publishers, 1996.

Stiglitz, J. *Globalisation and Its Discontents*. Melbourne: Penquin, 2002.

Tomlinson, J. *Globalization and Culture*. Cambridge, UK: Polity Press, 1999.

Urry, J. *Consuming Places*. London: Routledge, 1995.

Waters, M. *Globalization*. London: Routledge, 1995.

Williams, R. *The Long Revolution*. London: Chatto and Windus, 1961.

———. *The Sociology of Culture*. New York: Schocken Books, 1982.

Williamson-Fien, J. "Constructing Asia: Foucauldian Explorations of Asian Studies in Australia." Unpublished PhD thesis, University of Queensland, 2000.

Yuen, E., D. Rose, and G. Katsiaficas, eds. *The Battle of Seattle: The New Challenge to Capitalist Globalization*. New York: Soft Skull Press, 2001.

# Chapter 2

# Globalizing the Young in the Age of Desire: Some Educational Policy Issues

Jane Kenway and Elizabeth Bullen

## Introduction

In discussing contemporary constructions of the young in the Minority World, or the overdeveloped countries of the West, this chapter draws particularly from theories of cultural globalization. It compares the competing resources for youthful identity building offered by the global corporate curriculum of consumer-media culture and that of schooling in corporatized education systems. It focuses on questions of pleasure, agency, and knowledge politics. In so doing, it will explain the difficulties education policy faces in gaining the consent of the young in the age of desire and points to the need for new and more sophisticated policy to help teachers to both enchant the classroom and problematize the corporate curriculum.

Parents, teachers, and policy makers are worried about today's young people. They are not what the young used to be, or should be, either at home or in the classroom. Teachers find that many young people have a "5D relationship" to schools. They are dissatisfied, disengaged, disaffected, disrespectful, and disruptive. When teachers try to explain this "5D relationship," they often blame the media, TV, advertising, computer games, the Internet, and more, generally, children's and youth popular culture (Kenway and Bullen, 2001).

A major issue for teachers and education systems is how to understand and engage these young people. Of equal importance is what and how to teach them in circumstances in which commercially produced children's culture and youth culture are hegemonic in young people's lives. It is our contention that in order to find out, teachers and education systems have to understand some of the big cultural and institutional patterns and shifts associated with the global market metanarrative, as these are now manifested economically, culturally, and politically. They must come to grips with what this means for young people's culture, adults' culture, and the cultures of schooling. Yet strangely, education systems, otherwise so responsive to certain economic imperatives of globalization, have made little attempt to understand what contemporary globalizing forces mean for the construction of youthful identities and the implications of such constructions for education. Rather, they have adopted a form of educational fundamentalism that shows an almost complete disregard for who the young are and might become.

Over the last two decades, education policy makers have witnessed the economic and technological turmoil of globalization and the associated restructuring (and destructuring) of the state and much institutional life. They have seen and overseen major political moves away from the welfare state and toward the values of the neoliberal and corporatized state. In a climate of global change and tax dollars being channeled to fund corporate welfare, prison camps, and militarism, education policy makers in many Western education systems are now trying to steer the young and the future according to tightly scripted systems of management, measurement, and marketing. Technologies of control and technologies of choice come together in a mix of public-sector superego and private-sector id. The pincer movement of "audit culture" (Strathern, 2000) and "promotional culture" (Wernick, 1991) squeezes the liveliness from schools and turns them into places of disenchantment for students and teachers alike.

These forces exert enormous pressure on teachers and principals. Firmly under others' control, they feel out of control themselves. It is no surprise in this context that many teachers long wistfully for traditional authority relations between teacher and student, that their talk is informed by a nostalgic and deficit view of the young, or that they sometimes feel schools are merely holding pens for "5D" students. Paradoxically, teachers' sense of being out of control and in need of more control is mirrored in the policy agendas to which they are subject. These agendas reach for certainty in the age of uncertainty. They suffer particularly from what Giddens (1994) calls "radical doubt" and "burgeoning institutional reflexivity," which produces rapid cycles of policy change. Yet despite this, policy makers remain oblivious to the fact that "kids are not what they used to be," that this results in complicated and often difficult relationships among young people, adults, and schools, and that current practices of schooling need to pay serious attention to this issue if they are to re-engage young people in education. This claim points to the need for research on every-day education that takes cultural globalization seriously.

## Globalization

Globalization is clearly a very controversial process and concept. The recent avalanche of literature from various fields has attempted to disentangle its processes and pin down its meaning. In education policy, there is an emerging research base and set of literature on globalization (e.g., Currie and Newson, 1998; Stromquist and Monkman, 1999). Such research suggests that education policy sociology is moving beyond its "embedded statism" (Tomlinson, 1999: 104) wherein the nation-state is naturalized as the "political power container" and as a primary "source of cultural identity." It is now open to examining reconfigurations of time and space, creating new spatialities and mobilities. Thus, education policy sociology now attends to the educational responses to, engagements with, and expressions of global flows of trade, investment, wealth, labor, people, information, and ideas. It takes more seriously the permeability of borders and boundaries as well as the effects of this permeability on place/policy relationships.

This chapter complements such work, but comes to the issues from a somewhat different angle. It focuses on some subtle links among cultural, political, and economic globalization that have not figured much in educational discussion. It is concerned with the global culture industries—in particular the children's market and its global (although uneven) reach, which allows it not only to distribute cultural goods all over the world but also to commodify children's lives and identities (and their schooling) in highly ambiguous ways with benefits and costs to children and their education. We are not arguing that the transnational cultural economy invokes standardization and homogenization but rather that it involves "complex connectivity" (Tomlinson, 1999). Our view is that cultural globalization deterritorializes and hybridizes mundane places and institutions. In so doing, it complicates their relationship to the cultural practices, experiences, and identities of those who occupy them. Alongside this, it offers new transnational cultural spaces and identifications and new ways of imagined belonging. At the same time, it reconfigures certain geometries of power and re-inscribes others.

Markets, information technologies, and communication media together hold a powerful and privileged position in today's globalizing culture, society, and economy. Kincheloe (1997: 254, 259) calls the combination of corporate influence and technological innovation "techno-power" and argues that it has been the catalyst for "a new era of consumption." We call the cultural form that arises from this blend of consumption, communication media, and information technologies "consumer-media culture." Here we wish to put on the research agenda some questions about the globalization of education, about pleasure and power, and about the scripting of young people's identities and adult/child relationships in consumer-media culture in the age of desire.

The market motif is now the guiding metaphor of our times. Market modalities have moved into many areas of life once understood as commerce-free. Commerce-saturated information and communication technologies are vital global distributors of market ideologies. They help to spread market gospel about the benefits of consumption as a way of life. They spread images of desire. Indeed, according to Jean-François Lyotard's (1993) notion of the libidinal economy, they both exploit and are driven by desire. The market motif seeks to persuade us that consumption and pleasure are one.

*The Libidinal Economy* (Lyotard, 1993) draws on Marx and Freud to theorize the operations of desire in the economy. The libidinal economy consists of social and market structures and dispositions that release, channel, and exploit desires and feelings (intensities), but never fully control them. Lyotard clarifies the duplicitous nature of these intensities in both sustaining and subverting the libidinous economy. Paradoxically, desire persists only as long as it remains unsatisfied. Such duplicities and paradoxes are characteristic of all political economies. Thus, as Williams (1998: 60) explains in his interpretation of this proposition:

> In simple terms, the entrepreneurial side of the capitalist economic system, or Capital, sees the energy of each feeling or desire as an opportunity, as something to be exploited. But the regulative, systematic, side of Capital needs to bring these individual desires and feelings into the system, through the power of comparison of monetary value. Therefore, Capital has a death drive, the drive to bend everything to

a common measure, and an Eros, the drive to move into novel zones, to discover new opportunities.

To put it another way, "the point of the desire to invest in new desires and feelings is monetary profit, the very thing that will then reduce its power" (Williams, 1998: 60). Profitability comes at the expense, as it were, of diminishing the desirability of the product. As a product is assimilated into the marketplace, it eventually generates less profit as its novelty and, thus, desirability diminishes.

We suggest a comparable tension is at work in the interaction of the consumption practices and identity politics of the individual and, indeed, in postmodernity itself. Consumer-media culture increasingly provides the means by which people take up their identities and interact with the world. Desire here is a "lack" that the individual seeks to fill though consumption, but which can never be satisfied. This is perhaps nowhere more evident than in the children's market and in young people's consumption practices, where one fad or fashion rapidly succeeds another. More broadly, Lash (cited in Featherstone, 1992: 69) signals the impact of desire in postmodernity itself when he notes its "emphasis on primary processes (desire) rather than secondary (ego); upon images rather than words; upon the immersion of the spectator and investment of desire in the object as opposed to the maintenance of distance." What we see here then is "an aesthetic of desire, sensation and immediacy" (Featherstone, 1992: 69).

This cultural shift signals a loss of differentiation or what might be more appropriately called de-differentiation. De-differentiation can be defined as "the erosion, effacement and elision of established hierarchies—high and low culture, education and training, politics and show business—and the blurring of what were formerly clear-cut entities" (Brown, 1995: 106–7). Such de-differentiation is occurring in children's culture and in their education. Indeed, as we have argued elsewhere, advertising, entertainment, and education are hybridizing (Kenway and Bullen, 2001). At the same, there is an oppositional trend toward fragmentation and "tribalization." Here we are talking about two main, if very disaggregated, "tribes"—adults and young people.

Consumer-media culture is hybridizing and "tribalizing" our lives in many subtle and complex ways that educators and policy makers need to know about. Why? Because these counter-forces make for at least some aspects of the complicated and often difficult relationships between young people and schools mentioned earlier. We are talking about how tribalization and hybridization intermesh with the power and pleasure dynamics involved. We are talking about new equity issues that arise as young people's lives and psyches are flooded with commodities, images, and market dogma. We are talking about the corporate curriculum delivered via consumer-media culture and the legitimacy crisis it creates for schools, teachers, and any curriculum that seeks to define citizenship broadly and in multiple ways. And, finally, we are talking about the predicaments and possibilities all these generate for educational policy and pedagogy in the twenty-first century.

## Pleasure and Power in the Global Cultural Curriculum

In children's consumer-media culture, identities are formed and knowledge is produced and legitimated. In many ways, corporate pedagogues have become postmodern society's most successful teachers. Their pedagogies are voluptuous and are consumed hungrily by the young. The corporate curriculum has become the yardstick against which all other curricula are judged and found wanting. Finally, it contributes to some difficult intergenerational dynamics that are likely to intensify in our globalizing educational environment.

Children's and young people's culture/entertainment/advertising has its own aesthetic. It is flashy, fast, frenetic, fantastic, and fun. Kids respond to its fantasy elements and humor. They use this hybrid form as a cultural resource with their friends—as a form of peer literacy. They are also offered the notions that they can gratify their needs, wants, and desires or solve their problems through consumption. Most important for our purposes, young people are offered identities as pleasure-seeking, self-indulgent, autonomous, rational decision makers—in effect, as adult-like children. And, because there is much in consumer-media culture generally that adults see as being unfit for children, it comes to represent an aura of irresistible power and danger.

Young people are encouraged to live only in the present, to delight in the impertinent and the forbidden, and to transgress adult codes. This world where "kids rule" resembles Bakhtin's (1968) concept of the carnivalesque, which Lechte (1990:105) defines "as a make-believe overturning of the law and existing social norms." Such transgressions of the social order produce a pleasure that Barthes (1975) calls *jouissance*. Factored together, the concepts of the carnivalesque and *jouissance* are particularly salient to how we might begin to understand the construction of youthful identities by consumer-media culture and in regard to the libidinous economy. For although such culture is characterized by subversion, perversion, inversion, diversion, and disorder, these transgressions are highly regulated and ultimately reinforce the status quo. In other words, the carnivalesque is a form of "ordered disorder" designed to socialize children into consumer culture. Because the *jouissance* it evokes is a "pleasure without separation," and because it involves a "momentary loss of subjectivity" (Grace and Tobin, 1997: 177), it is undiscriminating and acritical.

Such pleasures as consumer-media culture evokes come with both benefits and costs to children and their education. With the aid of advertising and new media forms, the market has offered children consumption as a primary motivating life force and cultural artifacts with which to construct their dreams, set their priorities, and solve their problems. It has offered them the basis on which to build their group's commonalities and their sense of others' differences, and on which to establish their personhood. It is undeniable that the kids' market exploits and profits from children. But, by and large, it engages and satisfies them over and over again. In this sense, it is very much unlike schools.

A feature of children's culture, then, is the way in which adults and schoolteachers are constructed vis-à-vis kids. Bazalgette and Buckingham (1995: 7) argue that much children's and youth television is "designed precisely to exclude adults and their values." It inverts many ideas associated with adult culture and binds children together as an audience defined in opposition to adults. Children's and youth media construct parents and teachers as dull or too earnest, usually disapproving, slightly ridiculous and unworthy of emulation.

While they are occasionally heroic, generally parents and teachers are subjected to well-justified rebellion and rejection. Indeed, school is constructed as an old-fashioned, puritanical, drab, and overdisciplined place where, dreadfully or ridiculously, children must be governed by others or be self-restrained.

What are the flow-on effects of this situation for schools? In segmenting children from adults, entertainment from education, and pleasure from schools and teachers, the corporate curriculum may have created school students who expect and get no pleasure from the formal aspects of schooling; a cohort of students who do not expect adults to say anything worthwhile except in purely instrumental terms; who are unlikely to take seriously what schools tell them; and who are unlikely to construct their identities through schools. There is also a further downside when it comes to knowledge.

## The Knowledge Politics of Children's Pleasures

The *jouissance* that children derive from consumer culture is designed to ensure that they unreflexively consume rather than interpret such texts. *Jouissance* is about producing a surge of affect, not the reflexive pleasure of knowing. By its very nature, children's consumer-media culture seeks not to operate at this level of the rationality. As Lee (1993: 143) says of the postmodern aesthetic, children's media culture "invites a fascination, rather than a contemplation, of its contents; it celebrates surfaces and exteriors rather than looking for or claiming to embody (modernist) depth." It also "transforms all cultural content into objects for immediate consumption rather than texts of contemplative reception or detached and intellectual interpretation." Indeed, consumer-media culture blurs the boundaries between data, information, knowledge, entertainment, and advertising. It bombards children with simulations (images) and simulacra (signs), which often have no referents.

According to Baudrillard's (1983) concepts of simulation and simulacra, hyperreality results when the simulated images or models and signs presented by the media begin to determine reality and our perception of it rather than represent it. Kincheloe (1997) believes that the postmodern child cannot avoid the effects of the hyperreality produced by electronic media saturation. As he explains it, in postmodernity "media-produced models replace the real—simulated TV kids on sitcoms replace real-life children as models of childhood" (Kincheloe, 1997: 45). Giroux (1997: 53–54) makes the point that "Unlike the often hard-nosed, joyless reality of schooling, children's films provide a high-tech visual space where adventure and pleasure meet in a fantasy world of possibilities and a commercial sphere of consumerism and commodification." However, hyperreality is not solely about fantasy and imagination: "Disneyland is more 'real' than fantasy because it now provides the image on which America constructs itself" (Giroux, 1997: 55).

We may well ask, as Kinder (1991: 35) does, what of "the impact [on children] of seeing an imaginary world so full of rich visual signifiers before having encountered their referents or acquired verbal language"? The transgressive content of much contemporary television is often satirical in intent, but this is frequently lost on young children. Adults and teachers in *South Park*, for instance, are routinely depicted as simply foolish. Kellner

(1997) cites examples of 12-year-olds imitating violent and dangerous behavior represented in *Beavis and Butthead*. This is a not only a consequence of immature critical skills. Many younger children have yet to experience the reality that the satire inverts in order to critique it. When an absence of referential experience combines with the decontextualizing effect of hyperreality, the capacity of satire to successfully resist dominating discourses is neutralized. Its effect is dependent on knowledge of the reality satire inverts.

The more recent phenomenon of reality TV further blurs the boundaries between reality and hyperreality. In a discussion of reality television, Baudrillard (2001) comments on the "artificial microcosm" of a French equivalent to *Big Brother*.

> [T]he *Loft Story* is similar to Disneyland which gives the illusion of a real world, a world out-there, whereas both Disney's world and the world outside of it are mirror images of one another. All of the United States is [in] Disneyland. And we, in France, are all inside the *Loft*. No need to enter reality's virtual reproduction. We are already in it. The televisual universe is merely a holographic detail of the global reality.

Programming like *Big Brother* not only presents an illusion of lived reality, it involves the audience in a process of "interactive exclusion" that is also used in *Australian Idol, American Idol,* and their international equivalents. There is a comparable logic of exchange between audience and contestant that Ojajärvi identifies in the quiz show *The Weakest Link*. Ojajärvi (2001: 477) argues that *The Weakest Link* represents a "commodified form of play," the "main seduction" of which "is the dwindled and distorted potential space offered by its ultimate, destructive, and in the last analysis sado-masochistic logic of exchange" between participants. Teachers meanwhile are identifying schoolyard exclusion practices based on *Big Brother* and *The Weakest Link*.

When it comes to the difference and inequalities of "real life," the world that consumer-media culture presents to children is often already dehistoricized, a place where class, ethnic, sexuality, race, and gender struggles are ignored. Children are seldom offered the pleasures of reflexive knowing or a sense of agency derived from recognizing how their meanings, identities, and affective investments are produced. The potential pleasures of becoming informed and active citizens within the politics of consumption are usually overridden by the pleasures of fantasy. Further, the historically decontextualizing and self-referential processes of consumer-media culture also mean that the knowledge that children do acquire is contained within the bubble.

Seiter (1995: 134) concedes that in this regard, the utopianism of children's commercial television "can also serve to mask the fact that participation in the unity and community of entertainment has always been unequal, exclusionary. Entertainment's optimism about community can deny the real hardships discrimination creates."

Like Seiter, Jakubowicz et al. (1994) identify the racial, gender, and class hierarchies encoded in media simulations, noting the dominance of images of white boys and blonde girls. They acknowledge the improved representation of African Americans and Asian Americans in U.S. advertising—albeit confined to certain positions in the media text—and suggest that, with the easing of regulations on overseas content, this change has impacted positively on Australian commercial television. However, they also point out that minorities, including Southeast Asian, Aboriginal, Polynesian, and Maori groups, remain largely unrepresented on Australian TV in much the same way as American Indian and Hispanic actors have been excluded in the United States. Simulation of other ethnicities in Australian advertising is often stereotypical, with "almost no-one who looks like a southern European or Arab-Australian unless they are being parodied in some food ads" (Jakubowicz et al., 1994: 100).

Not surprisingly, the global corporate curriculum does not teach kids anything at all about how it is both produced and consumed. It screens from view the "night-time of the commodity"—the economic modes and practices associated with production and consumption. As Lee (1993: 15) explains:

> The ways in which commodities converge and collect in the market, their untarnished appearance as they emerge butterfly-like from the grubby chrysalis of production, the fact that they appear to speak only about themselves as objects and not about the social labor of their production is ultimately what constitutes the fetishism of commodities. The sphere of production is thus the night-time of the commodity: the mysterious economic dark side of social exploitation which is so effectively concealed in the dazzling glare of the market-place.

With regard to production, young people do not hear about exploited labor, Majority World sweatshops, child labor, corporate greed, and the corporate colonization of both public space and the popular psyche, let alone about corporate welfare and its negative implications for public services such as education. Equally, the corporate curriculum teaches no lessons about how consumption works; how consuming is equated with the good life; how advertising constructs their desires, identities, and values;

how other values of citizenship are pushed to one side. It is our view that schools should challenge the dominance of consumption as a way of life and help kids to find other satisfying codes to live by.

## Issues for Policy and Pedagogy

In our contemporary technologizing, marketizing, commodifying, hybridizing, tribalizing world, education policy makers face some moral dilemmas and urgent questions. Judging from the number of disaffected students, just managing, marketing, and measuring is not enough. So what general issues does the construction of youthful identities by consumer-media culture pose for education policies about pedagogy, curriculum, and school leadership? With regard to pedagogy, it leads us to ask how best to teach across the generation gap that exists among young people's culture and adults' culture. Indeed, we might ask, what can teachers learn about good teaching, pleasure, and the young from the corporate world? The curriculum issues that arise include the following: How can schools help students to explore the differences between information, advertising, entertainment, data, knowledge, and education? How can schools help the young to explore a sense of agency and citizenship beyond that made available through the media and consumption? How can school leaders best address the moral and educational dilemmas created by the competing pressures of school finance, corporate relations, and education? Overall, what is the role of education in the age of desire?

We are not in a position to answer all these questions here. Suffice is to say, schools might adopt a critical and ethical approach to consumer-media culture and their own relationship with it. They might become more reflexive about their collaboration with the corporate pedagogues. But, equally, they can take young people's pleasure and power seriously—which of course is to ask a great deal. Nonetheless, it is our view that the politics and pedagogies of engagement with consumer culture are vital for young people in schools. Several aspects of consumer culture are integral to such engagement: the cultural dimensions of the economy (the use of material goods as communicators), the economy of cultural goods (the market principles of supply, demand, capital accumulation, competition, and monopolization), and the "night-time of the commodity" (the concrete social relations involved in the production of commodities). Such political and pedagogical engagement recognizes the wide range of human motivations that consumer culture invokes. Students do need to understand how consumer culture works with and against them, and when and how to oppose it, to comprehend what else is possible and how these possibilities may be made real.

Schools have a responsibility to teach kids about what it means to be scripted within the global corporate curriculum and how they might re-script themselves differently as youthful global citizens. This is easier said than done. The challenge is to help young people to see the downside of media-consumer culture, the contradictory tensions within the libidinous economy, without destroying their pleasures in it; to combine the critical and ethical in ways that are pleasurable and empowering. Taking heed of how hybridization works in media-consumer culture means learning how to blend the playful and the earnest. To do so, we can begin with furthering our understanding of the 5D generation.

## References

Bakhtin, M. *Rabelais and His World*. Translated by H. Iswolsky. Cambridge: MIT Press, 1968.

Barthes, R. *The Pleasure of the Text*. Translated by R. Miller. New York: Hill and Wang, 1975.

Baudrillard, J. *Simulations*. Translated by P. Foss, P. Patton, and P. Beitchman. New York: Semiotext(e), 1983.

———. *Dust Breeding*. Ctheory 2001 [cited 29 September 2003]. Available from www.ctheory.net/text_file.asp?pick=293.

Bazalgette, C., and D. Buckingham. "The Invisible Audience." In *In Front of the Children: Screen Entertainment and Young Audiences*, edited by C. Bazalgette and D. Buckingham. London: British Film Institute, 1995.

Brown, S. *Postmodern Marketing*. London: Routledge, 1995.

Currie, J., and J. Newson, eds. *Universities and Globalisation: Critical Perspectives*. Thousand Oaks, CA: Sage Publications, 1998.

Featherstone, M. *Consumer Culture and Postmodernism*. London: Sage, 1992.

Giddens, A. *Beyond Left and Right: The Future of Radical Politics*. Stanford: Stanford University Press, 1994.

Giroux, H. "Are Disney Movies Good for Your Kids?" In *Kinder-Culture: The Corporate Construction of Childhood*, edited by S. Steinberg and J. Kincheloe. Boulder, CO: Westview Press, 1997.

Grace, D., and J. Tobin. "Carnival in the Classroom: Elementary Students Making Videos." In *Making a Place for Pleasure in Early Childhood Education*, edited by J. Tobin. New Haven: Yale University Press, 1997.

Jakubowicz, A., H. Goodall, J. Martin, T. Mitchell, L. Randall, and K. Seneviratne. *Racism, Ethnicity and the Media*. St. Leonards, Australia: Allen and Unwin, 1994.

Kellner, D. "Beavis and Butt-Head: No Future for Postmodern Youth." In *Kinder-Culture: The Corporate Construction of Childhood*, edited by S. Steinberg and J. Kincheloe. Boulder, CO: Westview Press, 1997.

Kenway, J., and E. Bullen. *Consuming Children: Education—Entertainment—Advertising*. Buckingham, UK: Open University Press, 2001.

Kincheloe, J. "McDonald's, Power, and Children: Ronald McDonald (Aka Ray Kroc) Does It All for You." In *Kinder-Culture: The Corporate Construction of Childhood*, edited by S. Steinberg and J. Kincheloe. Boulder, CO: Westview Press, 1997.

Kinder, M. *Playing with Power in Movies, Television and Video Games: From Muppet Babies to Teenage Mutant Ninja Turtles*. Berkeley: University of California Press, 1991.

Lechte, J. *Julia Kristeva*. London: Routledge, 1990.

Lee, M. *Consumer Culture Reborn: The Cultural Politics of Consumption*. London: Routledge, 1993.

Lyotard, J. F. *The Libidinal Economy*. Bloomington: Indiana University Press, 1993.

Ojajärvi, J. "The Weakest Link and the Commodification of Subjectivity by the Means of Play." *Cultural Values* 5, no. 4 (2001): 477–89.

Seiter, E. *Sold Separately: Children and Parents in Consumer Culture*. New Brunswick, NJ: Rutgers University Press, 1995.

Strathern, M., ed. *Audit Cultures: Anthropological Studies in Accountability, Ethics and the Academy*. London: Routledge, 2000.

Stromquist, N., and K. Monkman, eds. *Globalisation and Education: Integration and Contestation across Cultures*. Lanham, MD: Rowman and Littlefield, 2000.

Tomlinson, J. *Globalisation and Culture*. Cambridge, UK: Polity Press, 1999.

Wernick, A. *Promotional Culture*. London: Sage, 1991.

Williams, J. *Lyotard: Towards a Postmodern Philosophy*. Cambridge, UK: Polity Press, 1998.

# Chapter 3

# Cultural Pedagogies of Technology in a Globalized Economy

Helen Nixon

## Introduction

The new technologies of information and communication (ICTs) have been thoroughly implicated in some of the big cultural shifts associated with globalization. Innovations in the microchip, digitization, and computer networking have enabled the creation of global flows of capital that have given rise to transitions in the globalized *information* economy (Castells, 1996). ICTs have also been central to the global flows of people, ideas, signs, and images that have given form or substance to the global *cultural* economy (Appadurai, 1990). In this context, many nations across the globe have developed policies in relation to IT, telecommunications, and new media, mobilizing the cliché of "blurring boundaries" to restructure and destructure the relationship between policies governing the economy, culture, and education. In this process, the IT telecommunications industries have become central to economic policy; and multimedia software development has been foregrounded in cultural policy. ICTs have become key to the marketization of education internationally and central to debates about curriculum and pedagogy across all levels of education. Pressures to shift education into the "postindustriall" or "information" age come from multiple sources, and education sectors now face multiple and profound challenges that are still being debated and worked through.

In this chapter it is not my objective to focus on the impact of global-ization and ICTs on curriculum and pedagogy within institutionalized education. Rather, I examine changing relationship between the globalized IT, telecommunications, media, and culture industries and government economic, cultural, and education policies. The focus is on how these have together worked to produce cultural pedagogies of everyday life (Kellner, 1995) that associate ICTs with successful educational and social life trajectories. I explore how these cultural pedagogies have discursively yoked together a number of ideas about ICT-related education and na-tional productivity and constructed powerful public stories about national and individual success in a global cultural economy. However, I argue that there are discursive tensions and contradictions inherent in these pair-ings and these stories that point to ideological and political tensions about social power (Fairclough, 1992).

In public policy and media discourse, young people the world over are constructed as needing to be computer- and media-literate for the sake of their nation's future in the changing global economy. At the same time, these policies suggest that they need to participate as entrepreneurs in global IT, telecommunications, media industries, and cultures. The first goal—the creation of young clever and computer-literate workers—can potentially be achieved by mandating an appropriate curriculum within the public education system. In contrast, in order for young people to be-come global entrepreneurs and techno-tycoons, they need access to differ-ent kinds of cultural and symbolic capital (Bourdieu, 1986) than that which is available to all social groups or can be acquired within institu-tionalized education. The examination of ICTs and education discussed in this chapter highlights the powerful presence of new cultural pedagogies within a globalized cultural economy. At the same time, it suggests the necessity of planning for curriculum and pedagogy in formalized educa-tion that works with and against such cultural pedagogies.

## The Cultural Pedagogies of Media Culture

This chapter proceeds on the basis of theoretical assumptions drawn from educational sociologists (Bourdieu and Passeron, 1977), media theorists (Kellner, 1995) and cultural feminists (Luke, 1996) that the media per-form a public or cultural *pedagogic* function alongside the institutions of the family and the school. Accordingly, pedagogy is a broader concept than school-based teaching. Rather, pedagogy is:

redefined as a broader "articulatory concept," one allowing us to make connections between a diverse range of cultural production—from literature to licence plates, from media to maps—all of which continuously rewrite our sense of legitimate knowledge, subjectivity and social relations. (Morgan, 1993: 39–40)

The media today are central to such cultural production. We operate within a globalized, high-tech culture in which the media "contribute to educating us how to behave and what to think, feel, believe, fear, and desire—and what not to" (Kellner, 1995: 2). Understood from this perspective, the media are sources of stories and other symbolic forms that educate people about how to buy, consume, negotiate, and value commodities and services within everyday life. In this respect, the media function as one of the "pedagogies of everyday life" (Luke, 1996). They offer characters, plots, and textual forms "out of which plots can be formed of imagined lives" (Appadurai, 1990: 299). They provide the very materials out of which people forge their identities, make decisions, and take social actions that have material consequences.

Moreover, the media also act as cultural mediators in many arenas of social life, including institutionalized politics. They mediate the changes being effected through transitions in contemporary practices of globalization. They inform audiences about the present transition from a world constituted by print, film, and video to one that increasingly consists of multi-mediated mesh-worked computers and virtually invisible microprocessor-operated communications media and multiple forms of information collection, retrieval, and dissemination. Such mediation of changing media environments is carried out as part of the commercially motivated promotion and selling of computer hardware and software to homes, workplaces, or educational sites through advertising. Journalism also serves a key function in creating readers as publics who "need to know" about ICTs, new media, and their the potential social and cultural value.

The system of journalism is important precisely because it "connects readerships to other systems, such as those of politics, economics, and social control" (Hartley, 1995: 23). However, government departments also play a key role in the changing of media environments. Key ideas that emanate from government departments about the "meaning" of ICTs and the information economy for society are largely mediated to the public in press releases to the news media and in government-produced "information" brochures, websites, and various forms of advertising. In the large and complex repertoires of stories and images that constitute national and transnational mediascapes, "the world of commodities and the world of 'news' and politics are profoundly mixed" (Appadurai, 1990: 299). At the same time, new forms of pedagogy and new sites of education are created, promoted, and naturalized.

## ICTs and the Creation of a Clever and Competitive Nation

The early 1990s were important years in history for government responses to and expressions of the global cultural economy. For instance, in 1994 the Australian Labor government commissioned several reports about that nation's position in the global information economy (Commonwealth of Australia, 1994a, 1994b) and produced its first cultural policy, *Creative Nation* (Commonwealth of Australia, 1994c). The following is typical of the emphasis in commissioned reports on the need to harness the creative potential of Australians in relation to information networks in order to be competitive within the restructured globalized economy:

> Australia has a *competitive advantage* in its educated and skilled workforce, its rapidly strengthening business export culture, its multicultural population, and its proximity to large and growing markets. These opportunities demand that Australia harnesses its *creative potential* and ensures its population is well equipped to exploit the important role information networks are playing in our society. (Commonwealth of Australia, 1994a, italics added)

Such reports acknowledged that the achievement of this national economic goal would, however, require significant and widespread social and cultural change. It was envisaged that cultural attitudes as well as vast arenas of social life would need to change and adapt in line with the proposed shift to broadband service provision:

> To take full advantage of the technologies and services, industry and society will need to integrate them into the activities—a complete *re-engineering of processes* rather than just using new technologies to perform current tasks. [...] A real *commitment to change* will be necessary, in professional roles, organizational structures, and social and cultural attitudes. (Commonwealth of Australia, 1994b, italics added)

Education was thus explicitly linked with communications and culture in government rhetoric, and together these sectors were seen to make up "Australia's most successful export industries" (Commonwealth of Australia, 1994a). Moreover, moves were made to shape institutionalized education so that it supported the federal goal of re-engineering society for global competitiveness. Accordingly, ICTs were made central to debates not only about economic policy, but also to debates about education policy and education futures. At the same time, the federal government assumed the role of "educating" the public about the envisaged changes required in social and cultural attitudes. This pedagogic role was largely achieved through press releases and the creation of websites.

Successive governments, both neoliberal and neoconservative, have continued to place the new ICTs at the core of both economic *and* educational policy, consistently arguing that "as we move into the twenty-first century, economic, political and social processes will become increasingly knowledge and information based" (Alston, 1998). The following section examines the evolution and popularization of a nationwide online educational network known as EdNA, Education Network Australia. It is an example of how government policy about education, curriculum, and pedagogy in relation to ICTs has been shaped by the perceived imperatives of the global cultural economy.

## Government Policy and EdNA

After examining seven case-study countries, Selwyn and Brown (2000: 661) found that a common response to economic globalization was the creation of national information infrastructures. Government-funded educational networking initiatives were often an integral and pioneering feature in the production of such infrastructures. They provided the public subsidies to underwrite the development by private enterprise of these new technologies, often at huge cost to public education organizations, their staff, and students when they frequently performed below expectations, or completely failed. Similarly, soon after the production of reports proclaiming that Australia needed to become a networked nation, it was announced that the national government and the states and territories had agreed in principle to the development of Education Network Australia, or EdNA. The key objectives of EdNA indicated an amalgam of interests that combined academic/educational, social justice/public interest, and economic/commercial imperatives (Nixon, 1999). However, the stated objectives of EdNA most frequently referred to its anticipated economic outcomes. In particular, the stated goal was to coordinate and contain the costs of the use of interactive computer networks for educational purposes by state governments, nongovernment schools, the vocational and training sector, the higher education sector, and the adult and community education sectors.

By February 1996, an initial version of EdNA, managed by the Open Learning Technology Corporation, was made available for public access on the Internet. The newly stated aims of EdNA made more specific reference to what the network might mean for teachers and learners in the education sectors operating within a globalized world:

> One of the key aims of EdNA is to ensure that teachers and students throughout Australia are able to benefit fully from the information age. It will enable them to access and share information and ideas across the education sectors, across geographical borders and around the world. (EdNA, 1996)

The objectives of EdNA assumed the existence of a causal relationship between teachers' access to and the creative pedagogical use of the Internet. It was also implied that such changing pedagogical use of ICTs would automatically generate Australian-based, globally competitive, online education content that would in turn provide "the basis for an export industry in education software" (EdNA, 1996). Statements made by the Minister for Schools, Vocational Education, and Training at the official launch of EdNA in 1997 reinforced the message that the development and use of ICTs was central to ICT-related changes within society, especially the marketization of education within a globalized economy:

> These technologies are not just the latest but are tools to apply to *improving performance*. They help us *keep ahead of the game* and offer exciting possibilities for the way in which we learn, work and live together in our society. It is pleasing to see energy and commitment in all sectors of *the Australian education market* on this issue. (Ellison, 1997, italics added)

A discourse of marketing became central to the promotion of EdNA. Benefits of EdNA for the community, as described on its home page, included the provision of "one stop shop" for courses and programs online (EdNA, 1998). Assumed benefits for content providers included the claim that "EdNA is a significant Australian education marketplace [providing] access to markets." Finally, the benefits of EdNA for teachers, students, and parents were described using the language of positional advantage (Bridges, 1994). EdNA promised "to help teachers and students connect across Australia and internationally to find and use information and be smart about learning," as well as promising parents "a way to assist your child's learning from home" (EdNA, 1998). Hence the language of business and education, along with the shop, home, and the school, became interchangeable. The provision of an online educational service promised to provide competitive advantage to businesses, school communities, and households alike. At the same time, it was suggested that the pedagogies of teachers as well as parents would need to change if they were to provide educational success and improved life chances for young people. It was implied that the pedagogies of the new ICT-mediated media culture would assist the education of the younger generations in their living rooms and bedrooms at home.

The envisaged economic and educational opportunities provided by globalization have continued to maintain the government's focus on the development of a more productive national online education network into the twenty-first century. A key goal is to produce pedagogical change by enabling online curriculum delivery. To this effect, the EdNA Schools Advisory Group (2000) produced an "action plan" for education within the information economy whose objectives were to be achieved in part by the Schools Online Curriculum Content Initiative (SOCCI). The Ministerial Council of Education, Employment, Training and Youth Affairs (MCEETYA) instructed its ministerial companies Curriculum Corporation (curriculum materials) and education.au limited (electronic networks) to undertake feasibility studies into SOCCI. The emphasis was on investigating its potential contribution to the economy, to education, and to the production of skilled and knowledgeable workers and citizens for an unknown (and unknowable) future. In addition to providing a public subsidy for the private IT industry, SOCCI, it is argued, would

[m]ake a significant contribution to Australia's innovations agenda, in terms of: the *stimulation it will provide to ICT developers in Australia*; its synergy with work across the education sectors; and in terms of the knowledge, experience and skills it will develop in Australian students. (Schools Online Curriculum Content Initiative, 2001: 3, italics added)

In January 2001 the federal government announced its *Backing Australia's Ability: Innovation Action Plan* (Commonwealth of Australia, 2001), which promised AUS\$34.1 million in public funding for SOCCI for the period 2001–2006. An equivalent level of funding is anticipated from the states and territories. The "fixing" of knowledge on online packages contrasts with the dynamism of the technologies delivering never-ending changes. This contradiction is reflected in the goal for SOCCI, namely to supply "high quality educational content…so that Australian learners gain maximum benefits from the online revolution" (SOCCI, 2001: 3). The "fundamental educational values" that underpin the SOCCI plan include:

the value of learners… building on prior learning, and education as a foundation for active, productive participation in our democracy and community, with an imperative of developing habits, skills and understanding for such active participation. (SOCCI, 2001: 12)

The rearticulation of government economic, cultural, and education policy discourse is evident in the publicly funded stimulation of the IT industry undertaking through the evolution of a nationwide online education network. The preceding brief examination of these changes and continuity in politics, business, and education demonstrates the intimate relationship between national and global imperatives and the blurring of the distinctions between national and global boundaries. Government economic, cultural, and educational objectives are made manifest through these developments in ICTs. It also indicates how changing ideas about education and pedagogy have been discursively linked with changing the identities of young people to enhance their success within a "network society" (Castells, 1996). Within policy discourse it is young people who are creative. They possess intellectual and technological knowledge, understanding, and skills, and so will be key to the nation becoming favorably positioned within a competitive, globalized, high-tech cultural economy. Most important, much of this imagining of new forms of ICT-related education and pedagogy envisaged for the younger generation is conveyed to parents, teachers, and the general public through the press, television news, and government websites. The following section discusses how a slightly different message was relayed to the broader public in stories of successful young ICT-users that circulated in the news media during the same period (1996–2001).

## ICTs and Successful Life Trajectories in a Globalized World

I have argued that the cultural pedagogies of the media, advertising, and promotion, which operate on behalf of both institutional politics and the business sector (Kellner, 1995), have been key to the task of educating teachers and parents about how young people might best be prepared for participation in future national economic success within a global cultural economy. This section explores the operation of cultural pedagogies in media stories about one young entrepreneur's use of ICTs that worked alongside the governmental policy process described above. In relative terms, stories about children and youth do not rate highly in terms of their press "newsworthiness" (Jackson, 1993). However, since the mid-1990s, media stories about successful ICT-using children and youth have appeared in sections of newspapers devoted to business, computers, and high technology and in other popular media such as magazines. Moreover, some young people have been the subject of repeated stories about ICT-related educational, financial, and social success circulating in newspapers, magazines, and on radio and television (Nixon, 1999). As de Certeau (1984: 147) argues, such media narratives about children's successful ICT-related educational and social trajectories perform important cultural and ideological work in everyday life precisely because they are part of that "machinery by which a society represents itself in living beings and makes them its representations."

## Schoolboy and IT Company CEO Alex Hartman

Alex Hartman is a young person who has come to represent the idealized social subject of the postindustrial information society constructed as such in media stories about him that have circulated since 1996. Hartman was an urban schoolboy of 15 when news of his computer-related success first appeared in the national press (Bogle, 1996). My analysis of radio, television, newspaper, and magazine reports and websites 1996–2002 shows that Hartman's achievements have come to stand for what the dominant discourses of government policy held up to be an exemplar of the new generation. He is valued as having the attributes, skills, and competencies required by all young people in order to construct a "clever country" in the globalized information age.

On his website and in his published writing, Alex Hartman has also positioned himself this way. On an early version of his website home page he described himself as "the proud product of Sydney, Australia, the Olympic city" (Hartman, 1997a). He asked his readers to absorb the significance of a young man being taken on by the telecommunications company Telstra, a semi-government IT company, which bought from him the licence to use his Internet software product InfiNET as the user interface software for their BigPond Cable Network during 1998–1999. Similarly, in a feature article titled "True Blue in the Brave New Digital World" (Hartman, 1997b), published in a national newspaper on Australia Day, Hartman positioned himself as representative of his *generation* of youth as he explained the important place of ICTs in the nation's future.

> It is my generation of Australians, the teenagers of today, who will lead this nation into the next century. We are a generation of multicultural and diverse-thinking youths who will provide Australia with its first president and who will enable Australia to remain unique and identifiable through global communication revolutions and movements for internationality. (Hartman, 1997b: 9)

In this article Hartman (1997b: 9) explicitly posits the global information superhighway as potential component and index of *national* identity when he places it alongside the "legacy of dreamtimes, bushrangers, pioneers, diggers and bronzed lifesavers." Thus Hartman's story illustrates an understanding that national and global identities need to be understood in "relational" terms (Featherstone, 1993). Further, as Hartman's business expanded, media stories about him as a successful young *Australian* also emphasized the transnational and *global* elements of his life as a "jetsetting teenager [who] regularly commutes between Sydney, Beijing, and his office in San Francisco" (Tsavdaridis, 1999). Such discursive constructions worked to reinforce for media audiences the importance of young people projecting themselves into the global business arena in the interests of national economic success and in order to establish successful life trajectories.

A key feature of most media stories about Hartman has been the explicit connection made between his success at school and his success in the world of global business enterprise. This message is congruent with government policy rhetoric. The implication or "lesson" is that IT-literate students who work hard at school will also have a head start to success in the worlds of work and business. However, discursive slippage within the media stories illustrate political and ideological tensions about social power contained within these constructions (Fairclough, 1992).

At the age of 16, Hartman was reported to be "just another schoolboy" (Banaghan, 1996). However, far from being representative of other young Australians, he was reported to have "rare gifts" in academic and sporting pursuits (Bogle, 1996). Moreover, he attended a long-established, prestigious private school for boys and his house was described as being "on Sydney's North Shore," the home of the nation's elites. These media representations hint at the tensions inherent in neoliberal struggles against equality of opportunity, especially in relation to education and ICTs. Many societies are increasingly socially and economically divided due to the negative effects of the political and cultural economy of globalization (Australian Bureau of Statistics, 2000). Hartman's educational success was connected with a number of cultural signifiers of high income and social status. At the same time, he was also a hardworking employee and employer outside school. He worked on the weekends at a computer store to earn the capital he needed to launch his product and to employ his "team of 20 casual programmers and graphic designers—mostly university students—to write the software while he devotes his energy to concepts and strategies" (Bogle, 1996). However, the inherent contradiction here is that these achievements are hardly typical of 16-year-old school-boys, and they require knowledge and skills, as well as economic and social capital that are unlikely to be acquired within formal schooling.

Hartman's successful operation in both the worlds inside and outside school, and inside and outside the nation, are central structuring elements in the linguistic and visual semiotics of early news reports about him. In one story, Hartman (age 17) was represented in the photo caption as "Computer whiz-kid Alex Hartman…'I love school and I love business' " (Gibbs, 1997). Despite this yoking together discursively of success in school and in business, other aspects of the news story highlighted the contradictions inherent in this pairing. They pointed to the atypical nature of Hartman's access to the economic and cultural capital associated with the ICT-related business sector: "after initially struggling to find resources for his after-school business operation, Alex is now set to take on the world with the backing of huge computer companies including Apple and Packard Bell" (Gibbs, 1997: 3). Nonetheless, an implied connection between Hartman's success at school and his ICT-related success in the wider world continued to be a feature of media stories about him even after he had finished his formal schooling. Hartman was then typically described as a global tycoon and multimillionaire "whose empire began at school" (Tsavdaridis, 1999).

Although Hartman was successful at school, and although he gained university entrance qualifications, he achieved this without access to the kind of online curriculum and pedagogy envisaged for future young Australians in government policy. On the other hand, Hartman did have a good deal of prior knowledge, skills, and experience with ICTs, as well as powerful business and social contacts, which together assisted him to achieve national and global success. By senior secondary school, these prior skills, experiences, and contacts included having worked in a computer store at the age of 14, forming his own software company to produce an Internet product invented at age 14, outsourcing the work and employing university students as casual labor, explicitly aligning his goals with nationalist economic and cultural policy goals, and winning support from major transnational IT companies to assist him to establish an IT company that operated in a globally competitive environment.

By 2000, Hartman had won the National Career Achievement Category in the Young Australian of the Year Awards. He remained chief executive officer (CEO) of Amicus Software Company from 1995 until 2001, by which time he had sold his company, which by then had offices in Sydney, London, and San Francisco. That year, at the age of 21, he returned to Australia and took up the position of chair of the Youth Hub committee, part of the IT Skills Hub supported by major ITandT companies, but established with the financial support of the Commonwealth Department of Education, Science and Training (DEST) and the National Office for the Information Economy (NOIE). The Youth Hub website lists some of Hartman's current IT-related positions, which include founder of Mytek Pty. Ltd. computer services company; manager, technology at Gresham Advisory Partners, a leading merchant bank; joint CEO of Indicum Pty. Ltd., broker of IT consulting services; and columnist for a business news magazine. He also sits on the National Innovation Awareness Council, which reports to the federal minister for science and minister for industry, tourism, and resources.

Media stories about the young adult Hartman continue to play a cultural pedagogic role for his fellow citizens. They emphasize the centrality of ICT-related skills and knowledge to a successful educational and life trajectory in the global cultural economy. The media report that announced Hartman's new role as chair of the Youth Hub highlighted his authoritative position in regard to ICT-related national and individual success. His assumed authority on this topic was emphasized in the photograph's caption, which noted that "Mr. Hartman says IT skills will soon be seen as fundamental as literacy" (Foreshaw, 2001: 35).

This Youth Hub is a federal government initiative that has enlisted as its committee nine successful young people under the age of 25 who work in the IT professions. In his role as chair of the committee, Hartman has become an integral part of a government-funded national online initiative that performs a somewhat different function from EdNA and the Schools Online Curriculum Content Initiative discussed earlier. The Youth Hub, which aims to provide new forms of ICT-related pedagogy for the nation's youth, was conceived:

> to address the needs of today's youth as well as the future ITandT demands in Australia by engaging the longer-term source of supply—the youth market....
>
> Aimed at the 15 to 25 year old market, the Youth Hub provides a pathway for students to achieve a successful transition from school to further education, training and employment. (IT Skills Hub, 2001)

The main objective of the Youth Hub is to teach young people the value of a career in IT for the future of the nation as a basis for success in their future life. It also aims to inform young people about the kinds of skills and knowledge required to be successful in this sector of the business world:

> IT underpins every aspect of our lives from entertainment, transport, health, education, communication and industry. IT careers not only involve technology, but depend on creativity, commercial and marketing insight, project management capabilities, and an understanding of human behavior and needs.

> IT careers provide enormous long and short-term prospects, portability and excitement for young Australians. (IT Skills Hub, 2001)

However, the Youth Hub carries out its cultural pedagogic function using the language of consumer media culture to emphasize the differences rather than the similarities between industrial education provided in schools and postindustrial education acquired in the outside world. For example, the introduction to the "About Us" page of the Youth Hub website opens with the following:

> Brian Donovan, the CEO of the IT Skills Hub, does Iyengar yoga on Tuesday nights with his daughter, Kirsty. Alex Hartman, the Chairperson of the Youth Hub Committee, has seen the movie *The Matrix* 23 times. Want to find out more hard facts about what goes on behind closed doors? (IT Skills Hub, 2001)

Such enticements designed to encourage participation in informal communication and "personal" relationships are familiar in popular media culture. Similarly, the site "teaches lessons" to its young visitors about IT as a desirable and enjoyable career using a language and format familiar to print magazines and magazine-style radio and television programs. This can be seen in the invitation to "Party your way into an IT career" via the Dance Hub section of the site (which hosts a school Dance Party competition). Elsewhere it promises access to "Case Studies, to News and Events, to lifestyle stories and everything in between" when you register as a member of the Youth Hub.

## Conclusion

In this chapter, I have argued that today's high-tech media culture performs powerful pedagogic work on behalf of both institutionalized politics and the business sector. Although this pedagogic work supplements the pedagogic work of the family and the school, it may be becoming more dominant because of the pervasiveness of the media in all aspects of social life. The operation of such powerful pedagogies provides complex challenges for educators charged with the responsibility of constructing learning environments in the traditional sites of formalized schooling and higher education.

First, it illustrates the permeable borders that now exist among formalized education, government departments, and the market. Second, the operation of the cultural pedagogies of media culture is indicative of a shifting locus of "authority" in relation to education from public institutions to the commercial sector. Third, the pedagogies of global consumer media culture make problematic for educators the task of devising "new pedagogies" of critique and opposition in the context of the political and cultural economy of globalization. They produce enchanting enticements for children and young people that educators need to study, learn from, and exploit (see Kenway and Bullen, 2001, and this volume).

My analysis has drawn on two cases of the operation of cultural pedagogies in relation to ICTs and education to demonstrate how these have become not only *economically* but also *semiotically* bound up with the social construction of new visions of educated and productive transnational entrepreneurs and workers. This is partly due to the operation of flows of signs, ideas, and images enabled by a global cultural economy facilitated by ICTs and underwritten by government subsidies of public capital.

The two cases discussed in this chapter illustrate how media culture has served to naturalize the global cultural economy for the public. Media narratives like those associated with Alex Hartman assisted the project of nation building in a time of global competitiveness. Specifically, they have allowed the nation-state to represent itself through successful young people and make these young people its representatives who operate successfully on the global economic stage.

At the same time, however, these media representatives embody the discursive and ideological tensions inherent in attempts to tell stories about equality of opportunity in relation to education and ICTs in a society that is increasingly socially divided, due to the negative effects of the political and cultural economy of globalization.

Paradoxically, it is the very same global high-tech media culture that enables and performs such cultural pedagogic work about IT-related national and individual success that also exacerbates the differential access of Australians to IT-related economic and cultural capital.

# References

Alston, R. *Towards an Australian Strategy for the Information Economy.* July 29, 1998 [cited August 12, 1998]. Available from www.noie.gov.au.

Appadurai, A. "Disjuncture and Difference in the Global Cultural Economy." in *Global Culture. Nationalism, Globalization and Modernity*: edited by M. Featherstone, 295–310. London: Sage Publications, 1990.

Australian Bureau of Statistics. *Use of the Internet by Householders, Australia.* Vol. August (Cat. No. 8147.0). Canberra: Australian Government Printer, 2000.

Banaghan, M. "'Just Another Schoolboy,' the CEO Insists." *Business Review Weekly* 18, no. 5 (1996): 101.

Bogle, D. "Schoolboy's Gift for Geek-Free Internet." *The Weekend Australian*, October 19, 1996, 5.

Bourdieu, P. "The Forms of Capital." In *Handbook of Theory: Research for the Sociology of Education*, edited by J. Richardson, 241–58. New York: Greenwood Press, 1986.

Bourdieu, P., and J.-C. Passeron. *Reproduction in Education, Society and Culture.* London: Sage Publications, 1977.

Bridges, D. "Parents: Customers or Partners?" In *Education and the Market Place*, edited by D. Bridges and T. McLaughlin, 65–79. London: Falmer Press, 1994.

Castells, M. *The Rise of the Network Society. The Information Age: Economy, Society and Culture.* Vol. 1. Oxford: Blackwell, 1996.

Commonwealth of Australia. *Backing Australia's Ability: Innovation Action Plan*, 2001 [cited April 30 2002]. Available from http://backingaus.innovation.gov.au/.

———. *The Networked Nation*, ASTEC, 1994a [cited March 1996]. Available from www.erin.gov.au/astec/net_nation/meeting.html.

———. *Networking Australia's Future: The Final Report of the Broadcast Services Expert Group*, BSEG, 1994b [cited March 1996]. Available from www.dca.gov.au.

———. *Creative Nation: Commonwealth Cultural Policy.* DCA, Canberra: Australian Government Publisher, 1994c.

de Certeau, M. *The Practice of Everyday Life.* Translated by S. Rendall. Berkeley: University of California Press, 1984.

EdNA (DEETYA). *Introduction to EdNa* 1996 [cited April 1996]. From www.edna.edu.au (no longer available).

———.*About EdNA*, 1998 [cited September 1998]. From www.edna.edu.au/about (no longer available).

EdNA Schools Advisory Group. *Learning in an Online World: School Education Action Plan for the Information Economy*, 2000 [cited February 2002]. Available from www.edna.edu.au/publications.

Ellison, C. *Launch of the EdNa Directory Service. Mitchelton High School, Brisbane, Queensland* (media release), 1997 [cited March 1998]. Available from www.deetya.gov.au.

Fairclough, N. *Discourse and Social Change.* London: Polity Press, 1992.

Featherstone, M. "Global and Local Cultures." In *Mapping the Futures: Local Cultures, Global Change*, edited by J. Bird, B. Curtis, T. Putnam, G. Robertson, and L. Tickner, 169–87. London: Routledge, 1993.

Foreshaw, J. "Skills Hub in Drive to Attract Youth." *The Australian*, July 31, 2001, 35.

Gibbs, S. "Teen Tycoon's Big Bite of the Apple." *The Adelaide Advertiser*, July 9, 1997, 3.

Hartley, J. "Journalism and Modernity." *Australian Journal of Communication* 22, no. 2 (1995): 20–30.

Hartman, A. *So Who Is Alex Hartman?* 1997a [cited December 15, 1997]. From www.geko.net.au/~amicus.misc.staff/Alex_Hartman.html (no longer available).

———. "True Blue in the Brave New Digital World." *The Weekend Australian*, January 25–26, 1997

IT Skills Hub. *Youth Hub* 2001 [cited April 30, 2002]. From http: / / youth .itskillshub . com.au (no longer available).

Jackson, I. "Children of the Fourth Estate: Public Representations of Children and Childhood." *Journal of Australian Studies*, no. 36 (1993): 65–79.

Kellner, D. *Media Culture: Cultural Studies, Identity and Politics between the Modern and the Postmodern*. London: Routledge, 1995.

Kenway, J., and E. Bullen. *Consuming Children: Education—Entertainment—Advertising*. Buckingham, UK: Open University Press, 2001.

Luke, C., ed. *Feminisms and Pedagogies of Everyday Life*. Albany: State University of New York Press, 1996.

Morgan, R. "Transitions from English to Cultural Studies." *New Education* 15, no. 1 (1993): 2–48.

Nixon, H. "Creating a Clever, Computer-Literate Nation: A Cultural Study of the Media, Young People and New Technologies of Information and Communication in Australia 1994–1998." Unpublished Ph.D. thesis, University of Queensland, 1999.

Schools Online Curriculum Content Initiative (SOCCI). *Phase Two Plan 2001–2006*. 2001 [cited March 2002]. Available from http://socci.edna.edu.au/content/phase2.asp.

Selwyn, N., and P. Brown. "Education, Nation States and the Globalization of Information Networks." *Journal of Education Policy* 15, no. 6 (2000): 661–82.

Tsavdaridis, D. "The Computer Genius Who Has a Net Worth of Millions." *The Adelaide Advertiser*, July 10, 1999, 34.

# Chapter 4

# New Policies, New Possibilities?
# Adult Learners in the Global Economy

Sue Shore

## Introduction

The publication *The Learning Age: A Renaissance for a New Britain* Department for Education and Employment, (1998) typifies a period of intense interest in how adult learning may ameliorate the challenges of unemployment and social exclusion. In Europe (European Commission, 1996, 1997), the UK (DfES 2004), Canada (Human Resources Development Canada [HRDC], (2002), and Australia (ANTA, 2000a; 2000b), as well as within UNESCO (1996) and the OECD (2003), a wave of policy development and strategy formulation has centered around the opportunities for change. Indeed, for adults working in the new (multilingual) knowledge economies that purportedly epitomize contemporary working lives, such sentiments were crystallized in the British prime minister's (Tony Blair) new famous statement from *The Learning Age*: "[e]ducation is the best economic policy we have" (DfEE, 1998: 9).

The story goes something like this. New knowledge is necessary to expand a country's capacity to innovate and, paradoxically, to keep up with the growth in knowledges that accompany contemporary forms of globalization. New knowledge combined with enhanced social and economic inclusion promises to provide a competitive economic edge for countries. However, "knowing differently," as it is framed in these documents, does not necessarily presume a paradigmatic shift away from the "highly competitive "collecting" (Smith, 1999: 61) practices of the West, nor does it guarantee that uneven patterns of accumulation of wealth will be disrupted. In the knowledge economy, "knowing" is something to be captured and reworked as a commodity. Hence, innovation in education and training policies, pedagogies, and politics is a very different form of lifework than "imagination" (Appadurai, 1996; Morrison, 1992). The latter, can create policy making processes that explicitly situate the aims and purposes of such policies as inherently embedded in the racialized production of knowledge. This process is not devoid of articulations with specific localities and inflections of gender, financial security, sexuality, mobility, and/or age.

I make no claims that this chapter represents a global analysis of adult education policy making. The wave of policy making noted above is situated in a relatively narrow band of countries often collapsed to Western industrialized nations. It is work in this context that serves as the focus of this chapter. Even with this caveat, such policy making is caught in a difficult bind. Adult education and training programs often promise a second chance for adult learners. This is a familiar promise that is nevertheless problematic to realize given the complicity of education systems in the suppression of marginalized knowledges.

In this chapter, I explore how policy making processes, constituted by and through naming practices rooted in a racialized imagination, did not acknowledge the degree to which particular representations of whiteness guided the assumptions of successful and productive citizenship. I frame whiteness as a discursive system of pressures and forces that shapes the conditions of policy making at the same time as it disguises its actions. I suggest that invitations to participate in education make it harder to analyze such overtures as racialized systems of learning because their connections with whiteness are so obscured. Exploring the effects of policy making on possibilities for adult learners via these articulations, rather than neoliberal notions of individualism, market-driven choice, progress, and endless possibility, requires a different kind of starting place from one that presents the knowledge economy as a benign force. Indeed, some contemporary discourses of globalization further exacerbate the challenge of understanding these connections.

This chapter elaborates on the above insights by foregrounding the racialized construction of education systems and the "forgotten" connections among whiteness, globalization, and contemporary concerns for social inclusion. I move from these connections to examine features of two Australian Government Inquiries into *adult community education* (hereafter called ACE). Key features of these inquiries resonate with adult education and training policies, pedagogies, and politics in other regions. The aim of this analysis is to recuperate theoretical storylines that might help to show, in concrete ways, how reports and policies produced from the inquiries, participant submissions to the inquiries, and indeed the rules guiding participation promoted hope for all citizens at the same time as they elided the racialized landscape on to which these hopes were being mapped. In closing, I point to the effects these features had on the construction of opportunity for learners.

## "Remembering" the Racialized Culture of Globalization

My principal concern here is with relations between adult education policy making, the flow of knowledge(s) made possible by, indeed produced through repeated reference to the global within policy making. Particular assumptions about subjectivities underpin these policies. In developing this understanding of how such subjectivities are represented in policy making I am indebted to Edward Said (1993), Toni Morrison (1992), Ann Stoler (1995) and Ghassan Hage (1998). Each acknowledges the material patterns of inequality produced by and through research that is unaware of its racialized premises. Further, each also provides insights into how a racialized other is often the basis for constituting humanistic white identities.

Building on this body of work, I argue that there is a place for a different form of reflexivity in policy making. Reflexivity may activate a racialized imagination in such a way that policy-makers can no longer ignore the "white in the I" that travels below the surface of public policies that seek social inclusion. However, there are problems with this approach. Reflexivity of this kind is in danger of flagging a problem and then proceeding to ignore it by doing nothing about the material conditions it flags. At the same time, using policy texts and recorded transcripts of formal inquiries as the basis of my argument can present a disembodied version of policy activism. The text acts as the final word and erases the day-to-day resistances of educators as policy activists in the production of those texts. It is not my intention to suggest or produce either of these as effects of this chapter. Rather, I aim to unsettle the naturalness with which *published* policy texts have produced adult learning subjects anchored in the logics of empire while the connections and their effects are never articulated as such.

The naturalness of such policy making may be unsettled via "contrapuntal readings" (Said, 1993: 78). This pedagogical move involves the reading of a text in and against the political and historical contexts that produced it. Contrapuntal readings situate racialized landscapes at the center of contemporary policy analysis (Singh and Greenlaw, 1998), even when it appears that those landscapes are consigned to a long-forgotten past. The racialized roots of contemporary policy making texts become more apparent when one begins from the premise that globalization is an extension of colonial expansion and a continuation of the "civilizing" mission of the West. At the same time it signifies new cultural, economic and political relations among nations. There can be no examination of globalization without a corresponding understanding of the articulations between the project of modernity, the racialized nature of discourses of progress, and the extent to which the motif of movement—of knowledge(s), bodies, labor, commodities, and capital—has supplanted the concept of imperial reach (Winant 1994). Such a slippage in terminology makes it increasingly difficult to chart the relational ways in which self-mastery for adult learners is always and already a racial project.

The policy making setting I focus on in this chapter is articulated with globalizing tendencies to achieve economic productivity and the control and regulation of populations within and across nations. These impulses are not new. Education and training are embedded in a discursive system that delineates the parameters of success in the world. In adult education and training, this occurs via a set of references to lifelong learning, opportunity, and reinvention of the self. In policy making, it occurs through the referents of innovation, competition, and the capacity to increasingly expand knowledge. As Said (1993: 61) notes, these "references come with attitudes—about rule, control, profit, and enhancement and sustainability." They are not prescribed explicitly; rather, they are embedded in the cultural identity of "the" adult learner in such a way that it is almost impossible to speak of adult learning without mentioning such attitudes and references.

Furthermore, Richard Dyer (1997), Ann Stoler (1995), and Ghassan Hage (1998) have charted the articulations between whiteness and key ideals such as progress, freedom, agency, and possibility. Hage (1998: 20) argues that Whiteness is a "fantasy position of cultural dominance born out of the history of European expansion" constructed to sustain the no-tion of a nation-state governed by White multiculturalist practices imbued with inclusionary gestures based on tolerance of the Other. Such tolerance is, however, premised on the assumption that a particular kind of body serves as the norm against which all others are "tolerated." Education and training programs promise to serve the critical role in reducing the disso-nance between the fantasy position and that which is tolerated by provid-ing the curricula content to achieve accumulations that are supposed to successively close the gap.

I am loathe to suggest that Whiteness is a monolithic discursive forma-tion with predictable effects. However, many non-white peoples have suggested it certainly feels like this at times. This is a point worth remem-bering if a claim for reflexivity is to be taken seriously. Achieving white-ness was never a "secure bourgeois project" (Stoler, 1995: 99) of colonialism. It involved struggles within gendered and classed locations that were also imbued with expectations of how sexuality should be prac-ticed. Similarly, globalization is often portrayed as a monolithic and homogeneous construct when this is not the case.

Contemporary globalization is linked to the extension of earlier logics of empire (Appadurai, 1996; Winant, 1994). The effects of such logics framed colonial moments as always and only stories that made objects of the colonized rather than deeply implicating in the lives of the colonizers. Merging perspectives on whiteness with globalization provides a way of seeing how colonial practices of naming, defining, regulating, and classi-fying have constituted the structures of attitude and reference by which contemporary bureaucracies operate. In this context, educational policy making identifies, indeed constructs, social and economic crises such as unemployment, welfare, and "illiteracy." At the same time, policy is as-signed the role of developing structures and processes to alleviate social anxieties about these crises.

Reflexive approaches to globalization cannot ignore its articulations with racism and colonialism or gloss over the epistemological differences between sharing culture and appropriating it. Knowledge-"collecting" practices are linked to the theft of land, which acts as a brake on the de-velopment of community productivity (Smith 1999). Appadurai (1996: 31) reminds us that imagining globalization differently could achieve at least two things. First, it could render visible the *common experiences* of repressed workers, gender violence, and the (im)possibility of parity of living conditions when set against the optimism of the flow of objects, images, ideas, and people. Second, it could provide a different vantage point from which to understand policy making as a special practice of the imagination. Ignoring the possibilities of imagining and knowing differently means the colonial structuring of contemporary attitudes and references in education systems are left unexamined. Yet this is arguably the site where these practices have had most effect.

## Redefining Adult Learning: A Work in Progress

Political systems around the world have drawn on key words such as competition, innovation, social inclusion, and flexibility in their efforts to situate nations as viable economic entities in the global order. Moreover, "seeing" and "naming" practices are the means by which "the West" removes ambiguity at the same time as it asserts ownership of land, and other "commodities" such as knowledge (Smith, 1999). ACE provision has always been something of an indefinable unruly educational category. If people found it difficult to explain the complexities of vocational and workplace learning in relation to the compulsory schooling sector, the web of relations within ACE added even more ambiguity.

Many of the practices of "seeing and naming" were activated during a series of inquiries and reviews into ACE in Australia. Three particular features of inquiries, bearing the hallmarks of "rituals white empowerment" (Hage, 1998: 241), helped define ACE and at the same time consolidate the field as a sector governed by assumptions of whiteness. The naming and capturing of the field, the (re)presenting of adult learning profiles, and, the inscribing of appropriate participation are described in the following sections.

## Naming and Capturing the Field

Defining ACE was achieved via two government inquiries conducted in 1991 (Senate Employment, Education and Training References Committee [SEETRC], 1991a) and during 1996–1997 (SEETRC 1996–1997). Following standard parliamentary procedures the two Committees called for written submissions and witness statements. Generally, parliamentary inquiries operate in highly structured contexts. For example, in Australia all submissions and statements are audiotaped and transcribed as Hansard data and thus become a public record of proceedings. On occasions, written submissions were classified as confidential and hence not available in the public record. These submissions and transcripts provided the substantive data for this chapter, combined with reports and policies produced from the findings of the hearings.

Each Committee produced a report of ITS findings. The first report, *Come in Cinderella* (referred to hereafter as *Cinderella,* SEETRC, 1991b), was followed by the release of the first national policy on adult and community education Ministerial Council for Employment Education, Training and Youth Affairs [MCEETYA], 1993). *Beyond Cinderella* (SEETRC, 1997), the second report, was followed by the release of the second national policy (MCEETYA, 1997). A third document, *Ministerial Declaration on Adult Community Education* (MCEETYA, 2002), derived from a leaner process of consultation, was national in nature but relegated to the status of a "declaration" rather than a national policy. The three documents mark an intensive period of review and attention to ACE in Australia.

*Cinderella* described ACE as a sector that was "consumer-driven," "non-compulsory," was flexible, allowed learners to "enter and leave" as they required, and focused on the *pedagogical* opportunities available to individuals (SEETRC, 1991b: 7). Prior to 1990, ACE consisted of a loose conglomeration of providers involved in an ambiguously defined range of activities, supported by varied forms of public and private funding and imbued with a culture of philanthropy. *Cinderella* called for tighter, more systematic approaches to provision, increased funding that would be accompanied by increased administration of activities, and greater recognition of the sector and its contribution to national goals of social and economic progress. *Cinderella* reiterated the preference for lifelong learning (SEETRC, 1991b: 7, 16), noting that a country "serious about our economic and social justice goals, ...must get serious about adult community education" (SEETRC, 1991b: 160). The national policy produced from this Inquiry was the vehicle for "getting serious" about ACE (MCEETYA, 1993).

*Beyond Cinderella* determined the extent to which ACE had improved as a result of the initiatives emerging from the *Cinderella* report. In the first public hearing in Canberra in 1996, the chair noted that the committee had a particular challenge:

> what is a definition of adult education and whether there is any mileage in trying to pursue that one when we could be out there forever and still not come up with some better definition of it. (SEETRC, 1996–1977: 15)

Subsequently, she reminded witnesses of the problems associated with determining policy about something when "every time you get hold of it, it is gone again" (SEETRC, 1996–1997: 454). *Beyond Cinderella* (SEETRC, 1997) challenged the vocational/nonvocational binary often invoked to represent educational contributions. It noted:

> [t]wo basic orientations to education and training. ...the need of people to develop and maintain technical and professional skills to ensure an internationally competitive workforce...[and] broader social, cultural and personal values concerned with the enrichment of communities and the fulfillment of human lives. (SEETRC, 1997: 5)

Despite the recognition of two orientations, and an unwillingness to subscribe to one or other pairs, the "orientations" were put under pressure by the pragmatic need to "get serious" about *economic* productivity. The role of community education in economic productivity had always been problematic, being largely ignored prior to the 1990s. During the two inquiries, this role was increasingly foregrounded as an important goal of ACE and therefore the need for ACE to be a recognizable component of the national training system. Not twelve pages into the transcript of the first hearing in 1996, a prominent advocate claimed, in response to a question on structure, that ACE could be likened to "a small business sector" (SEETRC, 1996–1997: 12). Indeed it was the capture of ACE by the wider national system that enabled a consumer rationality to permeate the management of the sector. This motif was supported and encouraged by committee questions and researcher/practitioner responses.

The tenor of the inquiries shifted from "the emergence of ACE" in 1991, to the role of ACE in a learning society in 1997, and then to ACE's "dynamic, diverse and responsive role" (MCEETYA, 1997: 1) role in bridging a "knowledge gap" by 2001. By 1997, a series of quality assurance and accountability measures had been established as part of enhanced regulation of the national training system. Recommendations 2–6 and 11 of *Beyond Cinderella* were directed at effecting this restructuring and placing responsibility for ACE within this frame of reference. Pragmatically registration of providers, standards of quality for provision, and discrete categories of training to address different market needs were among the key mechanisms guiding ACE management (MCEETYA, 1997). By 2001, the goal of putting ACE in place had been effectively achieved via policy and funding relations. However, other processes were also at work to achieve an even deeper integration of ACE within the "civilizing" mission of education. The intention to "recognize" the role of ACE had far-reaching effects given the pressure of accountability management. The chair encapsulated the mood well in a hearing in Hobart:

"We cannot expect the government to be funding things that are ill defined, particularly in terms of being accountable to the taxpayer for the use of taxpayers' dollars" (SEETRC, 1996–1997: 181–2).

A taken-for-granted assumption pervaded the first Inquiry and was even more evident during the second. The ambiguity of the ACE sector was problematic. It needed to be identified and classified. It needed a name to distinguish it from other forms of delivery. It needed pathways to lead to these other forms of provision. Its goals, purposes, and contributions to articulation needed to be formally ratified, particularly in relation to the training system. Clarity in each of these areas was necessary in order to ensure its growth and viability as a distinct sector within the overall domain of education and training. Paradoxically, the viability of ACE was premised on gaining parity at the same time as its distinctiveness—messy ambiguity—was removed.

## (Re)Presenting Adult Learning Profiles

The process of putting ACE, in its place was accompanied by similar moves to define learners. The claims of ACE as a responsive and inclusive sector well situated to bridge knowledge gaps, its capacity to provide access to formal systems of education and training or work, and increasing demands for accountability meant that "efficient" public spending was a recurring priority during inquiries. Given these parameters, particular discursive tactics were employed to foreground learner profiles and the aims and purposes of provision across witness statements, submissions, and committee questioning.

The range of provision and diverse aims and purposes often meant that everyone and everything could be included under the umbrella of ACE. This included productive training for unemployed people; support for single mothers; creative and productive activities for the elderly; provision for rural and remote communities; and concerns for literacy and numeracy provision for youth, bilingual people, Indigenous people, and a range of other groups. Many witness statements protested the narrow focus on vocational learning, and were supported by comments from the committee in the second inquiry. At the same time, witnesses also suggested that people looking for work *would* be helped by participation in ACE. Few challenged the belief that ACE programs could make a difference if given adequate funding and improved infrastructure. In those areas of provision where the under-represented in training and the marginalized in the community were the focus, a common profile emerged of underconfident learners and people with limited language, literacy, and personal or life skills. Nevertheless, the tone of contributions, from committee members and ACE practitioners and researchers alike, reinscribed the necessity of a pool of "good" workers and citizens, constituted through ACE programs. With additional finance and infrastructure those people deemed unready or unable to move into formal systems of work could be either better prepared or at least engaged in productive activities. Such responses reinforced the view that a productive society, and *successful* ACE learners, needed to be protected from the destabilizing effects of *un*productive, *un*enterprising, lackluster "internal enemies" (Stoler, 1995: 96) of the nation-state. From this perspective, witnesses, educators with the best of intentions, consolidated the position that the *Beyond Cinderella* committee had inscribed in its earlier comments on the vocational/nonvocational divide. Neither group saw the implicit assumptions of enterprising white subjectivity informing decisions about ACE learner profiles. They did not connect these issues to a "flexible superior positionality" (Smith 1999: 60) that rejects one form of bias (the vocational/nonvocational divide) while ignoring the extent to which it valorizes enterprising subjects as the hallmark of ACE productivity.

Advocates for ACE were in a difficult bind. ACE programs were often marginalized, underfunded, and generally unimportant in the wider scheme of the economic and political concerns of the day. The public hearings provided an opportunity to change this. They consolidated public knowledge of the field, at least in education circles. As a result, government attention to and knowledge of ACE increased. Hence, research projects on pathways, barriers, and possibilities in ACE have featured prominently as a strand in national research funding. Contributing to this was the commissioned projects managed by the National Center for Vocational Education Research (www.ncver.edu.au) as well as Recommendation 11 (increased research funding) and Recommendations 12 and 18 promoting "best practice" projects for seniors and Indigenous people, respectively (SEETRC, 1997).

However, the hearings also consolidated the view that the possibilities in ACE were endless. ACE was constructed as having the power to be a springboard for social change. Agency for learners was operationalized through the overt framing of "human" characteristics of possibility and progress. Paradoxically, Whiteness, as a set of discursive practices, parallels this endless possibility, exemplifying "a need to always be everything and nothing, literally overwhelmingly present and yet apparently absent"

(Dyer, 1997: 39). During the inquiries and across subsequent reports and policies, numerous references were premised on a responsive approach to all cultures; nevertheless, the underlying tenet of "inclusion" was premised on a "fantasy" of tolerance and control. this rendered unspeakable the assumptions of whiteness underpinning the invitation of inclusion.

*Inscribing Appropriate Participation*

Capturing and profiling ACE and its participants were critical elements in knowing and suturing it in place in relation to other sectors. Equally important, these responses resonated with other policy processes that framed under-represented groups as deficient in the innovative knowledges needed for the future. They needed access to education and training to improve their employability prospects (DfES, 2003).

During 1991–2001, the submissions and consultations redefined the object of attention away from opportunities for adults with "special needs" (MCEETYA 1993), to strengthening responsiveness to target group needs (MCEETYA, 1997), and then to promoting community capacity building (MCEETYA, 2002). Each successive document intensified the framework and the necessary mechanisms to instantiate *participation into the "mainstream"* as the goal of ACE. At the same time, it collapsed ACE into lifelong learning. Via repeated incantations of participation, pathways, and access to learning, the policy making process emerged as a form of "constant purification" (Stoler, 1995) across ACE programs. Enterprising agentic subjectivity became the hallmark of program outcomes. These outcomes were aligned with administrative guidelines for naming and knowing *what* ACE was, *how* it could be named and known and in relation to what, *what* its outcomes were, and *how* they would be measured. This could be achieved through exposure to program content, skill development, and funding mechanisms that were closely articulated with the goals for economic productivity flagged in the policies. Registration of providers, quality assurance, and funding against prescribed national outcomes were now everyday requirements of the management of government-funded programs. At the same time, representations of ACE were woven into a wider and more powerful discourse of "social war" (Stoler, 1995: 96) that established insistent policing techniques to increase participation by marginalized groups under-represented in education and training.

Three issues characterized developments over this period. ACE was named, "client" profiles were established, and specific expectations of participation were institutionalized under the guise of accountability to the tax-paying public. Pressure to upskill was accompanied by exhortations to *register* for education and training, to always be *participating* in systems that would *recognize* learning, and to *become* lifelong learners. Officials recognized early on that existing systems were not perfect. One committee member, in response to concerns about the effectiveness of the system by an Indigenous witness during the first inquiry, commented, "I do not see why you are so worried about having a white bureaucratic system imposed on you, [it] does not work anyway with us" (SEETRC, 1991a: 485). The paradox of this comment aside, what this committee member refused to acknowledge was that education systems are deeply imbricated in "structures of attitude and reference" (Said, 1993: 62) that reward increasing accumulations of whiteness. The response displayed a level of "dysconsciousness":

> an uncritical habit of mind (including perspectives, attitudes, assumptions and beliefs) that justifies inequality and exploitation by accepting the existing order of things as given.... It is not the *absence* of consciousness (that is not unconsciousness) but an *impaired* consciousness or distorted way of thinking about race as compared to, for example, "critical consciousness." (King, cited in Rain, 2000: 78–79; emphasis in original)

Repeated invitations and enticements to take up pathways, and even more strongly worded mandates to participate, sustain the notion of rewards. The very real barriers and challenges that still exist for marginalized groups in wider society were ignored.

Social inclusion as a policy concept obscured the assimilationist tendencies inherent in such invitations. Viewed via a different imagination, the mapping of ACE was an exercise in reinscribing a system of "topping up" rather than engagement across cultures. Moreover for non-white learners, and many women and working class people, their success within these systems was rarely acknowledged as anything other than an accumulation of learned rather than owned behaviours. Hence, their "acquired competence" was always suspect, always open to challenge as "white but not quite" (Stoler, 1995: 102). Despite promises of social change and individual success, an invitation to participate in such systems of social training is therefore a two-edged sword for such participants.

During the last decade, participation become a code word for harnessing diversity within a discursive system of policy making that "forgot" its racialized construction. These claims may seem somewhat totalizing, erasing the specificity and particularity of ACE practices and ignoring the committed and strategic efforts of educators globally as they seek to work in and against these regimes. Yes, I am tempted, often, to modulate my claims. This would mean inserting "some" white people. I would emphasize that my claims about whiteness impact on non-white people as well, given that I view whiteness as a discursive system in which we are all imbricated. I would also say that "white privilege" can potentially demonize whiteness. I am drawn to soften the impact of my claims, lest I be accused of demonizing. Despite these desires, I resist precisely because these moderations *do* dilute the argument that contemporary systems of education *are* steeped in colonialism. They *do* discriminate—albeit differentially—and white people *are* privileged, albeit differentially, within these processes.

By 1997, ACE was described as an "educational chameleon" modifying the nature of its presence according to the environment in which it finds itself" (SEETRC, 1997: 18). Such a perspective resonates powerfully with the "protean" (Stoler, 1995: 105) construction of whiteness. This promotes "an individual and a universal subject...a stress on the display of spirit while maintaining a position of invisibility; in short, a need to always be everything and nothing, literally overwhelmingly present and yet apparently absent" (Dyer 1997: 39).

## Contrapuntal Readings: Not Just an Add-on

The analysis I offer here has been prompted by Dyer's (1997: 14) interest in seeing the specificity of whiteness, even when the text itself is not trying to show it to you, doesn't even know that it is there to be shown." There are many ways to chart the discursive patterns within texts produced from government inquiries into ACE. I hesitate to name the three features of the Inquiries identified as "white practices" in some deterministic sense. Nevertheless, such features are exemplary instances of *"rituals of White empowerment*—seasonal festivals where White Australians renew the belief in their possession of the power to talk and make decisions" about the other (Hage, 1998: 241, emphasis in original).

The effect of these rituals is to narrow learning opportunities for funded provision other than those that accord with articulated pathways planned for adult learners as enterprising productive workers. Following this line of reasoning, it is possible, indeed important, to observe that a particular totalizing form of ACE *was* constructed, *was* reinforced by national policies and strategies, and *did* come to dictate the formal boundaries of ACE as a *policy construct*. The distinctions among a policy construct, its effect on narrowing funding opportunities, and the ongoing activities in which many policy activists and learners continue to engage, funded or not, are also important. Many activities continue to take place beyond these funding parameters.

Edward Said's (1993) work has attracted controversy particularly where it is in danger of portraying an overly hegemonic approach to the constitution of the Orient and indeed "the West." In this chapter, I have attempted to show how discourses of progress and possibility, long held to be the reference points by which education and training are secured to government policy making, have parallels with practices of social training common in colonial times. Contemporary efforts to develop a "clever country" (SEETRC, 1997: 160), to fashion outcomes of "effective citizenship, teamwork and personal goals" (SEETRC, 1997: 9), and to "achiev[e] community capacity building through community ownership" (MCEETYA, 2002: 1) have *un*surprising parallels with the practices of "self-mastery" mobilized to endorse social training in colonial times (Stoler, 1995).

The premises on which these inquiries were based encouraged a policy making process that reinscribed an individualistic, apolitical model of education that could be "responsive" to a group that was becoming increasingly "dangerous" in terms of its power to erode the base of productive citizenship. By these means, discourses of innovation and competition enabled a white self to be sutured into the profile of the successful ACE learner. This discursive work is often invisible to policy-makers, researchers, and educators whose policy making logic (at one level reasonably so) is concerned with the access adults have to opportunities for work and financial security. A contrapuntal reading of these assumptions moves back into the construction of subjectivity that underpins the humanistic enterprise of education. Such readings show that the logics of innovation and competition in contemporary policy making may "underestimate such motive forces in history as profit, ambition, ideas, the sheer love of power, and... the fact that history is... a complex interaction between uneven economies, societies, and ideologies" (Said, 1983: 222).

This is the challenge for educators as globalization becomes both the rationale for the changes occurring across educational policies, pedagogies and politics and the reason for understanding these changes. Given the ways in which globalization is imbricated in the economic and cultural histories of colonialism, it is not surprising that globalization discourses

New Policies, New Possibilities?

operate in complex and often none too subtle ways to recuperate particular kinds of subjectivity via projects of adult community education and life-long learning. These projects are located in a complex milieu that does not always acknowledge the racialized culture of education and training landscapes. This includes the tacit assumptions about (white) subjectivity, the discursive collapsing of categories of race and capacity, the silence about whiteness, and at the same time recuperations of whiteness as generic human capacity. The instantiation of differences, attitudes, and references from formal systems provide a means by which ACE is relocated into a racialized framework that resists its articulations with colonialism. Indeed, in contemporary times the explicit intention is to articulate such qualities with a global need for competition. Hence, the global becomes the reason for change.

Policy making can be usefully informed by contrapuntal readings and for our imaginations to be aware and open to such readings. To be involved in the policy making process means asking difficult questions that challenge the ways in which new and improved forms of colonialism are recuperated in the enterprising innovative education systems at the heart of contemporary policy making. Subscribing to lifelong learning policies does not mean that we also have to subscribe to the language of racism that flows beneath its surface. If there are possibilities for rupturing the fault lines of "dysconsciousness," there are also possibilities for reinscribing racialized discourses and practices.

# References

Appadurai, A. *Modernity at Large: Cultural Dimensions of Globalisation.* Minneapolis: University of Minnesota Press, 1996.
ANTA. *A National Marketing Strategy for Vet: Meeting Client Needs* Australian National Training Authority, Brisbane, 2000a [cited October 18, 2002]. Available from www.anta.gov.au/images/publications/nationalMarketingStrategyMeetingClientNeeds.pdf.
———. *Shaping our Future: National Strategy for Vocational Education and Training 2004–2010.* Australian National Training Authority, Brisbane, 2000b [cited February 4, 2004]. Available from www.anta.gov.au/images/publications/national_strategy_final.pdf.
Department for Education and Employment. (DfEE). *The Skills Strategy White Paper: 21st Century Skills: Realising Our Potential. Invididuals, Employers, Nation.* 2003 [cited February 4, 2004]. Available from www.dfes.gov.uk/skillsstrategy/.
———. *The Learning Age: A Renaissance for a New Britain* 1998 [cited October 18, 2002]. Available from www.lifelong learning.co.uk/greenpaper/.

Dyer, R. *White*. London: Routledge, 1997.

European Commission. *Teaching and Learning: Towards the Learning Society. White Paper on Education and Training*. Luxembourg: Office for the Official Publications of the European Communities, 1996.

———. *Accomplishing Europe through Education and Training*. 1997 [cited January, 2004]. Available from http://europa.eu.int/comm./education/doc/other/reflex/home _en. html.

Hage, G. *White Nation: Fantasies of White Supremacy in a Multicultural Society*. Annandale, Australia: Pluto Press, 1998.

Hoogvelt, A. *Globalization and the Postcolonial World: The New Political Economy of Development*. 2nd ed. Baltimore: John Hopkins University Press, 2001.

Human Resources Development Canada (HDRC). *Knowledge Matters: Skills and Learning for Canadians: Canada's Innovation Strategy*. Hull Quebec: HDRC, 2002.

Ministerial Council for Employment, Education, Training and Youth Affairs (MCEETYA). *National Policy: Adult Community Education*. Carlton South, Australia: MCEETYA, 1993.

———. *National Policy: Adult Community Education*. Carlton South, Australia: Department of Training and Education, 1997.

———. *Ministerial Declaration on Adult Community Education*. Carlton South, Australia: Department of Education, 2002.

Morrison, T. *Playing in the Dark: Whiteness and the Literary Imagination*. Cambridge: Harvard University Press, 1992.

OECD. *Beyond Rhetoric: Adult Learning Policies and Practices*. Paris: OECD, 2003.

Rain, F. Is the Benign Really Harmless? Deconstructing Some "Benign" Manifestations of Operationalised White Privilege. In *White Reign Deploying Whiteness in America*. Edited by J. Kincheloe, S. Steinberg, N. Rodriguez and R. Chennault. New York: St Martin's Griffin, 2000.

Said, E. *The World, the Text and the Critic*. Cambridge: Harvard University Press, 1983.

———. *Culture and Imperialism*. London: Vintage, 1993.

Senate Employment, Education and Training References Committee (SEETRC). *Reference Inquiry into Adult and Community Education. Official Hansard Reports*. Vol. 1–12. Canberra, Australia: Commonwealth of Australia, 1991a.

———. *Come in Cinderella. The Emergence of Adult and Community Education*. Canberra, Australia: Commonwealth of Australia, 1991b.

———. *Reference: Developments in Adult and Community Education in Australia since 1991. Official Hansard Reports*. Vols. 1–10. Canberra, Australia: Senate Printing Unit, 1996–1997.

———. *Beyond Cinderella: Towards a Learning Society*. Canberra, Australia: Senate Publications Unit, 1997.

Singh, M., and J. Greenlaw. "Postcolonial Theory in the Literature Classroom: Contrapuntal Readings." *Theory into Practice* 37, no. 3 (1998): 193–202.

Smith, L. *Decolonizing Methodologies: Research and Indigenous Peoples*. London: Zed Books and Dunedin: University of Otago Press, 1999.

Stoler, A. *Race and the Education of Desire: Foucault's History of Sexuality and the Colonial Order of Things*. Durham: Duke University Press, 1995.

UNESCO. *Learning: The Treasure Within. Report to UNESCO of the International Commission on Education for the Twenty-First Century*. Paris: UNESCO Publishing, 1996.

Whitelock, D., ed. *The Vision Splendid: Adult Education in Australia: W. G. K. Duncan's 1944 Report and Commentaries*. Adelaide, Australia: University of Adelaide, 1973.

Winant, H. "Racial Formation and Hegemony: Global and Local Developments." In *Racism, Modernity and Identity: On the Western Front*, edited by A. Rattansi and S. Westood. Cambridge and Oxford: Polity Press: 266–289. 1994.

# Chapter 5

# Globalizing the Rustbelt and Public Schools

Pat Thomson

## Introduction

While politicians, social scientists, and welfare agencies argue about whether there has been an increase in poverty during the last decade or so, who is at the bottom of the socioeconomic league table, and whether the current income support and public housing policies have provided a hedge against extreme hardship, there *is* agreement among them that social inequality, the gap between the rich and poor, has increased significantly over the last decade. Inequalities in many countries of both the Majority and Minority Worlds are much more than they used to be. There is also general agreement that this socioeconomic gap is manifest in increased social-spatial polarization within cities and regions as well as between them, with increased concentrations of ethnically, linguistically, and culturally diverse people in particular places now struggling to retain dignity, health, and hope.

In this chapter, I argue that the historical, ideological, and localizing practices of neoliberal globalism are producing urban polarization and poverty that are manifested in one instance in the creation of a "rustbelt city." Specifically, this chapter explains how a combination of public policies emanating from the ideological and political project of neoliberal globalism for governing techno-economies and changing demographies has turned the Australian provincial capital of Adelaide into a rustbelt city (Thomson, 1999a, 1999b, 2000). Drawing on research undertaken for

*Schooling the Rustbelt Kids* (Thomson, 2002), I provide a very brief summary of how the rustbelt and the marginalization of residents within the city appears in rustbelt schools, comparing this with the context-free approach of education policy.

## Producing a Rustbelt City

On most social and economic measures, South Australia is now the poorest state in Australia, having very marked geographies of poverty (Baum, Stimson, O'Connor, Mullins, and Davies, 1999; Carson and Martin, 2001). The lowest income postcodes in the state and in the nation are isolated in the northwest and north of the city (Lloyd, Harding, and Greenwell, 2001). This chapter is about Adelaide, but, while it is particularly situated, its themes have a broader take. It speaks to, and of, many similar locations made poor in these times.

### What Is a Rustbelt?

A "rustbelt" is a relic of the industrial era. Like a "rustbowl," it is a region that was once heavily industrialized but now is the site of old factories that are antiquated and have a very limited future. In common parlance, the rustbelt refers to a geographical area in which particular kinds of dirty, assembly-line manufacturers once produced significant wealth and many unskilled, semi-skilled, and skilled blue-collar jobs. The plant is now technologically obsolete, and the business economically struggling or collapsed entirely.

In many parts of the Minority, overdeveloped, or (so-called) advanced world, such manufacturers have gone offshore, leaving not only their factories and machines, but also their labor force, idle and, literally and metaphorically, rusting. In the press in the United States, the rustbelt is often the binary other of the "sunbelt"; an area with new high-tech industries such as Palo Alto, California, also known as Silicon Valley. Rustbelts and sunbelts are inevitably spatially kept worlds apart, with the detritus of the economic order out of sight of the latest incarnation of neoliberal and/or neoconservativee globalism.

Rustbelts are associated with some of the changes that go under the catchall label of globalization. Dirty and sluggish industrial-age manufacturers have transmogrified into fast capitalist enterprises that thrive in the crucible of deregulated national currencies, lowered tariffs, and digitized infrastructures, which enable the steerage from quite a distance of semi-autonomous devolved plants and networks of subcontractors (Wiseman, 1998). These fast capitalist enterprises move from country to country seeking the cheapest labor and highest government inducements. The places that they leave behind are stripped of identity and hope (Appadurai, 1996). Rustbelt residents are locked into the local, teased by globally produced images of the good life that others lead (Bauman, 1998), and forced to define themselves into new "service identities" in order to find low-paid and insecure work (Allen, Massey, and Cochrane, 2000).

Figure 5.1: Views of the rustbelt

Coalitions of neoliberal and neoconservative governments have opted for "lean and mean" policy regimes as one way to manage what they argue to be the near achievement of the ideal *unfettered market*. These policy regimes involve reduced public services, increased competition between publicly managed services, the wholesale lease and sale of government utilities and assets, increased levies on citizen-consumers, fewer taxes to support public social and economic well-being, more consumerism, and more freedoms for private interests. This policy agenda plays out in various ways in different states and regions around the globe. It takes a particularly harsh turn in the rustbelt.

## A Success Story Gone Sour

Nation-building governments once believed that the provision of affordable public health, housing, transport, and utilities supplemented the legally designated basic wage to provide a decent standard of living for the vast majority of their population, especially their citizens (Peel, 1995). In doing so they produced a relatively egalitarian society or were reasonably committed to this objective (Travers and Richardson, 1993). This particular policy "solution" for social and economic prosperity was made possible, in Australia, by a raft of national tariffs, industrial agreements, and fiscal and taxation regulations organized around the male blue-collar breadwinner. Other aspects of this specific national regime included unequal wages for women; Whites-only, English-only ethno-nationalist politics; and the denial of full citizenship to the Indigenous first-owners. This created a low-welfare, full-employment, highly isolationist national system that protected its citizens from the risks of social and economic insecurities (Smyth and Cass, 1998).

South Australia was a manufacturing success story in the 1950s and '60s. Large international companies were lured to the state by the ready supply of cheap labor produced through immigration and the postwar baby boom. They were generously supported by incentives or subsidies from public resources by government in the form of low-cost land and buildings; ready access to land, rail, and sea transport; and cut-price (state-owned) electricity, water, and gas. In this favorable climate, auto passenger, textile and footwear, whitegoods, and light engineering companies flourished. The state government also provided large tracts of public housing adjacent to designated manufacturing areas. This was not welfare housing: It was working-class housing (Hamnett and Freestone, 2000). This public housing not only constituted a state-subsidized building industry but also supported manufacturing industry with a labor force on tap to do the often required shift work and overtime. It was also a solution to the postwar housing shortage and formed a significant part of the system of benefits called the social wage. These designated industrial and public housing areas were located in some country regions in the west, northwest, north, and south of the city. The state government established a whole new satellite town.

By the 1980s the nation-state's apparatus for providing social and economic protection to its citizens was under attack. There were now serious industrial competitors from Asia and Europe for Australian manufacturing companies, whose relatively high prices saw them struggle for international market share. Many companies began to replace unskilled and semi-skilled labor with more advanced technologies. There was also domestic competition because, despite the regime of tariffs, there was a local market for imported products, affordable to those who had some disposable income. Some companies moved sections of their operations offshore, relocating them throughout Asia, and consolidated their national operations with differing goods being manufactured only on one site. When equal pay for women was finally achieved, it was not only within a highly gender-segmented labor market but at the very time when unemployment was on the rise. Despite efforts by the trade unions and governments to manage wages and maintain high levels of employment, national policy makers decided that a new approach was required. They reasoned that for Australia to be part of a restructured global economy it must literally and unilaterally open itself up to the world. The Hawke-Keating Labor government constructed the protection afforded to the Australian economy and its workers as "the problem." They began "the solution" by deregulating the currency and instituting the unilateral removal of tariffs.

In Adelaide, these global/local economic and political changes were made manifest in the landscape. General Motors abandoned its two postwar plants in the western suburbs and moved all operations to the more modern facilities in Elizabeth during the late '70s. In the south, Chrysler closed altogether, its operations being eventually taken over by Mitsubishi, which has remained on the verge of closure ever since, despite repeated public subsidies. Whitegoods manufacturers Simpson Pope, Phillips, and Kelvinator slimmed drastically, moving some operations to other states; introducing "labor saving," job elimination, production processes, and eventually closing altogether in the '90s. The wharves and rail yards dwindled away as their operations shifted to the eastern seaboard, and road transport expanded. Textile and footwear manufacturers closed and moved to Southeast Asia. Forster (1986) estimates that between 1974 and 1975 and 1981 and 1982 alone some 16,000 manufacturing jobs were lost. The sheer volume of this socioeconomic change was significant in a relatively small city-state. The economy began irrevocably to shift away from manufacturing toward services and other low-labor areas such as defense and gourmet food (Baum and Hassan, 1993).

At the same time the population of the city was changing. Families grew more diverse, as single-parent, blended, and reblended families became more common. Immigration slowed, as did the birth rate. Once younger than the Australian average, the South Australian population has now gotten older (Hugo, 1999). And, as the population on the west and northwest aged, areas of urban growth shifted to the outer city in the north and south. The introduction of a controlled, multiracial immigration program in the mid-1970s allowed refugees from Southeast Asia to emigrate and settle in the city. Many moved into the public housing in the northwest, once home to blue-collar, Anglo-Australian families. These postwar public housing estates were no longer just housing for the working class. They were still home to older workers, but also increasingly housed families who were sporadically employed, single parents dependent on government income support, and a variety of citizens in temporary crisis. In these neighborhoods, there was no longer enough paid work to go around, but people who lived in them saw daily the now-closed factories, in which work was once everyday life.

The global/local practices that produced the rustbelt were accompanied by a particular kind of spatially concentrated poverty. In summary, this poverty was constructed by (1) a postwar urban planning strategy to colocate public housing and industrial tracts, (2) decisions made by globalized manufacturing industries to move elsewhere, and (3) demographic changes in families and population. But other factors counted too. There was also the systematic deconstruction of the apparatus of the Australian social wage by the conservative agenda of the neoliberal state.

## The Newly Produced Poor Get Their Deserts

The notion of desert—those who profit from their efforts, and merit and deserve to be free from government interference—is one developed by Nozick (1974) but interpreted by the New Right to mean a minimalist approach to welfare in which those who are deserving are assisted only enough to help them get by. By the mid-1980s, people most in need of government support and services were increasingly concentrated in particular sections of Adelaide in which local governments could not achieve the "rate base" (local taxes) necessary to provide amenities similar to those in more affluent neighborhoods. It fell to state and national governments to change the infrastructure in these public housing tracts in the north, northwest, south, and west of the city, and in country regional centers, which once were home to profitable manufacturing ventures. The previous residents—young working families—had established sporting clubs, churches, and community organizations, and supported kindergartens and schools. The current residents—the unemployed, aging, and economically vulnerable—required different public services in the areas of health and welfare, good public transport, adult and community education, job creation programs, and a helping hand, rather than charity.

However, the state and federal governments of the 1980s and '90s did not deliver. The Hawke-Keating national government began to unpick the social wage, opting instead for neoliberalism's market-driven macroeconomic change combined with microeconomic restructuring and destructuring. This approach may be dubbed "economic reductionism" because its prime rationale was to reduce everything to a matter of economics and then to reduce economic support for public goods (Pusey, 1991). The federal government adopted the notion of targeted welfare, rather than universal provision, and introduced a range of charges for public services with low-cost or free services only for the most needy. It refused to support the South Australian state policy of public housing for workers, seeing such housing as state funding of welfare provision. They did, however, support strongly an active labor market education program, which provided many of the long-term unemployed with opportunities for further training. They also funded a plethora of special-purpose social justice programs in education, welfare, and health. Their critics, however, were not convinced about this contemporary agenda, and pointed to continuing increases in unemployment, failure to reduce the current account deficit, escalating foreign debt, and widening economic inequalities (Rees, Rodley, and Stillwell, 1993).

The South Australian Liberal party came to office in the early '90s on a wave of disappointment at the collapse of the state bank and at the continued failure of the state Labor government to bring back prosperity. The conservatives offered an agenda of privatizing state-owned utilities and cutting costs through the "rationalization" of public services.

Adopting a melange of neoliberal policies being globally dispersed via governments in New Zealand, the United States, and the United Kingdom (Kelsey, 1999; Mink, 1998; Pilcher and Wagg, 1996) and their counterparts in the neighboring state of Victoria (Webber and Crooks, 1996), this new conservative South Australian government oversaw radical change. Water, electricity, gas, ports, and the airport were leased to international consortia, and public-sector services such as maintenance, construction, research and development, telecommunications, and mail were outsourced. The result was significant reductions in government employment (Spoehr, 1999), and the public-sector was forced to adopt the orthodoxies of "funder-purchaser-provider" models within a culture of high political "spin." The "funder-purchaser-provider" model refers to a marketization mechanism whereby government makes policy, state agencies let service contracts and design compliance and audit requirements, and providers (such as schools and hospitals) implement and deliver (Thomson, 1998). The neoconservative and neoliberal government raised rents for public housing tenants who could ill afford these increases, escalated the sale of houses to occupants who were in long-term debt through bank loans, and initiated the redevelopment of public-housing estates by private developers in which most housing is ultimately privately owned. Successive public education budgets were slashed together with other community services such as health, libraries, the arts, and welfare.

The federal election of the Howard government in 1996 ushered in the full neoliberal and neoconservative agenda. With a commitment to the ideology of individualism rather than to the public good, federal policy makers systematically undermined the web of industrial agreements and benefits; increased levies for university and further education, health, housing, and pharmaceuticals; oversaw the sale of government infrastructure; and provided a range of measures to promote competition between families, service providers, and industry. Controversial policies around immigration, public funding for private schools, and new taxation on goods and services fostered high levels of debate that spurred community divisions. While an overriding commitment to reduce government interference was applied to business and the wealthy, at the same time new coercive regimes of "workfare" or employment in the public-sector and surveillance of those on welfare were designated as the lot of the poor. All of these things came together in rustbelt locations in particular ways.

## At Home in the Rustbelt

This combination of national and state government agendas and the moves by national and multinational companies to centralize their operations is manifest in the South Australian rustbelt.

There are *reduced and more expensive public services*, including, for example, fewer and less frequent buses, public school closures, increasingly stretched community health and welfare agencies, diminished adult and community education, and fewer teachers and police officers (Troy, 1999). There are *higher everyday costs*, for instance, rent, pharmaceuticals, public school "fees," fares, medical "gap" payments, petrol, books, and dentists. There are *fewer local services;* for example, banks are replaced by teller machines; independent petrol stations have closed; and small grocery shops and a raft of small local businesses have closed, unable to compete with large chains in shopping centers and to deal with the recent impost of bookkeeping in relation to the Goods and Services Tax. *Community agencies are stressed* with much greater demands for emergency assistance and increased crisis intervention. These *local issues have a lower public profile* because the national networking of print and electronic media has meant fewer journalists in South Australia to cover such events. There is also reduced national interest in these conditions and events, or in the most marginal state in Australia, unless the events are truly sensational. In rustbelt neighborhoods, that is, in those public housing areas in which there is a need for different, more, and improved services, there are now *less of the very things that could make a positive difference.*

Figure 5.2: Effects of the rustbelt

But globalized works produce seductive images of the good life achieved through conspicuous consumption. These marketing and public relations images entice many from all social strata to overextend their credit and to "keep up appearances" with their neighbors and friends (see Raduntz, this volume). For the poor in the rustbelt who must spend a greater proportion of their income on consumption—now a prime focus for government taxation—televised images offer visions of "possible lives" (Appadurai, 1996) that are unattainable to most. Instead there are overdue bills, the depressing and never-ending search for work in the corrupt and clean economy, diminishing support networks, and the rising cost of living. For some (surprisingly fewer than might be expected), this eventually becomes too much to bear with equanimity.

## Schools in the Rustbelt

Public schools serving rustbelt neighborhoods now work in a milieu more difficult than a decade or so ago. Public policy has shifted to one in which competition between schools and systems is encouraged (Marginson, 1997) and in which education is seen primarily as both an individual benefit and as necessary for the human capital to drive economic recovery (Taylor, Rivzi, Lingard, and Henry, 1997). Federal policies on public schooling place high priority on literacy, numeracy, and vocational education (Comber, Green, Lingard, and Luke, 1998). The former Liberal state government held each public school site accountable for improvements measured in tests and against criteria spelled out in annual reports. Naming and shaming are possible consequences. Public schools are given their operating budgets and told to be "flexible" in their use of labor and other resources, cost-efficient, and effective in delivering politically determined priorities determined centrally.

While the South Australian Liberal government recognized that schools in poor locations did need more support than those in more comfortable places, the redistribution of meager funds usually failed to compensate. The income available to public schools from parents and community resources varied significantly, and most rustbelt schools fell short of the kinds of facilities, equipment, and support staff necessary for them to really do what is expected of them, let alone what they would like to do. At the same time, the public education system seemed incapable of preventing significant teacher and administrator turnover in rustbelt schools, and it continued to churn out new reform documents inadequately supported by funding or capacity-building measures such as professional development. The effect of this neoliberal state policy approach is inherently exploitative, requiring educators to be "doing very much more with very much less." However, disadvantaged public schools daily face demands other than those created by the neo-economic policies driving the restructuring and destructuring of public education.

## Everyday Onslaughts

In the rustbelt, particular public school populations create specific and pressing demands. All public schools report increases in the numbers of families under considerable stress, as working-class and middle-class families alike experience the flow-on effects of neoliberal globalism—job insecurity, rising costs, and escalating anxiety.

It is the sheer concentration of adults and children who have been living on the edge for some years that produces a daily onslaught of counseling, conflict resolution, neighborhood mediation, advocacy with government and nongovernment agencies, inter- and intrapersonal crises, harassment, and bullying. Rustbelt schools not only have fewer resources, but they also have less time than other public schools to invest in curriculum and pedagogical reform because they have no option but to attend to these time-consuming and energy-draining poverty effects.

As well, many public schools in the rustbelt have very particular issues with which they must cope. A few near public hospitals have large number of parents who are seriously ill and require regular treatment, and they must deal with children who are often not only prime caregivers but are also afraid and worried. A few public schools are next to women's shelters and they face a stream of shocked and grieving children. Some have extraordinary levels of transience and nearly half of their school population changes during a year, wreaking havoc on class organization, budgets, and systematic learning.

Some are in neighborhoods with large numbers of recent refugees in which national disputation over immigration policy takes on difficult daily personas, while others support Indigenous students who continue to be over-represented in suspension and exclusion statistics, as well as the lowest achievement percentiles.

When material realities such as these have been recounted to federal policy makers, they have been quick to accuse rustbelt school advocates of excuse making. They point to heroic local and international "lighthouse" schools as proof that social context does not matter, and they initiate suicide prevention, anti-depression, and interagency projects as if the families involved can be easily diagnosed, treated, and case-managed separately from the their lives embedded in the rustbelt. The ongoing educational conundrum—how to shift school education from one that sorts, sifts, and rewards children with particular kinds of cultural, economic, and social capitals—is now made much more difficult to tackle. Rustbelt schools struggle on as isolated devolved units, with diminished time and resources, significant student and staff turnover, policy churn, vastly increased expectations and pressures, and fewer other government and nongovernment agencies with whom they can work.

For this to change, the daily realities of rustbelt schools, and the economic, cultural, social, and political production of the rustbelt in and as "neighborhoods," must be recognized. This complex ecology of poverty, stress, ill health, diminished resources, and greater demands must be made both visible and troubling to policy makers.

## New Directions?

In early 2002, a Labor government with the support of two former Liberal Party "Independents" claimed a fragile electoral victory in South Australia. The premier, Mike Rann, in a gesture designed to link him to Tony Blair in the UK, established a Ministry for Social Inclusion, a Social Inclusion Board, and a Social Inclusion unit. This is an expression of the lasting legacy of the former British imperial era of globalization that is still strongly represented in the Australian political consciousness (Shore, this volume). The two priorities are homelessness and early school leaving.

Both of these "targets" could be dealt with superficially. On the other hand, they could be powerful policy levers. A sophisticated policy problematization could take up how it is that the tangle of supranational, national, and state policies come together with multinational corporate decisions, neighborhoods, and families, and a stripped-down public school system. It could mobilize findings from research that show how schools are complicit in the production and reproduction of the low achievement of rustbelt children (Marks, McMillan, and Hillman, 2001), that Vocational Education and Training may not be all of the answer but rather only one part of it (Ball and Lamb, 2001), how young people decide in ways reminiscent of Willis's lads that they would rather be out of school than in it (Smyth et al., 2000), and how schools fear and face new curriculum challenges from globalized youth cultures (Kenway and Bullen, 2001) and "choice biographies"(Dwyer and Wyn, 2001).

The Labor government has made moves that could stabilize staffing and has promised to reduce class sizes in the early years in rustbelt schools. This is a promising start, and rustbelt schools are hopeful that once again they may be seen as doing important social justice work and be supported adequately in this endeavor. It remains to be seen whether this will be the case. Deep in the rustbelt, workers in the schools and community agencies that remain witness the local lived human consequences of globalization from above and help as best they can.

# References

Allen, J., D. Massey, and A. Cochrane. *Rethinking the Region*. London: Routledge, 2000.

Appadurai, A. *Modernity at Large: Cultural Dimensions of Globalisation*. Minneapolis: Minnesota Press, 1996.

Ball, K., and S. Lamb. *Participation and Achievement in Vet of Noncompleters of School. Lsay Report 20*. Melbourne: Australian Council for Educational Research, 2001.

Baum, S., and R. Hassan. "Economic Restructuring and Spatial Equity: A Case Study of Adelaide." *Australia New Zealand Journal of Sociology* 29, no. 2 (1993): 151–72.

Baum, S., R. Stimson, K. O'Connor, P. Mullins, and R. Davies. *Community Opportunity Opportunity and Vulnerability in Australia's Cities and Towns*. Melbourne: Australian Housing and Urban Research Institute, 1999.

Bauman, Z. *Globalisation: The Human Consequences*. New York: Columbia University Press, 1998.

Carson, E., and S. Martin. *Social Disadvantage in South Australia*. Adelaide: South Australian Council of Social Services and Social Policy Research Group, University of South Australia, 2001.

Comber, B., B. Green, B. Lingard, and A. Luke. "Literacy Debates and Public Education: A Question of 'Crisis'?" In *Going Public: Education Policy and Public Education in Australia*, edited by A. Reid. Canberra: Australian Curriculum Studies Association, 1998.

Dwyer, P., and J. Wynn. *Youth, Education and Risk:. Facing the Future*. London: Routledge Falmer, 2001.

Forster, C. "Economic Restructuring, Urban Policy and Patterns of Deprivation in Adelaide." *Australian Planner* 24, no. 6 (1986): 6–10.

Hamnett, S., and R. Freestone, eds. *The Australian Metropolis: A Planning History*. Sydney: Allen and Unwin, 2000.

Hugo, G. "South Australia's Population at the Turn of the Century." In *Beyond the Contract State: Ideas for Social and Economic Renewal in South Australia*, edited by J. Spoehr, 55–91. Adelaide, Australia: Wakefield Press, 1999.

Kelsey, J. *Reclaiming the Future: New Zealand and the Global Economy*. Wellington, New Zealand: Bridget Williams, 1999.

Kenway, J., and E. Bullen. *Consuming Children: Education—Entertain—ment—Advertising*. Buckingham, UK: Open University Press, 2001.

Lloyd, R., A. Harding, and H. Greenwell. "Worlds Apart: Postcodes with the Highest and Lowest Poverty Rates in Today's Australia." Paper presented at the National Social Policy Conference, Sydney, July 2001.

Marginson, S. *Markets in Education*. St. Leonards, Australia: Allen & Unwin, 1997.

Marks, G., J. McMillan, and K. Hillman. *Tertiary Education Performance: The Role of Students' Background and School Factors. Lsay Report 22.* Melbourne: Australian Council for Educational Research, 2001.

Mink, G. *Welfare's End.* Ithaca, NY: Cornell University Press. 1998.

Nozick, R. *Anarchy, State and Utopia.* Oxford: Blackwell, 1974.

Peel, M. *Good Times, Hard Times: The Past and Future in Elizabeth.* Melbourne: Melbourne University Press, 1995.

Pilcher, J., and S. Wagg, eds. *Thatcher's Children? Politics, Childhood and Society in the 1980s and 1990s.* London: Falmer, 1996.

Pusey, M. *Economic Rationalism in Canberra: A Nation Building State Changes Its Mind.* Cambridge, UK: Cambridge University Press, 1991.

Rees, S., G. Rodley, and F. Stillwell. *Beyond the Market: Alternatives to Economic Rationalism.* Leichhardt, Australia: Pluto Press, 1993.

Smyth, J., R. Hattam, J. Edwards, J. Cannon, S. Wurst, N. Wilson, and G. Shacklock. *Listen to Me, I'm Leaving: Early School Leaving in South Australian Secondary Schools.* Adelaide, Australia: Department of Education, Training and Employment, Senior Secondary Assessment Board of South Australia and Flinders Institute for the Study of Teaching, Flinders University, 2000.

Smyth, P., and Cass, B. eds, *Contesting the Australian Way: States, Markets and Civil Society.* Melbourne, Australia: Cambridge University Press, 1998.

Spoehr, J. *Beyond the Contract State.* Adelaide, Australia: Wakefield Press, 1999.

Taylor, S., F. Rivzi, B. Lingard, and M. Henry. *Educational Policy and the Politics of Change.* London: Routledge, 1997.

Thomson, P. Thoroughly modern management and a cruel accounting: The effect of public-sector reform on public education. In *Going Public: Education Policy and Public Education in Australia*, edited by A. Reid, 37–46. Canberra, Australia: Australian Curriculum Studies Association, 1998.

———. "Doing Justice: Stories of Everyday Life in Disadvantaged Schools and Neighbourhoods." unpublished PhD thesis, Deakin University, 1999a.

———. "That's Where My House Is." *Arena Magazine,* (1999b). no. 42, Aug–Sept (1999): 37–40

———. "Like Schools, Educational Disadvantage and 'Thisness.'" *Australian Educational Researcher,* 27, no. 3 (2000): 151–66.

———. *Schooling the Rustbelt Kids: Making the Difference in Changing Times.* Sydney, Australia: Allen and Unwin, 2002.

Travers, P., and S. Richardson. *Living Decently: Material Well-Being in Australia.* Melbourne: Oxford University Press, 1993.

Troy, P. *Serving the City: The Crisis in Australia's Urban Services.* Sydney: Pluto Press, 1999.

Webber, M., and M. Crooks, eds. *Putting the People Last: Government, Services and Rights in Victoria.* Melbourne: Hyland House, 1996.

Wiseman, J. *Global Nation? Australia and the Politics of Globalisation.* Melbourne: Cambridge University Press, 1998.

# Chapter 6

# International Trade in Education Services: Governing the Liberalization and Regulation of Private Enterprise

Christopher Ziguras

## Introduction

Education is being traded across national boundaries, and the number of students and institutions involved in this trade is growing rapidly. The international trade in education services is generally more commercialized and less regulated than education delivered within national boundaries. Governments have traditionally been concerned with the provision of education for their own local students as part of the nation-building role of the state. Today, students and educational institutions are increasingly internationally mobile, and their activities often escape the scrutiny of national-focused education policies. In the past decade, the provision of education across national borders has grown dramatically; however, the governmental frameworks through which such programs are regulated have yet to solidify, with many countries introducing new regulatory measures through the 1990s. In addition, governments are enmeshed in, and constrained by, existing and emergent regulatory structures and trade agreements at national, regional, and global levels.

While we should *never* treat education as a privately consumed commodity, we nonetheless have to consider how the international market for educational services is to be regulated. In particular, governments increasingly need to consider what social, educational, and economic objectives they want to encourage from the international trade in education, what principles should govern its regulation, and the best mechanisms to achieve these objectives. This chapter examines a range of arguments in favor and against further liberalization of trade in education services, which are motivating governments and lobby groups from many countries during World Trade Organization (WTO) negotiations. The chapter sets out the social and economic objectives that proponents of trade liberalization believe can be achieved by governments adopting the regulatory principles embodied in the General Agreement on Trade in Services (GATS), and outlines the major criticisms of the WTO framework. The chapter deals primarily with international trade in tertiary education, which, along with English-language programs, accounts for the vast majority of programs.

## Regulating International Trade in Education

Historically, the most common form of international trade in education involves students traveling to another country to study for a period of time. This is referred to as "consumption abroad," since the student travels abroad to study in the country where the supplier is located. Around the world, there are now nearly two million international students, nearly two-thirds of whom study in just six countries—the United States, the UK, Germany, France, Australia, and Japan. The number of international students studying in OECD countries has doubled over the past twenty years, with the largest increases in Australia, New Zealand, and the UK. The majority of foreign students in OECD countries are from Asia (41 percent) or Europe (36 percent) (OECD, 2002b: 3–5).

This form of international education is regulated in a number of ways. First, students wanting to travel abroad to study may need permission from their government in the form of a visa or permission to convert currency. These requirements are common in former socialist countries where governments see these measures as necessary to ensure that students return home after their studies rather than emigrate and contribute to an international brain drain. The second form of regulation students are likely to encounter is visa requirements of the country in which they intend to study. These requirements often include evidence of the students' capacity to support themselves financially during the course of their studies; health checks; and restrictions on their ability to do paid work while studying, on the length of time they may stay in the country, and on the types of institutions and programs in which they may enroll.

More recently, educational institutions have begun to offer programs to students in other countries through "cross-border delivery," where the provider and recipient of a service remain in their own countries and the student studies with the aid of postal and electronic communication with the institution. In international distance education and online education, teachers and students are able to remain in their own countries and communicate through post, fax, telephone, and the Internet. Because the educational institution is operating from outside the student's country, it is difficult for governments to regulate this form of international education, and most place no restrictions on it. Governments can only really restrict this mode of supply through postal or communications regulations, and, as a consequence, this is one of the least regulated forms of trade in education (WTO, 1998: 8).

Despite the massive hype surrounding global online education during the 1990s, students have not flocked to these programs and instead have preferred transnational programs that are offered jointly by a foreign university in conjunction with a local institution that is able to provide a campus, local teaching staff, a library, computer access, and other services needed by students (Davis, Olsen and Bohm, 2000; Flew, 1998; Ziguras and Rizvi, 2001). While the international mobility of students is a well-established and growing feature of higher education, the international mobility of institutions and courses on a large scale is a more novel phenomenon. "Transnational education" describes programs in which learners are located in a country other than the one in which the awarding institution is based (UNESCO and Council of Europe, 2000). This form of delivery is referred in the WTO framework as "commercial presence," while in Australia the term "offshore education" is also commonly used to describe such programs.

During the past decade, the transnational provision of education has increased dramatically, particularly in Europe and Southeast Asia, where British, Australian, and American institutions have been at the forefront of educational innovation, delivering programs through local partner organizations, such as private colleges, universities, and professional associations (Bennell and Pearce, 1998). Blight and West (GATE, 2000) estimate that demand for transnational education by a sample of Asian countries (excluding China) will rise to more than 480,000 students by 2020. British offshore programs enrolled around 140,000 students in 1996–97, nearly as many international students as were studying in the UK at tertiary level the same year: 199,000 (OECD, 2002b: 13).

The second largest provider of transnational education, Australia, had around 35,000 offshore students in 2001, predominantly located in Singapore, Hong Kong, Malaysia, and China (Kemp, 2001). The proportion of international students in Australian universities who were enrolled in distance and offshore programs is growing rapidly, from 18 percent in 1997 to 35 percent in 2001 (OECD, 2002b: 13). Transnational education is a key feature of the process of globalization of higher education, in which globally mobile programs operating as tradeable services, facilitated by information and communications technology, use innovative delivery modes and partnerships to respond to student demand fueled by the exigencies of the (multilingual) knowledge economy and the lifelong learning required to find work (McBurnie and Ziguras, 2001; Scott, 2000; van Damme, 2000).

The commercial presence of foreign educational institutions is regulated in a number of ways. First, many countries impose restrictions on the type of local partner institution; for example, whether a local university may offer joint programs with a foreign university, whether a local private college may jointly offer degree programs with a foreign university, whether a foreign institution may establish a wholly owned subsidiary, or whether ministerial approval is needed for branch campuses. Second, in addition to quality assurance and accreditation requirements of the institution's home country, such programs are usually subject to quality assurance measures in the host country, which are designed to ensure that the program's curriculum, teaching staff, facilities, and standards are equivalent to those in the institution's host country (Ziguras, 2001).

In addition to these forms of educational provision listed above, lecturers and teachers often travel abroad to teach students in other countries, and this form of trade in educational services is referred to (rather awkwardly) by the WTO as the "movement of natural persons." Regulatory mechanisms usually take the form of immigration restrictions, which often stipulate the types of foreign workers who are not allowed to be sponsored by a foreign corporation to provide a service and the maximum duration of their stay. Governments are usually motivated by a desire to see their own citizens employed in preference to foreign nationals, whereas multinational organizations value the ability to move their workforce between branches in different countries. In higher education, transnational providers move lecturers and senior administrative staff between campuses in various countries. Regulations governing the movement of "natural persons" usually do not differ between sectors of the economy, so employees of educational institutions are often treated in a similar manner to employees in any other service organization by governments that have committed to GATS (WTO, 1998: 8).

## The Liberalization Agenda

Discussion about international trade in higher education has become distinctly polarized in recent years, as proponents and opponents of trade liberalization focus their attention on the negotiations under the WTO's General Agreement on Trade in Services (GATS). GATS came into force in 1995, and the first major round of renegotiations of countries' voluntary commitments took place in 2003. With the dramatic politicization of all forms of international trade regulation resulting from the widespread reaction against unrestrained economic globalization, negotiations over the liberalization of educational services under GATS are very sensitive. One of the most widely debated areas is the liberalization of access to national education "markets" by foreign institutions either through cross-border supply or commercial presence.

All members of the WTO are signatories to GATS, which requires them to treat all other WTO member countries equally, promote transparency in trade regulation, and establish legal processes in each country for settling disputes (Colas and Gottlieb, 2001). In addition to these requirements, within the GATS agreement is a schedule of voluntary commitments made by each country in relation to particular groups of services. At its most basic level, GATS attempts to enable greater international trade in services by enhancing the transparency, or clarity, of existing measures affecting trade.

The commitments are in relation to two forms of "discrimination" that impede commercial activity (Snape, 1998). First, governments can choose to commit to allow unrestricted "market access," which means that they will not discriminate between existing providers and new entrants into a market. When governments commit to allowing unrestricted market access, they agree not to protect existing education providers from competition from new entrants. The government is agreeing not to limit the number of providers, the number of students they may enroll, the legal form of new entrants (cooperative organization, for-profit company, statutory organization, etc.), or the foreign ownership of providers. Second, governments can choose to commit to not discriminate between domestic and foreign providers of services, referred to as the "national treatment" principle. When governments commit to the national treatment provisions of GATS, they agree to treat foreign providers no worse than domestic providers. If a foreign provider wishes to supply educational programs, it should not be discriminated against in approvals processes, financial viability tests, quality assurance requirements, or the recognition of qualifications.

A first round of commitments was made by governments prior to GATS coming into force in 1995 or after this date in the case of countries such as China that have since joined the WTO. Few WTO members have made comprehensive commitments to liberalize trade in education so far, making education services one of the least liberalized services sectors in the GATS (OECD, 2002a). The second round of negotiations conclude in 2005. From October 2002, WTO member countries make requests for trade concessions from their trading partners, who will in turn make counter-requests and offers. These requests will likely focus on restrictions imposed by education "importing" (Majority World) countries, which "exporting" (Minority World) countries feel are adversely affecting the commercial activities of educational institutions from their country. Supporters of freer cross-border provision of higher education are optimistic about future liberalization and see the GATS framework as one means of achieving this (United States International Trade Commission, 1997: 4.11).

While recent attention has been focused on GATS, it is important to bear in mind that it is only one of several parallel processes resulting in the greater permeability of borders for mobile students, teachers, and educational institutions. Trade in education is also facilitated by regional and bilateral free-trade agreements, and often these have more far-reaching implications. For example, within the European Community and the Australia–New Zealand Closer Economic Relations Agreement, international students from member countries are treated in the same way as local students. This greatly enhances international student mobility within Europe and between Australia and New Zealand.

Discussion of trade liberalization and its effects on education has been distinctly polarized. On one side, governments and pro-trade lobby groups have produced assessments of what they see as the major barriers to unfettered trade in higher education, in order to clarify their priorities in future negotiations (United States International Trade Commission, 1997; WTO, 1998, 2000; GATE, 1999; APEC, 2001). These studies are very generalized surveys, and usually avoid making reference to specific barriers or the consequences of removing them. On the other side of the divide, there are warnings that the WTO is aiming to destroy public education on a global scale (Barlow and Robertson, 1996; Education International and Public Services International, 2000; Kelsey, 1997, 1999, 2000; Altbach, 2001; Wesselius, 2002). These accounts are similarly vague, in that they tend to make dire predictions without providing concrete case studies of past or future consequences of the commitments of GATS in particular countries. In the remainder of this chapter, I will set out the major lines of argument in favor and against further liberalization.

## Economic Benefits for Exporting Economies

International trade in education is clearly of benefit for the economies of the major exporting nations (largely Minority World nations), and the leading exporters of education generate significant foreign exchange income from trade in services, including the United States (US$10.3 billion), the UK ($3.8 billion), and Australia ($2.2 billion) (OECD, 2002b: 11). Exporting governments are quite open about their economic aims in pursuing more open borders. For example, the Australian government has stated that it intends to "pursue negotiations on education services in order to encourage liberalization commitments from WTO members and greater market access to sectors of our trading partners" (DETYA, 2000: 215).

While the rapid growth in the number of students traveling overseas to study is in part a consumer-driven response to local undersupply of places, it has also been fueled by the shortage of public funding facing many universities in exporting countries. This is perhaps most pronounced in Australian universities.

Australia has the second highest proportion of international students after Switzerland, and many universities are now financially dependent on fees from international students to supplement decreasing public funding. As a result, their budgets are extremely vulnerable to fluctuations in the international education market and the fate of inherently risky overseas commercial ventures. The economic dependence of Australian institutions and governments on revenue from international students makes them ardent advocates of trade liberalization. If international education were to be discouraged by governments, resulting in decreasing numbers of international students, the financial viability of many Australian universities would be threatened.

## Expanding Access to Education
## in Importing Countries

Proponents of educational trade argue that the growth in student and institutional mobility should be seen as a response to and expression of market forces. Unmet demand for education in one place leads students to study elsewhere where the supply is greater. Likewise, educational institutions often see the establishment of overseas operations as an alternative means of responding to unmet student demand in other countries (largely in the Majority World), thereby assisting in building educational capacity where the demand exists. The United States asserts that the presence of foreign education providers "increases the variety and amount of education services available to WTO members" (WTO, 1998: 1). Accordingly, the United States has argued that countries' policies on transnational education should "be reviewed and the restrictions liberalized to the greatest extent possible" (WTO, 1998: 2).

More recently, the United States has emphasized that the GATS does not threaten public education but instead is focused on expanding trade in private education and training, which, it argues, "will continue to supplement, not displace, public education systems" (WTO, 2000). Australia also argues that educational trade can expand both the number and range of educational options available to students. Similarly, Australia and New Zealand's recent negotiating proposals also recognize that governments play a significant role in the financing, delivery, and regulation of education, and support further liberalization in educational services as a means of supplementing and supporting the range of educational options provided by the state (WTO, 2001a, 2001b).

As demand for higher education has outstripped supply in many countries, growing numbers of students have traveled overseas to study, a form of trade that is difficult for governments to restrict. In some cases, governments have used selective recognition of foreign qualifications as one means of limiting the desirability of overseas study, but even these measures generally only apply to graduates who seek professional registration or employment in the public-sector. There are several issues arising from the growth in overseas study that concern importing governments. First, there are balance of trade implications, since these students take a considerable amount of money out of the country, which could otherwise be spent domestically. Second, overseas study does not assist in the development of increased local capacity that could redress the undersupply of university places. Third, many students who study overseas seek residency in the country in which they study, causing some governments to be concerned about the resulting "brain drain" of the highly educated to education exporting nations. In response to these issues, some governments have sought to promote transnational programs. Malaysia's approach provides a good example.

In 1995, the 20 percent of Malaysian students who were studying abroad cost the country around US$800 million in currency outflow, constituting nearly 12 percent of Malaysia's current account deficit (Silverman, 1996: 26). While part of the solution was to increase the capacity of public universities (Neville, 1998), the government saw the local private sector as the key means of reducing this currency outflow and in the long term of transforming Malaysia into a net exporter of higher education (Ismail, 1997). With the passage of the Private Higher Educational Institutions Act 1996, the government formally began to encourage the private sector to play a complementary role in the provision of higher education. As a result of these measures, by the end of 1999 the proportion of young Malaysians between seventeen and twenty-three years of age in higher education had increased dramatically to 22 percent, with 167,507 enrolled in public universities and an estimated 203,391 in private institutions, according to government figures (Johari, 2000: 8).

By 2000, there were eleven public higher educational institutions, seven new local private universities, three foreign university branch campuses, and more than 400 private colleges approved by the Malaysian government (Challenger Concept, 2000: 203–4, 218–24). Once established, foreign universities' branch campuses are subject to the same regulation as local private universities, and no substantial distinction is made in the legislation between other local and foreign private educational institutions. The presence of a large number of foreign programs in Malaysia has brought the expected trade benefits, and that country is already making progress in its quest to become a net exporter of higher education by 2020 (Malaysia, Government of, 1991), as the number of international students studying in Malaysia has grown rapidly. By moving away from consumption abroad to other modes of supply of education, Malaysia hopes that liberalization of trade will result in increased local capacity and therefore less need for students to travel abroad, leading to reduced imports and economic benefits resulting from a more highly educated domestic workforce.

Critics of trade liberalization point out that increased reliance on private and foreign providers will exacerbate social inequalities in access, particularly in developing countries. They fear that local public institutions may lose staff and students to wealthier, more commercially driven foreign providers, creating a two-tier system of higher education in developing countries. This threatens the well-being of public institutions with a commitment to serving the national interest and to teaching a broad range of courses that may not be commercially viable. Overall, they generally agree that capacity will be increased.

## The Dangers of Commercialization and Commodification

Educational trade raises concerns about the commodification and rationalization of education in both importing and exporting countries. GATS and other "free" trade agreements seek to create more freedom for private and foreign providers, which some see as challenging the role of the modern nation-state as the key provider of public education. Opponents see GATS as increasing the power of multinational institutions at the expense of public education providers and democratic control over education policies. In particular, public-sector organizations and trade unions have seen GATS as leading to increased pressure in favor of privatization of education (Altbach, 2001; Education International and Public Services International, 2000; Kelsey, 1997). While trade in educational services can respond to unmet student demand, the resulting supply is determined by the market and responds to the private needs, of employers and individual students rather than broader public needs; for example, for graduates in fields that are socially necessary but where there is little financial incentive for private investment by families in education, such as in the fields of nursing, teaching, or social work.

New Zealand researchers exploring the flow-on effects of higher student fees have summarized the tensions between *regulating the public good by means of market forces* and the benefits of *government subsidized private interests* that are at the heart of the debate; in the privatized education market,

> the quantity and mix of education services provided will be determined by decisions based on private benefits and costs. Spill over benefits to others will not enter into the decision making process of the consumers and sellers of such services because these benefits will not be relevant from their perspectives. Governments acting as

agents for society are able to take a societal perspective which will capture all costs and benefits relevant to society. Education may also be regarded as a merit good to which all citizens should have access regardless of their ability to pay. (Scott, 2000: 6)

The range of offerings may meet the needs of some students and some sections of the labor market, but are less likely to meet the perceived social and developmental needs of the nation. International students are more attracted than domestic students to programs in business and administration, information technology, engineering, and humanities and arts, but are less likely than local students to enroll in programs in education, science, and health (OECD, 2002b: 9).

Transnational education, in particular, challenges the modernist, industrial conception of public education as a central function of the nation-state because it is neither national nor provided by the state. A recent report on the development of transnational education, commissioned by European university rectors, dismissed "apocalyptic" visions, but nonetheless warned that "national autonomy and sovereignty in the domain of higher education (and tertiary education) have never before been challenged on such a scale" (Adam, 2001: 6–7). Such concerns are underlined by debates surrounding endeavors to liberalize privatized buying and selling of education services under GATS. One of the leading scholars of international education, Philip Altbach (2001), recently highlighted the inherent contradiction in which the drive to accumulate capital through the marketization of education undermines the education—its knowledge base, relationships, and practices—on which the realization of capital depends (see also Raduntz in this volume). He argues:

If higher education worldwide were subject to the strictures of the WTO, academe would be significantly altered. The idea that the university serves a broad public good would be weakened, and the universities would be subject to all of the commercial pressures of the marketplace—a marketplace enforced by international treaties and legal requirements.... Subjecting academe to the rigors of a WTO-enforced marketplace would destroy one of the most valuable institutions in any society. (Altbach, 2001: 75)

There is a widespread argument that trade liberalization, in the interests of efforts to promote private provision of education, inevitably treats education as a market commodity, thereby undermining academic traditions of free inquiry and university autonomy (AUCC, 2001). However, there is nothing, except perhaps their ideological commitment to the political project of neoliberal globalism, to stop a government from ensuring that private-sector institutions act in accordance with these traditions by stipulating conditions for registration. As long as these do not discriminate between local and foreign-based institutions or discriminate between private and public institutions, and have an explicit policy objective, GATS does not explicitly prevent this type of regulation at this stage.

Public institutions would also be threatened if a government's commitment to national treatment meant that it would have to fund—that is, publicly subsidize—all new private providers to the same extent that it funds existing public education providers. Because governments are prevented from putting caps on the number and size of private providers, it is argued, governments will put limits on public-sector funding instead while its funding for the private sector continues to grow. The Australian National Tertiary Education Union warns that:

> The implications of this are far reaching: flow-on claims for funding from other domestic private providers, reduction in grants to public institutions as governments seek to cap expenditure, increased likelihood of recourse to competitive tendering or voucher-based funding to ensure that there is no *discrimination* by government between public and private or domestic and foreign providers. (NTEU, 2001: 116)

Most countries state explicitly that their GATS commitments on education apply only to private education services, claiming that they can continue to distinguish, or discriminate, between public and private institutions in funding and regulation.

The agreement does not put pressure on governments to fund public and private institutions equally, and recent negotiating positions from the United States, Australia, and New Zealand have reaffirmed that these leading players and beneficiaries in pushing the liberalization of efforts to privatize education do not, in the short term, seek to diminish the state's capacity to provide public education (WTO, 2000, 2001a, 2001b). What is more likely is that a National Treatment commitment would mean that governments could not discriminate between local and foreign private education providers that are registered in their country for the purposes of funding.

For instance, Australia's current neoliberal government has not committed to national treatment for commercial presence because it wants to reserve the right to fund local and foreign providers differently, that is, creating an "exception" where it discriminates between private and public education providers (DFAT, 2001).

## Regulating Private Education

GATS and most regional and bilateral trade agreements discourage governments from regulating the private sector by restricting the number and size of providers or by discriminating between local and foreign providers. Instead, these agreements encourage governments to meet their policy objectives by implementing transparent processes for regulating the market, which apply equally to all providers. In education, this has generally entailed a shift from restrictions on commercial provision of education to a greater emphasis on the role of the state and educational authorities in assuring the quality of private education. Many governments in Southeast Asia have responded to the growth in transnational education by implementing quality assurance and accreditation requirements for private and public higher education providers, at least replacing inconsistent policies toward both local public institutions and foreign private institutions with internationally standardized procedural conceptions of quality (McBurnie and Ziguras, 2001). The threat posed by foreign providers has spurred these governments to improve the standards required of both local and foreign private providers. Proponents of trade liberalization argue that students and the public benefit from rigorous and transparent processes for licensing, recognizing, and accrediting private providers.

One impact of educational globalization is the increasing interdependence of governments in regulating cross-border economic activity, including transnational education, which clearly requires coordinated regulatory measures by more than one nation-state. Pressures against "exceptions" are effected and "harmonization" achieved through bilateral, regional, and various supranational cooperation mechanisms. Many such mechanisms are currently being explored in relation to transnational education (van Damme, 2000). Many national agencies are threatened by the need to "harmonize" standards. The Joint Declaration on Higher Education and the General Agreement on Trade in Services signed by the European University Association, the Association of Universities and Colleges of Canada, the American Council on Education and the (U.S.) Council for Higher Education Accreditation argues that GATS may undermine national prerogatives and put at risk "quality, integrity, accessibility and equity" (AUCC, 2001). It notes that signatory members are already committed to promoting education mobility "using conventions and agreements outside of a trade policy regime" and argues that any additional benefits of GATS are outweighed by the potential dangers. It urges member countries to make no commitments (or, where commitments have already been made, no further commitments) on postsecondary education under GATS.

The signatories to the joint statement and many other opponents of the GATS argue that the agreement threatens the ability of governments to regulate the private sector to pursue social policy objectives. There is widespread concern that "free" trade measures such as GATS and regional trade agreements will remove the power of the state to determine national education policies, and hamper the civic and nation-building functions of education. Anti-WTO manifestos often claim that the GATS principles of nondiscrimination regulation aim to prohibit all forms of business regulation in the services sector. The following statement is typical of these calls to action:

> The GATS aims to increase global trade in services by removing restrictions to trade in services. Such restrictions include government measures like professional standards, taxation policies, legislation to protect the environment or government policies to maintain public services. (Wesselius, 2002: 4)

However, these fears may or may not be unfounded. At least the preamble to the agreement explicitly recognizes "the right of Members to regulate, and to introduce new regulations, on the supply of services within their territories in order to meet national policy objectives." How this is to be achieved remains unclear. Tensions may arise between national policy objectives and trade liberalization if countries have made voluntary commitments in relation to market access or national treatment since they cannot introduce regulations that contradict their undertakings. Governments that have made full commitments, and this is only a minority of WTO members, are able to regulate in any way so long as they do not restrict foreign providers' access to the market or discriminate between domestic and foreign providers. In addition, a full commitment to national treatment and market access in a sector requires that governments must:

- Not restrict the number of foreign education providers, either through a quota or an economic means test or (arguably) restrict their student intakes
- Not restrict the type of legal entity required for a provider to operate
- Not limit the percentage of foreign ownership

- Ensure that qualification requirements and procedures, technical standards, and licensing requirements are not "more burdensome than necessary to ensure quality of service"

Countries that use these types of regulatory measures may be able to keep them in place by listing the relevant measures as "exceptions." So far, there have been no dispute settlement cases in the WTO based primarily on services (Colas and Gottlieb, 2001). Consequently, the meaning of some of the contestable terminology in the agreement has not been tested, and remains open to interpretation and further negotiations.

## International Cooperation and Cultural Diversity

Proponents of the liberalization of private interests in international educational trade argue that it can facilitate greater understanding of international issues and cultural diversity, although these are not part of the regulatory requirements. This is a major social benefit that is achieved through enhanced international mobility of students and educators and access to foreign teachers, institutions, and educational resources. Supporters of trade agreements claim that improved international cooperation and understanding may result from international education engagement, but have made no regulatory provisions requiring this. International education engagement is claimed to bring benefits at the level of ongoing social relationships, the exchange of knowledge across borders, and the experience of cross-cultural settings. This suggests that it should be possible to point to many examples of international political, social, and business links that endure for decades between classmates from different parts of the world or the impact that graduates of foreign programs have made in many areas of society in many countries. It is true that in a time of rapid global integration, the capacity to move between the global and various local levels of economic, intellectual, and social activity is becoming increasingly important.

Critics point out that the flow of international knowledge and understanding is as unbalanced as the trade figures. This is borne out by student mobility statistics. Within the OECD countries, there is an average of three incoming international students for every local student studying overseas. This statistic reflects the fact that most international students come from the poorer non-OECD countries of the Majority World. For the leading exporters from the Minority World, this ratio is much higher—UK

(9:1), the United States (15:1), and Australia (23:1) (OECD, 2002b: 6). An important question is whether local students in these Anglophone countries benefit from internationalized education. How much is the Anglophone world engaging with and learning about the rest of the world through international education? How much is it really a matter of making a profit from selling another commodity?

One approach to developing international programs that are attractive to students from different countries is to "globalize" the curriculum so that it is largely independent of the local context of the student (Ziguras and Rizvi, 2001). The hoped-for success of global online education, in particular, relies on it being able to develop curriculum that rather contradictorily, in the words of Bates and de los Santos (1997: 49) "is relevant to learners wherever they happen to reside." What are imagined to be, and marketed as, "globalized" curricula are generic, universalized programs produced in one location for global consumption. Their relevance to where students are located is an open question, given the reliance on removing specific references to local experiences and examples that may confuse or distract remote students and focusing on supposedly universal approaches that allegedly can be applied in any context. Transnational higher education has commonly involved educators from Minority World nations exporting their own locally developed curriculum, albeit with their local references removed (Kelly and Tak, 1998; McLaughlin, 1994; Wells, 1993). While removing location-specific content is claimed to be necessary to avoid "confusing" offshore students, in trying to universalize a course, education providers risk abstracting the curriculum from real-world contexts.

Some commentators are becoming concerned about the impact of large-scale transnational provision in importing countries. Dhanarajan, director of the Commonwealth of Learning, an international distance education body, warns that the nation-building role of higher education may be being undermined by "a mismatch between offshore curricula and local hopes of building national cohesion, maintaining cultural identity and addressing local resource needs" (Guttman, 2000). Not surprisingly, this tendency toward globalized curricula has led to a growing level of criticism of transnational programs by international agencies. For example, UNESCO's assistant director-general of education, Jacques Hallak, warned that "the danger is that companies selling education outside their frontiers will attempt to impose the same standards everywhere, and this will dissociate education from the social, cultural and political origins of a country" (quoted in James, 2000: 19). These critics argue that such supposedly decontextualized "globalized" curricula reflect a particular view of what is claimed to be "universal" that is informed by the geographical and social location of the curriculum developer, which is typically the Minority World. That is, the implicit social values of the exporting countries will inform curriculum, and the social and cultural context in which students live will be largely ignored by such courses.

Some critics of the liberalization of trade for private education enterprises argue that the WTO framework focuses on education as a commercial service, and thereby it undermines the capacity of governments to shape the cultural and social dimensions of education. The Association of University Staff of New Zealand, one of the few countries that has committed fully to "free" trade in higher education, lamented that the WTO treats education

> purely as a commercial, tradable commodity. There is no recognition of its role as a means of nation-building; a local storehouse of knowledge; the vehicle to transmit culture and language; the pre-requisite for a vibrant democracy and a contest of ideas; a source of innovation and change; or a desirable activity per se. (Kelsey, 1999)

The GATS does not explicitly prevent governments from implementing policies and nor does its regulatory measures steer the private education entrepreneurs in order to achieve particular social and cultural objectives.

## Conclusion

Much of the debate over the liberalization of trading regulations governing the marketization of education through private enterprises has centered on the erosion of national sovereignty and the cost-benefits of privatization. Neoliberal advocates encourage governments to take on a more assertive role in shaping, regulating, and subsidizing private education providers to develop curriculum that addresses local cultural, social, and human capital development needs. There has been a lack of debate over the types of regulation the WTO and governments should institutionalize to ensure that the international trade in education serves the social, cultural, and economic interests of the countries involved. This debate should include discussion of the formation of national and international regulations for building a local educational capacity in those countries of the Majority World where it is needed most. An ideological struggle rages between neoliberal advocates of liberalizing the trading regulations governing the marketization of education through private enterprises ("free" trade) and those who condemn the commodification of public education and the public subsidization of private profit-making. The future of international education is quietly being reshaped by those who are making the trade agreements, while the debates are proceeding elsewhere. This is a point around which could be formed a global/local education community to engage in the work, ideas, and debates concerning the design and promotion of various forms of international global/local education.

## References

Adam, S. *Transnational Education Project Report and Recommendations.* Brussels: Confederation of European Union Rectors' Conferences, 2001.

Altbach, P. G. "Higher Education and the WTO: Globalization Run Amok." *International Higher Education*, no. 23 (2001): 65–83.

APEC. *"Measures Affecting Trade and Investment in Education Services in the Asia-Pacific Region: A Report to the APEC Group on Services."* Singapore: Asia Pacific Economic Cooperation Organization, 2001.

AUCC, ACE, EUA, and CHEA. *Joint Declaration on Higher Education and the General Agreement on Trade in Services.* Association of Universities and Colleges of Canada, American Council on Education, European University Association, Council for Higher Education Accreditation, 28 September 2001 [cited 15 May 2002]. Available from www.unige.ch/eua/En/Activities/WTO/declaration-final1.pdf.

Barlow, M., and H. Robertson. "Homogenization of Education." In *The Case against the Global Economy and for a Turn toward the Local.* edited by J. Mander and E. Goldsmith, 60–70. San Francisco: Sierra Club Books, 1996.

Bates, A., and J. de los Santos. "Crossing Boundaries: Making Global Distance Education a Reality." *Journal of Distance Education* 12, no. 1–2 (1997): 49–66.

Bennell, P., and T. Pearce. "The Internationalisation of Higher Education: Exporting Education to Developing and Transitional Economies." In *Institute of Development Studies Working Paper.* Brighton, UK: Institute of Development Studies, 1998.

Challenger Concept. *Education Guide Malaysia.* 6th ed. Petaling Jaya, Malaysia: Challenger Concept, 2000.

Colas, B., and R. Gottlieb. *Legal Opinion: GATS Impact on Education in Canada.* Toronto: Gottlieb and Pearson, 2001.

Davis, D., A. Olsen, and A. Bohm. *Transnational Education Providers, Partners and Policy: Challenges for Australian Institutions Offshore.* Canberra: IDP Education Australia, 2000.

DETYA. *Higher Education Report for the 2000 to 2002 Triennium.* Canberra, Australia: Department of Education, Training and Youth Affairs, 2000.

DFAT. *Australia's Trade: Outcomes and Objectives Statement.* Canberra, Australia: Department of Foreign Affairs and Trade, 2001.

Education International and Public Services International. *The WTO and the Millennium Round: What Is at Stake for Public Education.* Brussels: Education International, 2000.

Flew, T. "Hype and Hope at Virtual U." *Arena Magazine*, no. 38 (1998): 35–38.

GATE. *Trade in Transnational Education Services*. Washington, DC: Global Alliance for Transnational Education, 1999.

———. *Demand for Transnational Education in the Asia Pacific*. Washington, DC: Global Alliance for Transnational Education, 2000.

Guttman, C. "Offshore Threats." *UNESCO Courier* 2000, 35.

Ismail, R. "The Role of the Private Sector in Malaysian Education." In *Educational Challenges in Malaysia: Advances and Prospects*, edited by Z. Marshallsay, 135–52. Clayton: Monash Asia Institute, 1997.

James, B. "Does Profit Put Culture at Risk? UNESCO Chiefs See Profit Motive as Threat to Cultural Needs." *International Herald Tribune*, 16 October 2000, 17, 19.

Johari, B. M. "Higher Education Planning in Malaysia." *Education Quarterly*, July/August (2000): 7–12.

Kelly, M. E., and S. H. Tak. "Borderless Education and Teaching and Learning Cultures: The Case of Hong Kong." *Australian Universities' Review* 41, no. 1 (1998): 26–33.

Kelsey, J. "The Globalisation of Tertiary Education: Implications of GATS." In *Cultural Politics and the University*, edited by M. Peters, 66–88. Palmerston North, New Zealand: Dunmore Press, 1997.

———. *10 Reasons Why the General Agreement on Trade in Services (GATS) Is Bad for Public Education*. Association of University Staff of New Zealand, 1999 [cited 17 April 2001]. Available from http://aus.ac.nz/.

———. "Free Trade Trojan Horse." *Advocate: Journal of the National Tertiary Education Union* 7, no. 4 (2000): 5.

Kemp, D. *Media Release: International Student Numbers Reach Record High in 2000*. DETYA, 3 September 2001 [cited 12 November 2001]. Available from www.detya.gov.au/ministers/kemp/sept01/k209_030901.htm.

Lee, M. N. *Private Higher Education in Malaysia*. Penang: University Sains Malaysia School of Educational Studies, 1999.

Malaysia, Government of. *The Way Forward: Vision 2020*. Kuala Lumpur: Prime Minister's Office, 1991.

McBurnie, G., and C. Ziguras. "The Regulation of Transnational Higher Education in Southeast Asia: Case Studies of Hong Kong, Malaysia and Australia." *Higher Education* 42, no. 1 (2001): 85–105.

McLaughlin, D. "Contrasts in Learning in Asia and the Pacific." *Pacific-Asian Education* 6, no. 2 (1994): 41–50.

Neville, W. "Restructuring Tertiary Education in Malaysia: The Nature and Implications of Policy." *Higher Education Policy* 11, no. 4 (1998): 257–80.

NTEU. *The General Agreement on Trade in Services: Implications for the Domestic Regulation of Higher Education and Professional Accreditation*. Melbourne: National Tertiary Education Union, 2001.

OECD. *Current Commitments under the GATS in Educational Services. Backgound Document Prepared for the OECD/U.S. Forum on Trade in Educational Services*. Paris: Organization for Economic Cooperation and Development, 2002a.

———. *Indicators on Internationalisation and Trade of Post-Secondary Education. Background Document Prepared for the OECD/U.S. Forum on Trade in Educational Ser-*

*vices, Washington, DC, 23–24 May 2002.* OECD, 2002b [cited 22 May 2002]. Available from www.oecd.org/pdf/M00029000/M00029606.pdf.

Scott, P. "Globalisation and Higher Education: Challenges for the 21st Century." *Journal of Studies in International Education* 4, no. 1 (2000): 3–10.

Scott, W., and H. Scott. *New Zealand University Funding over the Last Two Decades.* Wellington: Massey University College of Business and Association of University Staff of New Zealand, 2000.

Silverman, G. "Silence of the Lambs." *Far Eastern Economic Review,* November 14 (1996): 24–26.

Snape, R. "Reaching Effective Agreements Covering Services." In A. Kruger (ed.) *The WTO as an International Organization.* Chicago: University of Chicago Press, 1998.

UNESCO and Council of Europe. *Code of Good Practice in the Provision of Transnational Education.* Bucharest: UNESCO-CEPES, 2000.

United States International Trade Commission. *General Agreement on Trade in Services (GATS): Examination of Asia/Pacific Trading Partners' Schedules of Commitments.* Washington, DC: United States International Trade Commission, 1997.

van Damme, D. "Internationalization and Quality Assurance: Towards Worldwide Accreditation." *European Journal for Education, Law and Policy* 4 (2000): 1–20.

Wells, M. *The Export of Education: Exploitation or Technology Transfer.* Sydney: Research Institute for Asia and the Pacific, University of Sydney, 1993.

Wesselius, E. *Behind GATS 2000: Corporate Power at Work.* Amsterdam: Transnational Institute, 2002.

WTO. *Communication from the United States: Education Services.* World Trade Organization Council for Trade in Services, 1998.

———. *Communication from the United States—Higher (Tertiary) Education, Adult Education and Training.* Geneva: World Trade Organization Council for Trade in Services, 2000.

———. *Communication from Australia: Negotiating Proposal for Education Services (S/Css/W/110).* Geneva: World Trade Organization, 2001a.

———. *Communication from New Zealand: Negotiating Proposal for Education Services (S/Css/W/93).* Geneva: World Trade Organization, 2001b.

Ziguras, C. "Ensuring Quality across Borders." *Education Quarterly,* March/April (2001): 8–10.

Ziguras, C., and F. Rizvi. "Future Directions in International Online Education." In *Transnational Education: Australia Online,* edited by D. Davis and D. Meares, 151–64. Sydney, Australia: IDP Education Australia, 2001.

# Chapter 7

## Responsive Education: Enabling Transformative Engagements with Transitions in Global/National Imperatives

Michael Singh

### Introduction

Efforts to teach the rising generation of citizens about the changing imperatives of contemporary globalization call for a thoroughgoing reimagining and reworking of education. Somewhat more modestly, this chapters begins with an account of contested orientations to curriculum. In doing so, it seeks to make evident the global forces nation-states are attempting to mediate and mitigate and to suggest the limitations of prevailing responses. This provides a basis for generating new questions with respect to how and why education might respond to both. The rationale for an education that is responsive the changing national/global imperatives is situated within arguments about the construction of nonlinear narratives of flexible, multi-faceted global/national relationships. Selected aims of *responsive education* are illustrated through an exploration of the problems of teaching about the localizing, historical, and ideological practices of globalization that are now in transition. Finally, this chapter offers six overlapping and interrelated lens through which to learn about uneven and disjointed global/national flows that might be studied across the curriculum—vital learnings for the expanding and deepening the autonomy of national/global citizens in the spheres of their public and private life.

The underlying theme of this chapter is that the shift to responsive education, alluded by Singh, Kenway and Apple (this volume) may usefully be understood as a process of supplementation of existing forms of education rather than their wholesale replacement. This is similar to the supplementary changes effected with each new generation of information and communication technology. Changes in telephones, radio, cinema, television, video, computers, the internet, and multimedia devices have seen continuities in existing technologies, albeit reworked or otherwise brought forward, to make advantages of changed circumstances. Similarly, all forms of education institutionalized to produce a generation of workers to service the sociopolitical, cultural, and economic circumstances of the past are challenged by the changing imperatives of contemporary transitions in globalization. This includes the use of ever-advancing technologies to supplement the knowledge producing pedagogies to be found in communities, business, and politics. It is thus the case that responsive education struggles with existing constraints to construct transformative policies, pedagogies and politics that enable intergenerational engagements with changing global/national imperatives.

"Area" or "regional studies," as an example, has been under to pressure to change in response to changes in global relations of power. "Regional studies" was developed in response to government-industrial-military interests in the Minority World in addressing the globally dispersed Cold War struggles throughout strategic areas of the over-exploited Majority World. Since Deng Xiaoping's initiation of China's market socialism in 1978 and the collapse of the Soviet Union in 1989, there has been a struggle to reconstitute "Area studies" from a postcolonial perspective, one that recognizes the restructuring and destructuring of the central place European imperial powers once held throughout the world. However, the rising generation of national/global workers, citizens and learners need an education that responds to these changes by building on the achievements of area studies that made it possible for students to learn foreign languages, to study alternative worldviews, and to appreciate sociocultural change in marginalized regions of the Majority World (Appadurai, 1996: 16-18). Current approaches to education, as articulated, for example, in curriculum statements for schools (Curriculum Corporation, 2002), are responding by ensuring they include the study of specific geographic localities, their languages and multicultural consumerism as historical products effected by and responsive to contemporary global/national dynamics. Any and every site around the world can be studied in terms of how a given nation or specific locality mediates and mitigates practices of globalization from above and below. Typically, this involves giving national or culturally diverse forms to global products and services consumed locally; this helps to explain the rise of multiple Englishes throughout the world. As well, any nation or particular locality may be studied in terms of how past practices of globalization from above, such as Western European imperialism, underwrite contemporary contestation over education, policies, pedagogies, and politics. This applies irrespective of whether "locality" is identified by its constituents as a neighborhood, local government area, remote village, rural community, suburban fringe, or global city.

Unequal and contested curriculum orientations battle for precedence in the hearts and minds of educators and the public. The transition to responsive education bring to the fore numerous issues. For instance, these include public debates and curriculum contestations over providing students the vital learning to enable them to transgress the monocultural protectionism of White-nation, English-only politics in order to secure their economic well-being via the corporate multiculturalism of the world's multilingual knowledge economies. In addition to their importance in furthering democratic dialogues, these public contests help all citizens to understand and deal with the restructuring and destructuring of the global/national connections that arose, and continue from previous eras of globalization (Apple, 2001). The explanations given below of these contested curriculum orientations indicate how educators are positioned by such competing approaches and suggest how we might position our curriculum work within and against these contradictory and uncertain trajectories.

## Contested Curriculum Orientations

None of the following contested agendas for orienting the curriculum are without tensions or problems. Some may complacently rationalize a curriculum based on the *dominating* forms of globalization, for instance, readily accepting the extension of US/American global dominance; unsustainable consumerism; and promoting nostalgia for uncontested patriarchy and anthropocentrism. Others may favour a curriculum that feeds into some people's *resentment* to the ideological, localizing, and historical transitions in contemporary globalization. They may be keen to nurture regressive parochialism and the backlash politics that uses the fear incited by neoliberal globalism to exploit people's alienation, marginalization, and disaffection. However, governments wanting to learn and wanting to enable their citizens to learn how to respond productively to changes in global/national imperatives are orienting the curriculum around *transformative projects*. Such strong governments invest in responsive education to enable their public and private institutions, as well as their citizens, to engage in a whole-of-society *transformation, in continuity* with the values of *community well-being* enacted through the global/national cultural flows of risks, power, knowledge, capital, people, technology, and information (Castells, 1997: 357). Transformative project curricula develop through appropriating the material resources of hope. This involves identifying, affirming, and elaborating the contradictions evident in both the resentment and dominating agenda that suggest transformative possibilities.

Despite the growth in studies of the popular multicultural industry and political economy of the United States, Appadurai (1996: 31) claims that "the United States [of America] is no longer the puppeteer of a world system of images but is only one node of a complex trans-national construction of imaginary landscapes." In contrast, many people around the world experience contemporary globalization as Americanization. The view that globalization is now a product of the world's only super-ordinate power has been substantially reinforced by the terrorizing wars of revenge following the criminal attacks made in New York and Washington on September 11, 2001. The networked villages of the globe are now subject to symbolic and linguistic domination by some aspects of the American culture, economy, and military. These compete with, challenge, and generally seek to overpower the production and distribution of all other identity-forming codes throughout the world. Here it should be noted that there is a substantial divide between those who belong to the networked villages of the globe and those that do not. The superhighway that tracks through these Internet-linked global/local villages is signposted by American corporate cultural logos. Furthering U.S. cultural, linguistic, and economic imperialism is a deliberate and explicit strategy of its foreign policy (Morley and Robins, 1995). For instance, the heavily state-subsidized motion picture industry continues to provide export-led advertising for American consumer products and media imaginings of how the good life might be lived. American entertainment and media exports promote U.S. political, economic, and cultural interests at home and abroad. Joining its economic strength with the control of information technology to shape people's identities and the public opinions of the world continues to be essential to maintaining the international power of the United States.

There is concern that the state is relinquishing many of its institutional capacities for protecting its citizens' public and private autonomy, forgoing its capacity for their socioeconomic security in the face of the uncertainties of global/local market forces. Women, indigenous people, and immigrants along with gay and lesbian communities also struggle to sustain a public consciousness of the state's history of repression. In the face of the neoliberal project of globalism, regressive parochial education grounds itself in the politics of resentment as a sanctuary against the uncertainties of "globalization from above" (Falk, 1999: 161–62). The withdrawal of the state from underwriting societal risk protection has been compensated for by the state-based incitement of fears of racialized Others. These reproduce the ethno-nationalist identity that was once associated with the protectionist nation-state. For instance, regressive parochial education engages with local texts, discourses, knowledge to win converts to ethno-nationalism; valorizes White-nation, English-only politics; and returns to the mythic projects of racist purification and patriarchy. Much of the tarnished monoculture of Whites-only politics seems to have long ceased to have symbolic relevance and meaning. However, from the 1980s onwards, the White-nation, English-only movement has been variously reconstituted in waves of resentment politics directed against bilingual education, multifaith religious studies, multicultural education, and studies of Asia and Africa.

This resentment politics is stimulated by the global/national restructuring and destructuring of the world economy and its failure to address the miseries of the poor and marginalized. However, it strikes out against racialized others rather than the agents imposing "globalization from above." Ironically, while resentment politics has built on grassroots discontent, it nonetheless serves the interests of neoliberal globalism. The causes for the loss of public social and economic security are displaced onto alienated and disaffected communities inciting the fears needed to foster chauvinistic and xenophobic identities. To deflect attention from the state's disinvestment in its citizen's educational security, it vilifies cultural and linguistic differences and proactive social movements against patriarchy and ecologically unsustainable economic overdevelopment. Regressive parochial education redefines the legitimacy and authenticity of the nation-state around exclusionary political criteria: racism, White ethno-nationalism, chauvinism, xenophobia, and "mean-stream" resentment politics. Governments in the Minority World have used this reactive social movement to mask the negative sociocultural and economic consequences of their commitment to neoliberal globalism. In part the appeal of regressive parochial education can be attributed to the erosion of the protectionist umbrellas of the nation-state, the Cold War superpower alignments, and the Western European imperial infrastructure—legacies of previous eras of globalization.

Not all citizens are convinced that education must succumb to the interests of this neoliberal and neoconservative alliance, let alone abandon students' identity formation and sense of agency as national/global citizens to alienation and disaffection. There is another position for educators to take. To better prepare students for lives where they will have to deal with, on a day-to-day basis, the imperatives of globalization, these educators contest the emptiness of dominating and resentment curriculum perspectives manifested in narrow, short-term considerations. Instead, they seek to develop new *transformative curricula* from latent possibilities current within both.

However, those educators who prefer exploring curriculum possibilities that respond to the social, cultural, ecological, and economical imperatives that are global as much as they are national or even local also find their efforts being challenged by the dominating and resentment curriculum perspectives with which they compete (see Morris this volume). In part, this is because they look to the corporate world for ideas about making teaching/learning pleasurable and critically engaging and for creating mesh-worked modes for accessing (across and through more permeable boundaries) and producing (rather than managing, controlling, or harvesting) funds of community knowledges (see Kenway and Bullen, this volume). The global proportions of the problems now confronting this dangerous and endangered world are informing struggles to shift the focus of education, beyond the interests of the neoliberal state. As Lynton Brown (this volume) argues, this shift to responsive education invites the testing of innovative pedagogies for developing students as knowledge producers.

These emerging transformative curriculum projects offer the potential for a new generation of integrated, national reconstruction projects. To move beyond the predatory society inspired by neoliberalism requires that state to build and preserve public and private spaces where, for example, a new anti-patriarchal cosmological consciousness might be debated and associated practices enacted (Castells, 1997: 357–61). These debates focus on reconstructing the family on an egalitarian basis, degendering societal institutions, using science and technology for sustaining ecological and multiculturally diverse forms of life (rather than their patriarchal domination of women and the environment), and integrating humanity and nature on the basis of a sociobiological identity. Aspects of this project emerge from a critically analysis of resentment politics and its manifestations in regressive parochial education. This involves critically engaging the underlying crises of state, civil society, and the economy created by the restructuring and destructuring borne of neoliberal globalism that trigger reactive and defensive social movements. While the neoliberal state and capitalist organizations may dominate and shape human society, those informed and active national/global citizens engaged in shaping "green and purple" eco-cultural codes represent significant policy actors mobilizing responsive education.

## Rationale for Responsive Education

If all curriculum is a matter of storytelling, of locating students' lives in a trajectory from past and present to future, then what reasons might justify the telling of multiple stories about the ideological, localizing, and historical practices of globalization? Nonlinear curriculum narratives about the complexities of global/national connectivities allow for student explorations of change and its legitimacy, as well as continuity, discontinuity, and the inherent uncertainties. This involves studying the differentiated, uneven, and often disjointed positioning of varying entities in global/national relations of power. The point that globalization is experienced differently by different individuals and communities; national societies; the world system of relationships among nation-states and, between them and multinational corporations; the organizations of national/global civil society; and humankind and relationship with the planet (Roberston, 1992). Globalization carries the "prospect of benefits as well as disadvantages" for all of them (Curriculum Corporation, 2002: 5).

Meaningful engaging curriculum narratives provide students with the opportunity to analyse, interpret, and comprehend the multifaceted dimensions of globalization. For instance, narratives associated with individual actors might construct the local ordering and disordering arising from the practices of globalization in ways that differ from narratives about individuals in othersettings. And these are likely to differ from the stories told by the group of eight nation-states (G8) that control international monetary instruments and exchanges and to differ yet again from the tales told by the world's only super-ordinate power, the United States (Appadurai, 1996: 33). Similarly, the narratives associated with the experiences of global civil society, transnational nongovernment organizations (e.g., Amnesty International) and subordinated nation-states constitute the practices of "globalization from below" that differ from those associated with the networks of transnational capitalist corporations that capture, filter, and distribute global/national flows. These sorts of narratives enable students to situate themselves self-consciously and tactically within the interdependent, multilayered practices of ecological, economic, cultural, and socio-political globalization/localization.

Curriculum narratives centered on dated articulations of global/national connectivities are now being reassessed in the light of the concern that the imperatives of contemporary globalization require a different educational response. For instance, histories that were once written and studied to glorify the British empire or the longevity of projects to construct Whites-only nation-states now have to answer new questions. Such questions might include how has the failure of ethno-nationalism as a socially integrative force hindered the establishment of democracies based on the sovereignty of citizens. In a number of countries, the corporate vision and division articulated in the nineteenth century and reproduced in classrooms throughout the twentieth century called for Whites-only nation-states cleansed of the admixture of all non-European peoples, Indigenous and immigrant alike. Despite assertions by White ethno-nationalists, imaginings of these emerging nation-states of the Minority World as ethnically, linguistically, and culturally homogenous are breaking down under the global flows of people from all around the Majority World.

Responsive educators are now posing new questions for history and history students to answer. For instance, how does the historical record explain the growing admixture of White ethno-nationalists cosmopolitan nationalists? What does the historical evidence reveal about the failed sociopolitical experiments of constructing Whites-only nation-states in the Minority World that that now make it possible, but difficult to pursue a cosmopolitical trajectory that invests sovereignty in citizenship and not ethnicity or gender? This involves revisiting evidence from and about the past in ways that answers questions about the imperatives of contemporary globalization. This is pulling the history of different nation-states in quite contradictory directions to that projected by and for White-nation, English-only politics. Now the histories of these nation-states have to be told anew in the light the failed sociopolitical project to create a Whites-only, ethno-nationalist fortress exclusive of the admixture of peoples from the Majority World.

The complacent, nostalgic, or even resentful curriculum narratives of ethno-nationalists are being reassessed in response to the growth of supra-national organizations and transnational movements that have made some (but certainly not all) aspects of the borders of nation-states relatively po-rous. Wars and trade are key aspects of contemporary studies of transna-tional relations. Economic matters are important to learning about various forms of transnational relations and the ways in which they are subject to multicultural contingencies and codings. Corporate multiculturalism has become an explicit feature of national/global politics, with multilingual knowledge economies structuring and shaping interactions between na-tion-states. The national/global market economy manufactures and regu-lates multicultural consumerism. Multi-ethnicity and multilingualism remain central elements in the foreign policies of the Minority World na-tion-states and their domestic formation as spaces of transnational cos-mopolitanism.

Increasingly, individual citizens and workers are thinking in complex terms, both favourable and otherwise, about the global/national economy and the ecological sustainability of the planet Earth. For individuals, glob-alization involves the problems and benefits of coming into intimate con-tacts with hybridized forms of multicultural life. In an increasingly globalized world, individuals are becoming self-conscious of changing civilizational, societal, ethnic, linguistic, and regional engagements in which their lives are already embedded. Individuals perceive and con-struct their local experiences of the national/global (dis)order in different ways, including those who refuse to accept that the practices of globaliza-tion are changing their world. Negative reactions by ethno-nationalists are expressed in efforts to resuscitate the White-nation, English-only politics of monocultural and economic protectionism. No matter how tortuous, these reactions themselves are constitutive of the contradictory develop-ments of globalization and necessitate engagement through responsive education (Roberston, 1992: 26). While individuals may make "rational" decisions to maximize whatever they calculate to be their private self-interests, we are also necessarily rule followers responsive to socio-cultural norms and contractual constraints borne of claims for reciprocity (De Landa, 1997: 19). Some, most notably those involved in the ecologi-cal, gay/lesbian, and women's movements, are able to tactically engage in

the multicultural production of collective values and the institutionalization of processes that challenge anthropocentrism and patriarchy.

The ethno-nationalist curriculum narratives of the twentieth century are
being revised in recognition of the nation-state, and humanity more generally as being a manifold, interconnected community of our imaginings.
Efforts to increase students' consciousness of worldwide interdependence,
of the complex connectivities in their lives, are sharpening their understanding of humanity's shared trajectory with the Earth. De Landa (1997:
20) and Diamond (1998) offer a dimension to responsive education that
incorporates flows of organic materials—plants, animals, germs, and
genes—that continue to affect the history of the world's ecosystems.
European colonialism is one of the means by which the genes of many
nonhuman species, especially parasitic entities, have invaded and con-
quered the world's ecosystems (Crossby, 1986).

The reproduction of ethno-nationalist curriculum narratives is seriously
flawed because it fails to provide an education that responds to the imperatives of the multidimensional, real-world national/global connectivities. This failure to meet the vital learnings that could enable students to
engage with the driving forces of globalization points to the need to rework and create a new generation of responsive education.

## Reworking the Aims of Responsive Education

Educators testing possibilities for re-articulating socially critical approaches to teaching about the ideological, historical, and localizing practices of globalization are confronted with competing curriculum
orientations. Some orientations, such as those given to complacency, nostalgia, or event resentment, draw on the weight of the neo-conservative
ethno-nationalist state for their legitimation. However, Crossby (1986),
De Landa (1997), Diamond (1998), and Wong (1997) have identified a
number of problems relevant to all curriculum perspectives. Their insights
into these problems provide one basis for regenerating the aims of a responsive education.

First, developing a nonteleological, nonlinear approach to teaching
about the transitions in global/national imperatives is required for the following reasons. History does not flow in a straight line as if it is inevitably
and necessarily leading to some predetermined good. On the contrary, De
Landa (1997: 16) argues that "at each bifurcation alternative stable states
were possible, and once actualized, they coexisted and interacted with one

another." In explaining practices of change, continuity, and legitimation, historians struggle to avoid creating a sense that what occurred was absolutely the only necessary or natural eventuality. Instead, they prefer to show "the multiple possibilities always open at particular historical moments... alternative paths could have been taken at any of several junctures" (Wong, 1997: 3). The focus shifts to making restrained suggestions about less than certain possibilities for the future, replacing as outmoded the idea of "progressive" accumulation toward some known "positive" or "inevitable" outcome. At the very least such fatalism robs citizens of any agency or power they might have. Historical events are then explained by the mutually stimulating dynamics of conflict and competition interacting with institutional norms and organizations to intensify the accumulation of knowledge needed to realize new technologies of power (De Landa, 1997: 20).

Consideration of chronology provides a second reason for making education responsive to the imperatives of our times. The task of establishing "periods" of globalization is fraught with difficulties where it reinforces mistaken views about fixed stages of human progress. Not all educators see history as different phases involving progressive developmental steps. It is not the case that each subsequent phase is necessarily an improvement on the previous stage. Instead, they argue that each new phase adds to those that already exist. Thus, ethno-nationalism is not left in the past but comes to coexist and interact with efforts to invest democracy in the sovereignty of citizens (De Landa, 1997: 15–21). In other words, rather than advancing in stages of increased perfection, successive developments accumulate different types and layers of geological, biological, and linguistic flows. These do not form completely new, closed phases distinct unto themselves. Instead, they result in complex coexistences and complicating interactions of different kinds. Each new layer of accumulated materials multiplies the reservoir of contested options for future coexistence and interactions. Curriculum narratives about globalization are a case in point here. It is difficult to characterize the history of globalization in terms of a single linear trajectory, as does Hopkins (2002: 1–10). He sees a movement from "archaic globalization" (prior to 1500s), through "proto-globalization" (beginning in 1600), and "modern globalization" (from 1800 onward) to "post-colonial globalization" (from the 1950s onwards). Rather than a succession of neat stages, the history of globalization involves a series of overlapping and interacting sequences, wherein one era co-exists with others that it nurtures, absorbs, and complements. And this varies from place to place, people to people.

Just like historians, responsive educators also face a third challenge, namely the problem of abandoning the flawed and biased Euro-American Minority World view of globalization and the Earth's history. This involves dislodging Euro-American capitalism and state formation from their privileged position for thematizing world history. It also means avoiding the privileging of Euro-American categories for analyzing the dynamics of historical change. Please note, this does not mean forsaking them altogether but rather engaging them contrapuntally with the themes and categories voiced by others (Wong, 1997: 2). The privileging and centring of Euro-American perspectives stems from a faulty

> belief in "western civilization" as the main dynamic force in world history and the embodiment of all that is good and progressive in human societies and ways of thought. Such a view is bound to downplay or dismiss both the role and the importance of other traditions and societies; indeed the experience of the majority of the world's people. (Ponting, 2001: 1)

According to the Curriculum Corporation (2002: 3), "For centuries, Europeans considered themselves to be at the world's center.... These Eurocentric views and images still persist." An illustration of this Euro-American perspective comes from the director-general of the World Trade Organization, Supachai Panitchpakdi, and his co-author Mark Clifford (2002: 7–9), who claim that China has not only remained "cocooned" and "insular" but has also "proved unable to change" and "discouraged innovation," and therefore it has had to be "pried open" by external forces, most recently the WTO. In order to replace Euro-American forms of global/national history it is strategically important to engage Majority World interpretations and analyses on an equal basis. In China's case there is considerable evidence of a long history of global engagements, albeit not necessarily on terms that served or privileged Euro-American interests (Waley-Cohen, 1999). Moreover, the historical records show that many elements of Euro-American "civilization" were developed by and imported from the peoples of the Majority World (Bernal, 1987). To avoid a Euro-American approach to global/national history, one that is obsessed with and glorifies the Minority World, the focus could perhaps move beyond interactions between the Minority and Majority Worlds to examine interactions between the different peoples of the Majority World.

There is a fourth challenge to responsive educators, namely addressing the politics of exclusion as it relates to a host of non-human actors in curriculum narratives. What would it mean for education to leave anthropocentrism behind? The ecological debates over unsustainable overdevelopment invite educators to address the idea that humans have responsibilities for the natural world. The world's ecology is of value to us because of the human need to protect the diversity of life for its own sake, not because it can provide profitable yields. In a world of complex connectivities, all things matter. Just as an Earth that contained only humans and their products would rapidly become a dead world, humans owe much of our history, present and future, to other living creatures and non-living entities (Crossby, 1986; Diamond, 1998; De Landa, 1997). In a world of fast food, fast capital, and fast communications, integrating humanity into the "glacial time" (Castell, 1997: 358) of the Earth's ecology is necessary to advancing an education that is responsive to a cosmological consciousness.

Fourth, educators also face the challenge of racism and patriarchy that are grounded in biological assumptions about genetic deficiency and innate differences in intelligence among people, between women and men, and in relation to people's sexual orientation. Racism and patriarchy are used, privately and publicly, to rationalize people's dispossession of private or public autonomy. Besides being loathsome, such sexist, homophobic, and racist explanations are wrong. For instance, Donald Horne's (1964) used the concept "the lucky country" to criticize Australia's ethnonationalist elites, dismissing them as dependent, second-hand and second-rate. The term "the lucky country" was explicitly used to question the claims made by ethno-nationalist elites that they deserve credit for building a literate, industrial, democratic state based on metals and food production in Australia. However, rather than create such a society here, ethno-nationalists

> imported all of the elements from outside Australia: the livestock, all of the crops (except for macadamia nuts), the metallurgical knowledge, the steam engines, the guns, the alphabet, the political institutions, even germs. All these were the end products of 10,000 years of development in Eurasian environments. (Diamond, 1998: 321)

Responsive educators are now engaging with "forms of language devised by and for, and to represent the worldview and experiences of groups formerly without the power to create language, make interpretations, or control meaning" (Lakoff, 2000: 91). Not only are disempowered groups such as women, transnational bilingual communities, gays/lesbians, and Indigenous people claiming the power to name themselves and to reject their naming by ethno-nationalist patriarchs, they are claiming the authority to narrate history's truth claims. It is their efforts to narrate the curriculum that provide a basis for White ethno-nationalist efforts to incite fear and hatefulness. They once possessed the unilateral, unambiguous power to use education (and other means) to create language, make interpretations, or control the meaning of women, sexuality, and Other races. Attempts to interrupt or even redistribute power, to move it away from the privileged White-nation patriarchal power structure that incites White ethno-nationalist vitriol, vilification, and hate crimes.

Thus, attempts to teach the history of the global/local connections of Minority World nation-states from the multiple, contested, and contradictory perspectives of the people of and from the Majority World raise difficult problems concerning the use of language:

> Language is important to how we understand and respond to global issues.... The words and images used to describe the world... often reflect culturally dominant values, and how the world appears to the most powerful groups and nations. (Curriculum Corporation, 2002: 3)

In the nineteenth century, the British Foreign Office developed the terms the "Far East," the "Middle East," and the "Near East" for areas of concern to its military command. These terms contain two major errors (Ponting, 2001: 10–11). First, Greece is situated as part of Europe, whereas for most of its history it had been part of the world centered to its east rather than that to its west. Second, despite its inclusion, Iran has historically been differentiated from the region to its west and has had as many contacts with the regions to its east as elsewhere. Likewise, Diamond (1998: 18) argues that the terms "progress," "civilization," and the "rise of civilization" all "convey the false impression that civilization is good, tribal hunter-gatherers are miserable, and history for the past 13,000 years has involved progress toward greater human happiness." Similarly, terms such as "classical" and "medieval" represent particular Western Euro-American views that distort the history of the Majority World. To this list the Curriculum Corporation (2002: 4) adds Euro-American terms such as "developed" and "Third World." The point here is to use this language to pursue education tasks of preparing the rising generation of citizens to participate in the democratic processes of public argumentation. Such public debates aim to critically deconstruct assumptions about the power and privilege informing these concepts.

Fifth, because past events continue to impact on people's lives, their livelihood, their well-being, and their world view, history necessarily invites moral and political evaluations about the merits and demerits of particular systems, governments, or people. People make moral reflections on the past in order to learn to make ethical judgments about the present and to make publicly justifiable designs for the future. How might students learn to make ethical judgments about history in a thoughtful, sensitive, consistent, and thorough way? What frame of reference, standards and evidence might they use? How might students deal with opposing viewpoints? Pedagogically, Abernethy (2000: 387) proposes gathering the different perspectives of the critics and defenders of an historical event, (re)constructing the debates between them, and then examining and critiquing each side's evidence, logic, standards, and visions of what might have happened should the events under discussion not occurred. In effect, enables student-as-citizens learn to engage in the democratic processes required of national/global citizens. After identifying points of agreement, points of disagreement are likely to cover various issues. These include the use, definition, and measurement of terms, as well as the selection of frames of reference for comparing changing global/national power relations. Further, these disagreements are likely to encompass differing emphasizes given to the subjective and objective aspects of the designated historical situation, as much as the differing interpretations given to the intentions and consequences of the actions of the major agents of historical change. Debates such as these are part of education's response to the need for deepening and extending democracy nationally and globally. With the aims of responsive education in mind, what vital learnings *for* life might enable students' transformative engagements with transitions in global/national imperatives.

## Responding to Disjunctive National/Global Flows: Vital Learnings across the Curriculum

Appadurai (1996: 27–47) conceptualizes the political and cultural economy of globalization around five "scapes," namely the national/global flows of technology, media, people, finances, and knowledge. Each of these scapes is subject to its own political, informational, and techno-environmental vulnerabilities, constraints, and incentives at the same time that each acts as a risk, constraint, and parameter on the movements of the others. The national/global relationships among these cultural flows are unpredictable due in part to differences in their speed, scale, and volume. Each of these overlapping flows provides a lens through which to study these disjointed and differentiated national/global flows of power, raising questions about democratizing supranational organizations. Thus, for example, the cross-border, nonlinear flows of *technologies* might be studied in terms of the restless movements of skilled and highly educated *people*, along with the production, distribution, and dissemination of *media* images worldwide. Similarly, the speed with which *money* moves around the world and the contestation over the meanings of key *ideas* could be investigated along with the languages in which knowledge is expressed and legitimated.

Against the competitive and coercive forces of corporate (mis)management and economic reductionism discussed in Chapter 1 of this book, responsive educators are exploring the vital learnings for engaging disjointed global/national flows. Vital learnings about the transitions in globalization include studying each of the interdependent, nonsequential "global/local flows" identified below and engaging students in deconstructing the disjunctive relationships among them.

The five disjointed global/national/local flows identified below focus vital learnings across the curriculum about the ideological, historical, and localizing practices of globalization. These may be studied through considerations of the *risks* to the world and the opportunities these create for global/national citizenship and the democratization of international governance. Among the risks yet to be resolved are world poverty, the transnational spread of diseases, the destruction of local/global ecologies, international terrorism, and unsustainable overconsumption. These threats are sustained not in the least because of the interactive spiraling effects of these risks with the forces of neoliberal globalism, as much as contested interpretations of what the sustainability of ecological and multicultural diversity means in practice. In response to the risks confronting the world as a whole, there has emerged proactive global/national "movements that seek to alleviate suffering across national boundaries" (Appadurai, 1996: 50, 168). Transnational women's organizations and "green" biopolitical agencies constitute a framework for producing and disseminating an alternative multicultural code for addressing global/national risks that is giving rise to the press for democratizing the transnational order of governance.

These global/national risks now concern humanity as a whole, and therefore invite exploration of proactive social movements, organizations of national/global civil society, and the prospects of "globalization from below" (Falk, 1999). The nation-state's claims to prosperity no longer coincide with the security of its citizens. Although much work has been invested in undermining the confidence of citizens in the nation-state, there has been no significant attenuation as many have been agents of globalization from above. This is especially the case given the role of Minority World governments in meditating and mitigating contemporary global/local restructuring and destructuring.

Beck (2000: 38–41) provides but one view of these global/national risks. First, there is the technological-industrial destruction of ecological and multicultural diversity. The incalculable dangers and unpredictable consequences caused by affluence include the ozone hole, the greenhouse effect, language extinction and knowledge death, genetic engineering, and reproductive medical technologies. Second, there are the dangers of destroying ecological and multicultural diversity evident in the poverty caused by multifaceted, globally structured socioeconomic injustices, including the interrelated and interdependent issues of population growth and loss of linguistic, species, and genetic resources. Third, there are the dangers posed by terroristic use of nuclear, chemical, and biological weapons of mass, regional, or national/global destruction, and the failure to address underlying causes. These risks resonate with those identified by the Curriculum Corporation (2002: 5): local/global poverty and inequality; debt in over-exploited nation-states; "mad cow" disease, SARS, and the HIV/AIDS pandemic; the pollution of water and atmosphere; and the destruction of ecological and multicultural diversity and the extinction of species. Vital learnings *for* life engages students in producing knowledge and developing skills to address these risks.

Vital learnings about the historical, ideological, and localizing practices of globalization could engage students in studying the interdependent, nonsequential "global/national mega-money flows." The "financescapes" describes the disposition of "currency markets, national stock exchanges, and commodity speculations [to] move mega-monies through national turnstiles at blinding speed" (Appadurai, 1996: 34–35). The economic framing of globalization is the prevailing perspective used by neoliberals to debate its practices. The density of international trade and the national/global mesh-working of finance and the money flows have now been allowed to escape the control of nation-states, despite proposals for a tax on the electronic transfer of all monies. In the world's multilingual knowledge economies, it is the knowledge available in humanity's 6,000 different languages that is now the focus of struggles over intellectual property rights, market share, biopiracy, and wealth creation. Languages—as the repository for knowledge of ecological and patriarchal critiques as much as technological and multicultural commodities—are what makes it possible for human beings to achieve so much across the generations (Singh, Kell, and Pandian, 2002). If for no other reason, the problem of language extinction raises key concerns about the death of knowledge that is important to the world's multilingual knowledge economies. For instance, the extinction of a local language means the death of intimate knowledge of that habitat—its land, water, plants, and animals—and therefore a loss to postindustrial technological, ecological, and multicultural ventures of knowledge that could be really useful for learning how to interact with ecosystems more wisely. In a world of globally dispersed linguistically diverse niche markets, a monolingual, English-only knowledge economy is an anti-market mechanism, that deprives film companies, telecommunications corporations, travel agencies, and art impressarios access to the deterritorialized markets that thrive around transnational populations (Appadurai, 1996: 49).

Vital learnings about the transitions in globalization might focus on the interdependent, nonsequential "global/local linguistic flows." Linguistic flows or "ideoscapes" refers to the production of knowledge, ideas, keywords, and narratives as well as to the "ideologies of states and the counter-ideologies of movements explicitly oriented to capturing state power or a piece of it" (Appudrai, 1996: 36). An important curriculum concern is to effect a transition from the knowledge management modes of education to the knowledge producing modes of responsive education. The former is exemplified by the reinvention of the decontextualized, supposedly reusable "learning" packages. The latter involves educational innovators using advancing technologies to create proximal and extended vital learning communities that generate shared funds of knowledge. The global national flows of these linguistic materials, including ideas about globalization, provide the dynamism for generating new linguistic forms and syntactic constructions. In comparison, regressive parochialism, for example, seeks unsuccessfully to create a rigid and unchanging (standardized) English, leading to the death of *othered* languages (De Landa, 1997: 20).

Vital learnings about the transitions in global/national imperatives could also engage students in deconstructing the disjunctive relationships between energy flows or "technoscape." The interdependent, nonsequential "global/national energy flows" refers to the fluid (re)configuration of postindustrial markets involved in technology, "both high and low, both mechanical and informational, [that] now move at high speeds across various kinds of previously impervious boundaries" (Appadurai, 1996: 34). The revolution in the ever-advancing *technologies for human interaction, knowledge production, and community formation* is having a dramatic impact on people's lives. For instance, they have now broken the need to have people to work and study together in a given place (Beck, 2000: 18). Further, while once there may have been a competitive advantage in the concentration of knowledge—intellectual resources—in the English language, second-generation multilingual-multi-script digital technology now makes it much easier for many different languages to enter and establish distributed and networked markets worldwide. Responsive education is concerned to study the powerful pedagogies enacted in and through these technologies for meaning making, identity formation, and emotional support.

Vital learnings about the historical, ideological, and localizing practices of globalization could engage students in deconstructing the disjunctive relationships between organic flows or "ethnoscape." Interdependent, nonsequential "global/national organic flows" refer to the transnational exchanges involved in the movements of peoples and invite acknowledgment of the racialization of practices of globalization (see Shore this volume). The movement of individuals and groups of tourists, immigrants, refugees, exiles, guest workers, students, business people and others constitutes "an essential feature of the world [and] affects the politics of (and between) nations to a hitherto unprecedented degree" (Appadurai, 1996: 33). Across the globe, immigrants struggle for acceptance as makers and representatives of transnational popular multiculture at the same time as they are acting against xenophobia (Beck, 2000: 89–90). People are less and less tied exclusively to monocultural identities or a particular geographical space, although a sense of placeable bonding remains very important. This transnational mobility does not mean any transcendence of biological and cultural racisms; it can be used to trigger exclusionary resentment politics. However, more people are linked into the symbolic circuits of transnational trade. Because multiculturalism is now a defining feature of Minority World nation-states, it is not something from which White ethno-nationalists can opt out. However, people who continue to imagine nation in the exclusionary politics of Whites-only, English-only, continue to find it difficult to cope with normal features of democratic cosmopolitics. Responsive education works with people who continue to image their national community in ethno-nationalist terms to develop a sense of national community in terms of sovereign citizenship.

Vital learnings that enable students' transformative engagement with the transitions in globalization could focus on the interdependent, nonsequential "mediascapes." The "global/national media flows" refers to both "the electronic capabilities to produce and disseminate information... and to the images of the world created by these media" (Appadurai, 1996: 35). Enabling students to differentiate between info-tainment and edu-tainment is an important part of their vital learnings about the pleasures of consumption and production (see Kenway and Bullen, this volume). The nation-state's political sovereignty over the national/global information network has been limited, but censorship has not been totally curtailed. The stream of media images produced by the global/national, postindustrial cultural market is producing a symbolic world that is canceling the equation of the state with the nation and citizens' identity. Cultural globalization is producing transcultural lifestyles, symbols, and identities such as watching the same television programs, wearing brand-name clothes, listening and dancing to similar music, smoking common drugs, and identifying with converging cultural symbols. For instance, "satellites make it possible to overcome all national and class boundaries, to plant the carefully devised glitter of White America in the hearts of people around the world" (Beck, 2000: 43). This White American globalization does not mean that the world is becoming culturally homogeneous, although the coercion demonstrated by the American wars around the world do have a powerful effect in this direction. Nevertheless, the consequences of the practices of cultural globalization are multiple and contradictory; there is a growing multicultural market involving the production worldwide of multilingual and multi-ethnic symbols. The media is, however, achieving a consciousness whereby people are increasingly aware of the world as being a single place needing a new order of educational responsiveness to global/national ecological frailties.

## Conclusion

The shift from complacency, nostalgia, and resentment mobilized by neoliberal globalism to an education that is responsive to the imperatives of contemporary globalization involves practices of supplementation. The cultural institutionalization of neoliberal globalism in education is unlikely to be replaced in the foreseeable future. Given the articulation of the power of the neoliberal state with market forces over the education of national/global publics, the challenge for educators is to bring forward an agenda for responsive education, reworking it to enable their students to make advantages of the transitions in the ideological, historical, and localizing practices of globalization. The challenge for all forms of education institutionalized is to identify the imperatives whose trajectory is likely to prevail during the course of their students' lives, so as to revivify, perhaps even re-enchant, education with its life-giving meaning. Curriculum engagement and pedagogies of enablement provide students with the agency, pleasure, and power to produce real and worthwhile knowledge about and with the resources of contemporary globalization.

The risks created by neoliberal globalism and resentment politics may be pessimistically taught as threats representing dangerous socially, culturally, and economically explosive hazards. However, while enskilling students to make analyses of the sociocultural, ecological, and economic imperatives of globalization and the despair that this engenders, responsive education is concerned that they be explicitly taught to mine these changes for resources of hope, for instance for the multicultural codes needed to nurture an eco-cultural identity. Responsive education is not only concerned to engage students in investigating the risks posed by the ideological project of "globalization from above" and to enable them, construct in this project opportunities for innovation, making the nodes within the alienation and disaffection of resentment politics available for creative, constructive community formation. It is also important to recognize and investigate the ways in which responsive education is constrained by the dominating regulatory regime of neoliberal globalism within which it inescapably and necessarily operates. However, global/national restructuring and destructuring has opened up possibilities for innovative ways of reframing the role of education. Such responses to the risks of neoliberal globalism are less an extension to curriculum work than they are suggestions for the fundamental reworking of education. This means restoring the capacity of education for enabling students to respond to and engage with the ethical dilemmas and investment risks the world now faces.

# References

Abernethy, D. *The Dynamics of Global Dominance: European Overseas Empires*. New Haven, CT: Yale University Press, 2000.

Appadurai, A. *Modernity at Large: Cultural Dimensions of Globalisation*. Minneapolis: University of Minnesota Press, 1996.

Apple, M. *Educating the "Right" Way: Markets, Standards, God and Inequality*. New York: Routledge Falmer, 2001.

Beck, U. *What Is Globalization?* Cambridge, UK: Polity Press, 2000.

Bernal, M. *Black Athena: The Afroasiatic Roots of Classical Civilisation*. London: Vintage, 1987.

Castells, M. *The Power of Identity*. Oxford: Blackwell, 1997.

Crossby, A. *Ecological Imperialism: The Biological Expansion of Europe*. Cambridge: Cambridge University Press, 1986.

Curriculum Corporation. *Global Perspectives: A Statement on Global Education for Australian Schools*. Carlton South, Australia: Curriculum Corporation, 2002.

De Landa, M. *A Thousand Years of Non-Linear History*. New York: Swerve, 1997.

Diamond, J. *Guns, Germs and Steel: A Short History of Everybody for the Last 13,000 Years*. London: Vintage, 1998.

Falk, R. *Predatory Globalization: A Critique*. Cambridge, UK: Polity Press, 1999.

Hopkins, A. ed. *Globalization in World History*. London: Pimlico, 2002.

Horne, D. *The Lucky Country*. Harmondsworth, UK: Penguin, 1964.

Lakoff, R. *The Language War*. Berkeley: University of California Press, 2000.

Morley, D., and K. Robins. *Spaces of Identity: Global Media, Electronic Landscapes and Cultural Boundaries*. London: Routledge, 1995.

Panitchpakdi, S., and M. Clifford. *China and the WTO: Changing China, Changing World Trade*. Singapore: John Wiley, 2002.

Ponting, C. *World History: A New Perspective*. London: Pimlico, 2001.

Robertson, R. *Globalization: Social Theory and Global Culture*. London: Sage Publications, 1992.

Singh, M., P. Kell, and A. Pandian. *Appropriating English: Innovation in the Global Business of English Language Teaching*. New York: Peter Lang, 2002.

Waley-Cohen, J. *The Sextants of Beijing: Global Currents in Chinese History*. New York: Norton, 1999.

Wong, R. *China Transformed: Historical Change and the Limits of European Experience*. Ithaca, NY: Cornell University Press, 1997.

## Acknowledgments

This chapter is the result of work undertaken as part of an Australian Research Council funded project. It benefited from discussions with the participants and contributors to the national project on Teaching Regional and Global History in Schools initiated by the Federal Department of Education, Science and Training. Thanks also to Linda and Benjamin, as always, for their time during which research for this chapter was undertaken.

# Chapter 8

# Performing Pedagogy and the (Re)construction of Global/Local Selves

Gayle Morris

## Introduction

> You know this neighbour in Kensington, everyday called me "sister." "Hey sister," he'd say, everyday when he see me. Then I find out he thinks I'm a nun, because of my hijab (points to her hijab). All students in the class break out into uproarious laughter, particularly the Muslim women.

Like many recent refugees, Faduumo, a young, single mother from Somalia, represents and embodies the changing fabric of diversity in Australia. The above anecdote, shared in her English as a Second Language (ESL) class, provides a glimpse into her daily life and how "others," in this instance a neighbor, see her. Identity development for both Faduumo and her neighbour is performed as diverse others interact across significant social and cultural divisions within the community. Thus, for Faduumo, migration entails not just physical dislocation, that is to say, a dislocation of place, but also a dislocation of self (Swirsky, 1999).

Contemporary adult English as a Second Language (ESL) classrooms mirror the increasing presence of adult learners, like Faduumo, from around the globe, as globalizing processes of migration bring different cultures into contact and collision. This has profound implications for education since such movements of people bring to the surface difference and the particular. Edwards and Usher (1998: 160) argue that

> globalisation, by surfacing the locatedness of each and all, highlights the significance of location and the practices of locating. [They refer to this as] "(dis)location", a conception that provides a useful, non-essentialising metaphorical resource

through which to analyse, understand and develop changes in pedagogy in conditions of globalisation.

This space of (dis)location in their view constitutes what Brah (cited in Edwards and Usher, 1998: 160) terms "diaspora space—a space which marks the intersectionality of contemporary conditions of transmigrancy of people, capital, commodities and culture."

The account offered here of the mediation and mitigation of contemporary transitions in the historical, ideological, and localizing practices of globalization is situated in the context of pedagogy. It draws selectively from data drawn from ethnographic work, including interviews with recent Somali refugees and their teachers and from extensive classroom observations in adult ESL literacy classroom undertaken in 1999. While the original research considered the multiple ways that learner identities were dynamically constructed and contested and how these constructions provide the resources through which individuals' identities and experiences are shaped (Beckett and Morris, 2001; Morris and Beckett, 2003), this chapter contributes to a broader discussion about education and globalization and the global/local nexus of identities in classrooms. I consider the extent to which current adult pedagogy engages with the range of embodied identities present in the classroom and how educators might create more possibilities and find ways of working with students' trans-national or global/local identity formation.

Where previous work has emphasized the discursive forms of socially approved identities that students display (Canagarajah, 1993; Norton Peirce, 1995; Pennycook, 2001), this chapter argues that the sociocultural formation of identity is even more significant when this formation is regarded as a *self*-construction of identity, that is, adults' intentionality, articulated through embodied action, including, but not reducible to speech actions (Beckett and Morris, 2001). This is an important key to rethinking pedagogy in globalized times. What is required is a more dynamic means to engage with diversity and a variety of discourses and practices, and in three ways this chapter will explore how.

I begin by discussing identity and second language acquisition, and I then move to a discussion of embodiment and difference, where the body takes center stage in the discussion of identity and language. Finally, I consider how certain experiences embody *vital learnings,* and how this knowledge can be confirmed and harnessed to enrich the teaching/learning context. Throughout this chapter, I "flesh out" the fieldwork evidence by drawing on relevant theoretical resources to illustrate the range of identity issues that these adult learners and teachers respond to. As I analyze and discuss in this chapter, however, identities and difference are multiple, diverse, and interrelated. The story of "identities" is to be "taken" many ways.

## (Re)presenting Global/Local Selves: Identity and Second Language Acquisition

> I suppose that if one had to identify one of the most telling factors in the relatively short-lived, if intense, history of studies in second language acquisition, it would have to be the consistent anonymising, if not the actual eclipsing, of the learner. (Candlin, 2000: xiii)

In recent years, second language theory, of which ESL is a part, has come under attack for its problematic constructions of learners and their languages as "otherness." While there have been advancements in linguistic understanding, Pennycook (2001: 144) observes, "little has been said about learners as people; the contexts of learning or the politics of language learning more generally." Peirce (1995: 19) argues that "second language educators have not adequately considered social identity in their conceptualizations of second language learners, nor how the relations of power affect students' identity formation, nor the socio-political interactions that occur within and against the language-learning context." Pennycook (1998) attributes this legacy to the pervasive "White/mainstream" (see Shore in this volume) positivist models and approaches to language teaching/learning that tend to regard difficult questions of "difference" as unimportant in understanding aspects of cognition. Despite the development of alternative or even innovative models of language acquisition, approaches to these issues in the teaching of English to Speakers of "Othered" Languages (TESOL) have worked with superficial and fixated concepts of both in terms of "culture," which in turn has then been defined as an overly deterministic category. For Canagarajah (1999) as well as Singh, Kell, and Pandian (2002), this view of cultural fixity "is part of a long history of colonial othering that has rendered the cultures of learners of English as a second language as fixed, traditional, exotic, and strange" (Pennycook, 2001: 145). In contrast, Anglo-ethnic cultures associated with different varieties of English in the United States of America, Britain, and Australia are unexplored movements of (post)modernity and normalcy.

The TESOL construction of the ESL learner as Other overlooks the possibilities that these students have multiple identities drawn from multiple resources. Such a flat and deterministic view of culture, identity, and difference is indeed all too shallow. Not only does it deal in very superficial ways with culture and identity, it also deals with limited forms of difference. Nevertheless, there are educators who take seriously the need to work more directly with learners as embodied subjects. For example, Peirce (1995) and McKay and Wong (1996) share an interest in identity and how ESL students negotiate their way through multiple discourses. While their findings move beyond the clichéd representation of learners as a kind of "generic, ahistorical stick figure" (McKay and Wong, 1996: 603), identity remains overly deterministic.

Despite her emphasis on agency, Peirce (1995), for instance, employs the single identity markers of *caregiver* or *multicultural citizen*. Similarly, McKay and Wong (1996: 583) develop a taxonomy of identify formation around notions of the *colonized, racialized,* and *model minority*, which they recognize "do not possess more than an ad hoc status." In both of these accounts, learner agency and context are downplayed, thereby perpetuating dominating constructions of the passivity and acquiescence of ESL learners. Such discourse-driven analyses of ESL learners are susceptible to two problems. They are reductive in that the "conscious action" (the conative) is minimized, and, related to that, learners' actual social and the affective experiences are similarly ignored (Beckett and Morris, 2001: 38). Their findings challenge the reductionist tendencies of much second language acquisition theory and practice, yet their efforts to (re)present the ESL learner as complex and multiple slip dangerously back into essentialism.

Thesen (1997) draws educators' attention to the way much discourse analyses neglect individual agency and ignore how identities are shaped by practices of labeling and relabeling. Discourses inevitably frame what can be said, exclude other discourses, and seek to subsume other possibilities for the development of identity. Yet all discourses are subject to contestation and change; hence, educators are now working to avoid treating "ESL" and "literacy" identities and discourses as if they are for-ever stable, fixed, and unitary. Where "discourse" is employed as a one-way process, O'Loughlin (1998: 290) suggests that this constructs subjects and bodies that "are *normalized* though discursive intervention, such that the bodies can no longer speak or have their experiences heard or interpreted." Hager (1999: 67), like O'Loughlin, remains unconvinced that "languaging and being languaged is a sufficient account of the variety and depth of our encounters with the world around us." Language alone is not sufficient for accounting for human experience, nor are subjects merely an effect of discourse. In other words:

> Language affects how we view the world, and how we make sense of the experiences we have. But it is also true that much of what we experience remains unnamed, and cannot be reduced to its articulated meanings. I urge people to be receptive and attentive to the inarticulate too, not just what is named. (Thayer-Bacon ,cited in Beckett and Hager, 2002: 167)

Anything less than a deep and variegated account of "languaging" and "being languaged" fails to attend the complexities of ESL in practice. Notions of ESL-ness and literacy/illiteracy appeal to an understanding of language and culture as merely a "representation," as opposed to actually "being-in-the-world" (Csordas, 1994). There seems to be a preference to deal with the world at the level of signification and not in conjunction with the material objects themselves. Yet the two are mutually imbricated. As Crossley suggests in his analysis of Merleau-Ponty's work on perception, "discourse itself is a fleshy process...they belong to each other as do legs and walking" (1995: 51).

## "Fixing" Identities

There are educators who acknowledge that questions of identity are closely linked to language and who recognize the importance of considering pedagogical responses to multiple forms of difference. The data presented in this section and those that follow serve to illustrate how learner identities are enacted in the ESL literacy classroom. This evidence allows for an exploration of the work of identity construction and maintenance as evidenced through classroom discourse. The first instance comes from an interview with Sharufa, a refugee from Somalia who recounts her very first day in an ESL literacy class in Brunswick. The second account is drawn from one of many classroom observations.

> There was an old lady at the club in "Brunswick," but she learned Somali in Somalia. When she came to Australia she didn't know any English but when she see the words she can say it, "One" whatever, and when she write, she's faster than us. She say [talking about her teacher], "Except Halima saying all the words, she knows everything. What about you, you all from Somalia!" Because there four or five of us from the same country she teacher saying "you're from the same country." When you don't know anything the teacher saying "what the hell is wrong with my student" so I want to learn more. (Sharufa)

Sharufa draws the attention of educators to the way in which the relationships between identity and English language learning, between the language learner and the larger sociopolitical world, powerfully manifest themselves in a contemporary ESL literacy-learning context. In doing so, Sharufa provides educators with three "takes" on identity as ascribed to self and others through discourse. First, Halima is constructed as a "knowing" student, whose literacy in the Somali language facilitates her classroom performance in English. Second, the teacher is constructed as an "authority," in terms of her interpretation that *"saying,"* English oracy, equates with *"knows everything,"* that is knowledge. Third, the teacher constructs the "other" Somali learners through her assumptions of "sameness" and, in doing so, diminishes the historical, social, and cultural differences among Somali learners. However, as already noted, identities and difference are multiple, diverse, and interrelated.

For many of the women interviewees, their cultural identities have not developed in a "straight unbroken line, from some fixed origin" (Hall, 1998: 225). Rather, their identities are marked by discontinuity, differences, and social displacement. As well as there being many points of similarity, there are also critical points of deep and significant difference that constitute "what we really are" and "what we have become." In this view, cultural identities are understood as simultaneously involving a matter of "becoming" as well as of "being." Hall (1998: 225) highlights the complexities of cultural identities, arguing that:

> Cultural identities come from somewhere, have histories. But, like everything else which historical, they undergo constant transformation. Far from being eternally fixed in some essentialist past, they are subject to continuous "play" of history, culture and power...cultural identity is a matter of "becoming" as well as of "being." It belongs to the future as much as to the past.

"Immigrant," "ethnic minority," "migrant," and "refugee" identities cannot be viewed as fixed states of "being"; they are continually being shaped within and through everyday interactions with the social world. More often than not, Majority World migrants' reasons for entry or residence in the Minority World resist strict typologies and underscore the shortcomings of *any* monolithic casting of migration or types of migrants. Their multiple identities intersect with social, class, gender, and generational identities. Cultural identities can be regarded as the hybridization of these beings, becomings, and have beens.

There is a resonance in this instance with Thesen's (1997) account of the identity issues confronting black students undertaking first-year studies at a South African University. Thesen used the analytical categories of *discourse* and *voice* to examine the intersection between the individual and the social. In doing so, Thesen was attempting to reinsert, or at least construct, the perspective of the *individual in context* that recognizes the social envelope in which literacy events take place and the way discourses create insiders and outsiders in the educational process. Her analysis questioned whether a reliance on discourse theory alone could account for the complexities that emerged from the interviews. Thesen's (1997: 504) interviews demonstrated coherent but often tentative accounts of "emergent identity" across different contexts in which students were agentive, that is, "making choices about where to merge and where to resist, assessing whether a strategy is working or not." In this respect, many of the students displayed a strategic awareness of identity boundaries that shifted over time. This commitment to exploring "identity in movement" (Thesen 1997: 506) invites the further extension of the range of identity markers than has previously been included or permitted in educational debates that explore identity at a particular point in time and place. This extends beyond conventional categories of gender, ethnicity, and language to allow for the emergence of additional categories: rural-urban transitions, migration, religious literacy practices, and a strong oral transition. In this way, the analysis of language and identities can distinguish between identity categories that are "brought along" and those that are "brought about" (Makoni, cited in Thesen 1997: 506), suggesting the need to attend to how adult ESL learners make choices when negotiating their identities.

The women I interviewed showed awareness of the historical, social, cultural, political, and ideological relations of particular systems of knowledge and social practice. This knowledge is generated by the need to locate oneself and make sense of frequent transitions in and across social and cultural contexts. The life that is lived after migration is different, not simply in terms of a dislocation of place, culture, language, and the events they lived out. Within that different life, a different identity, a different self, is reconstructed within a body occupying a new space.

## "Performing" Identities

In this second instance, the attention of educators turns to actual bodies and actual performances in the classroom. On the day of the observation, the students were preparing for a two-week work experience placement; this is a response to and expression of neoliberal globalism (see Radunz in this volume). This is the final lesson drawn from a course manual designed to systematically direct teachers' preparation of ESL learners for work experience. What follows is part of a discussion between Elaine (teacher) and Hawa, Faadumo, and Maria (students). The objective of this lesson is to foster a greater sense of what is expected of these ESL students while on work placement.

Elaine      What's a positive attitude?
Hawa       It's a…

*Before Hawa finishes her response, Elaine continues…*

Elaine      Not negative, you smile. If the man asks you to do something you smile, look happy. They are doing you a favour. Look happy, look excited!
Faadumo    Do I have to go? (on work experience)

*Several other students almost in unison make similar requests.*

Elaine      You have to. You have no choice.
*Hawa*      Why no pay? Why not $1 for 1 hour. I don't care. 20 cents.

*The teacher doesn't respond and continues the lesson by having individual students read line by line characteristics associated with "good worker" from their course book.*

Maria       "Do" learn and absorb as much as possible and always keep your goal in mind.

*The teacher interjects.*

Elaine      You all have hopes and dreams. Think of this as one way of meeting it.

*Students continue to read. This time the "Do" refers to "not getting involved in office politics." Several exchanges in first language, a few shrugs and shaking of heads. The teacher "senses" that perhaps the meaning is not clear and attempts to clarify.*

Elaine      Office politics, you know, "he said, she said…" don't get involved. Keep your private lives private. No one wants to hear about…maybe a little is okay.

Lankshear (1997) argues that industrial education is a modernist institution characterized by "spaces of enclosure," such as the textbook, the classroom, and the curriculum. These spaces work to enclose meaning and experience through a fixed curriculum that is transmitted in classrooms where the textbook is the paradigm form of authority. In this classroom instance, the learners' task is to represent the singular and definitive version of the "good worker" that is "contained" in the course manual prepared by state authorities to maximize the chances of meshing the student/worker relationship. Questions about the potential exploitation of student labor are ignored; possibilities of learning from students' expression of resistance silently overlooked. The teacher's task, as the state's embodied authority, is to ensure that students' interpretation of the text's meaning accurately reflects the preferred reading proposed by the state and to contain all other possibilities. Both textbook and teacher work to ensure that the adult learners are discursively "kept in their place" as prescribed by neoliberal globalism.

Yet the learners in this instance, as in the preceding account, work in ways that call this space for enclosing them into a world of unpaid labor into question. They question the underlying assumption about the fixity of the text(book) and the teacher as authoritative bearer of neoliberalism's preferred meaning through their active insertion of themselves into the dialogue. This is a situation where learners do not simply extract and represent meaning but rather actively collaborate in creating meaning and thus open up the potential to determine their own learning paths. They actively draw on knowledge and experiences beyond the walls of the classroom, which in this instance disrupts the normalizing tendency of teacher and text, bearers of the neoliberal project of creating closer linkages between education and the economy.

This classroom process discourages genuine participation from the ESL students as it fails to recognize or engage with the very real and substantive understanding, experiences, and skills they bring to the classroom and the funds of community knowledge they could access from there. Indeed, for these women learning has flourished in the interstices of family, community, and work life, shaped by their cultural, social, and historical circumstances. Where these funds of knowledge available through students' proximal and extended communities are acknowledged by educators, such learning offers a means with which to move the adult learners to fuller engagement and valued participation in ESL literacy classrooms. In other words, a re-reading of these classroom stories may open up a space through which to do pedagogy differently, in ways that do not close off the women's efforts to insert *themselves* and their own meaning-making into the text.

## "Embodied" Differences

Thus far, this discussion of identity and second language acquisition has suggested there are limitations to the reliance on discourse-driven analyses of identity (Thesen, 1997; Pennycook, 2001). Language educators often neglect the body as an epistemological site, preferring instead more rationalistic, abstracted, and immaterial understandings. As Hayles (1992) observes, this can be seen as part of the larger terrain of postmodernity and postmodernism in which the individual('s) body disappears in favor of discursive and linguistic constructions of fashion, deconstruction, signification, and virtual reality.

Recent work within philosophy, cognitive science, and social theory has argued persuasively that the body cannot be ignored but must be seen as intimately involved in processes of cognition and social activity. As an alternative to abstracted/ bodyless views of identity discussed previously, this foregrounds the body as a site of discursive and material identity construction (O'Loughlin, 1998; Beckett and Hager, 2002) in which emotional, physical, spiritual, and social knowledges are experienced and lived. McWilliam and Palmer (1996) suggest that the body might be understood as a seat of subjectivity and therefore seriously challenge educational theory and practice that continue to privilege "mind over body."

To speak of a "lived body," or a "mindful body" constitutes a significant departure from the traditional "mind/body" distinction. The "lived, mindful body" is understood to be an integrated being in which capability is ascribed to a body as a lived structure of experience. McLaren (1988: 58) uses the term "body/subject" as "a terrain of the flesh in which meaning is inscribed, constructed, and reconstituted." He goes on to argue that the embodied subject is the interface of the individual and society, the site of "enfleshed" subjectivity. That is, embodiment is at once material, individual, and social. After all, individuals' identities are constituted through the social shaping of bodies. Individual subjects with particular identities of gender, character, joy, understandings, and such like are the result of the immersion and transformation of bodies social relations of power.

Looking at identity, then, as something we *perform* through language rather than something *reflected* in language (Pennycook, 2001) but never reducible to speech actions helps educators move beyond the essentialized identities of much second language research and practice and enables the return of the body.

## "Embodied" Identities

The body re-emerges, not as a static signifier of identity or as a surface onto which identities are inscribed but as a place where students' (and educators') identities are re/generated and embodied. However persuasive the arguments are for seeing the body as constructed, the body always exceeds its construction in ways that cannot be described. The limits of inscription are usefully illustrated in the following instance where a teacher draws the attention of educators to the challenges and complexities of working with a diversity of trans-national learners in her daily practice:

So this Muslim woman, she would wear the hijab. She didn't wear anything across her face, her face was exposed and we went, as I said, used public transport and everything was fine. Several months later, she has become more and more strict, and now she wears a full veil, right over the top of her face, you can't even see her eyes. It's just a black gauze right over the top, she wears gloves as well…. One day when we were walking down the stairs and I was just next to her, and I thought I could ask her, and I said, "Look, how come only six months ago you came with me on public transport and you showed your face and that was no problem and now, you've got it totally covered?" And she said, "Well, I'm closer now to my religion, I'm more…I'm a better person now because I do this." Now for someone like you and I, that is just… how on earth can we possibly understand what stage each of these people are at and how do you know you're offending people. I said to her, "Aren't you worried about what people think of you?" I mean I could, because she knows me very well, so I could push the limits a little bit. I said to her, "Look, to look at you, you are very frightening. If someone on the street looks at you they would be very frightened and if there's anybody that doesn't like Muslims you're the person they're going to attack." I said, "Aren't you worried about that?" She said, "Oh no." I said, "You could have something underneath your dress, you could have a weapon and people would be frightened of that." And she was totally; she just thought there was no need for her to worry.

But it seems to be the opposite to what they're trying to achieve. In their own country where everybody wears, dresses like this, they're not noticed. Yet if they're not wanting to be noticed, they do the absolute opposite here in this culture, because they are noticed, by being so different from everyone else. And she said she wasn't concerned at all. With her I could ask and she was pretty open with me, and she just said oh, that was what she wanted to do. I still find it really difficult, you know, I try be as open as possible but sometimes I feel I must offend them by wearing what I wear or things that I say.

Of importance here is the tension that the female Muslim body evokes in the female Angloteacher's secular Christian body. It works at a number of levels. As the surface, the body is inscribed with meaning, quite literally "written on" by gender, ethnicity, and culture. In this instance, meaning for the teacher is tied to the surface or an external representation, and therefore the transition from hijab for full veil is implicated in how this learner is seen by her teacher.

The hijab is constructed as a reasonable or acceptable marker of difference, whereas the veil becomes a potent representation of the "other" frightening and threatening. The "material" transformation challenges the teacher's comfort with, and understanding of, this ESL learner—Muslin, woman, Somali—which derived from seeing that learner's identity as enduring in nature, continuing, and unitary.

Here, the adult learner (re)presents a very different version of culture, one that is lived, where knowledge, beliefs, and experiences are located in the body, where the body is the medium for having a world. Kamalkhani's (2001) research into the experiences of Muslim women in postmigration contexts and the relevance of those experiences in terms of identity making found that Somali refugee women in exile in a secular Minority World society expressed a strong wish to maintain their Islamic beliefs even more than in their home country.

In part, this may be attributed to the need to publicly demarcate religious boundaries and to assert an identity under global threat where previously in Somalia there was little need to do so. This is also manifested in the ongoing Qur'anic education of their children, attendance at Islamic schools, and varying degrees of religious practice, including the renegotiation of dress. The discourse that the teacher employs makes it difficult to understand the learner's individual body practices the body is treated obliquely as a symbol for something else, which acts to distance us from the individual's everyday embodied experiences.

This rubs up against the teacher's assumption that "Muslims" want to blend in, be unnoticed, and her confusion about why in this instance the student chooses to be fully veiled and therefore a more potent public visible representation of Islam.

But of significance to the argument being developed in this chapter is that she fundamentally misrecognizes the Somali woman's agency, that is, what the student wants to happen, how she acts upon her world purposively and reflectively and, in doing so, reiterates and remakes the world in which she lives in circumstances where she may consider different courses of action possible and desirable.

## Performing Pedagogy: Changing Performances of Learning and Teaching

What arises from these instances are accounts of "active bodies" constructing and reconstructing their sense of self and occasionally resisting the construction of themselves by teachers and textbooks that mediate and could mitigate the authority of the neoliberal state. They are not simply subject to external agency but are simultaneously agents in their own social construction of their world and their place in it. We begin to see how different components of adult learners' identities can be understood as dimensions of existence expressed by an active body. In the instances reported above, the adult learners' embodied knowledge and experience challenge the universalizing impulses of particular classroom practices and teacher discourse that privilege neoliberal globalism along with a representational epistemology.

By attending to the kinds of learners' identities that are constructed through pedagogical interaction in the classroom, educators may better be able to understand how the meaning of language and literacy acquisition for adults is influenced by their agency. We may construct learners' embodied knowledge and experiences not as distractions from English language learning but as necessarily constituting the very fabric of learning and the lives of learners.

Returning the notion of embodiment to center stage directs our attention to the complex realities of students' and teachers' embodiment in discursively constituted settings. As the instances above illustrate, placing the body at the center of analysis of identity and literacy allows different kinds of questions to emerge about the self, the individual in relation to others, and English literacy as a sociocultural practice. If embodied selves shape and are shaped along the way, it becomes important to attend to the performative aspects of teaching. An awareness of how teaching practices elicit or construct identities may well lead educators to perform differently.

By foregrounding embodiment, learners are presented in a much more complex vein as sociocultural beings. This enables a very different conceptualization of the learner as a knowing subject. It challenges the generic ahistorical "stick figure" prevalent in dominating conceptualizations of second language learners and encourages educators to explore pedagogies for giving a productive life to ESL learners' knowledge that comes with the complexity, incompleteness, discontinuity and multiplicity that are inextricably tied up with living in a world with difference. Such acceptance requires educators to revise the conceptual frameworks that currently shape their work. But as McCarthy and Dimitriades (2000: 203) argue, any strategy that seeks to address these challenges calls forth

> a recognition that our difference of race, gender, and nation are merely the starting points for new solidarities and new alliances, not the terminal stations for depositing our agency and identities or the extinguishing of hope and possibility.

The notion of learner as presented in the chapter necessitates a more holistic conceptualization of adult literacy learners within second language contexts. This means giving full regard to the emotional and somatic aspects of learning, in addition to the cognitive. This enables educators to retrieve and reveal agency and offer a way to better connect learners' funds of experiential and community knowledges with classroom practices. Such a perspective, even as it argues for the importance of agency, does not see discourses and relations of power as amenable to quick intervention. However, a committed attempt to understand these adult learners as complex, multidimensional adults, and the classroom, especially the ESL classroom, as a contestatory discursive site is needed.

## Conclusion

Classrooms are but one instance of the "little habitats—where aspects of globalization seep in at different rates, in different colours, contours, and guises" (Luke and Luke, 2000: 291). I have attempted to show conceptually and empirically that ESL literacy students bring to the classroom context substantial cognitive, social, affective, and physical understandings, and that their understandings, experiences, skills, and knowledges are under-recognized by well-meaning teachers. In doing so it has shown the multiple ways that identities are dynamically constructed and contested, and how these constructions provide the resources through which individuals' identities are experienced, shaped and unfold. This chapter explored how the learners' social and cultural conditions not only shape their understanding of experience, but also how certain experiences embody vital learnings, and how this knowledge can be confirmed and harnessed to enrich the teaching and learning context. In each of the instances presented in this chapter, I suggested a re-reading of such stories in a manner which foregrounds the body to stimulate a re-thinking of pedagogy. They provide situated examples of the very possibility of difference, and illustrate the lived ways in which neo-liberal education policies and practices are not one-dimensional.

The challenge lies in being attentive to embodied differences in ways which do not simply "re-other" those bodies and their voices that are marginalized by a reliance on discourses as markers of difference, and to develop pedagogical practices resonant with the trans-national diasporic spaces created by contemporary shifts in globalization. The challenge to educators is to see the classroom as a space in which identities are unsettled rather than established, and reflected upon rather than wished away.

# References

Apple, M. "Between Neo-liberalism and Neo-conservatism: Education and Conservatism in a Global Context." In *Globalization and Education: Critical Perspectives*, edited by N. Burbules and A. Torrens. New York: Routledge: 2000.

Beckett, D. and P. Hager. *Life, Work and Learning: Practice in Postmodernity*. London: Routledge, 2002

Beckett, D., and G. Morris. "Ontological Performance: Bodies, Identities and Learning." *Studies in the Education of Adults* 33, no. 3 (2001): 35–48.

Burbules, N., and A. Torres, eds. *Globalization and Education: Critical Perspectives*. New York: Routledge, 2000.

Canagarajah, A. S. "Critical ethnography of a Sri Lanka classroom: Ambiguities in student opposition to reproduction through ESOL." *TESOL Quarterly,* 27, no.4 (1993): 601–626.

Canagarajah, A. *Resisting Linguistic Imperialism in English Teaching*. Oxford: Oxford University Press, 1999.

Candlin, C. "What Happens When Applied Linguistics Goes Critical?" In *Learning, Keeping and Using Language*, edited by M. Halliday, J. Gibbons and H. Nicholas, 461–86. Amsterdam: John Benjamins, 1990.

Crossley, N. "Merleau-Ponty, the Elusive Body and Carnal Sociology." *Body and Society* 1, no. 1 (1995): 43–64.

Csordas, T., ed. *Embodiment and Experience: The Existential Ground of Culture and Self*. Cambridge: Cambridge University Press, 1994.

Edwards, R. and R. Usher. "Moving Experiences: Globalization, Pedagogy and Experiential Learning." *Studies in Continuing Education* 31, no. 2 (1998): 159–174

Grosz, E. "Bodies and Knowledges: Feminism and the Crisis of Reason.: In *Feminist Epistemologies*, edited by L. Alcoff and E. Potter. New York: Routledge. 1993.

Hager, P. "Robin Usher on Experience." *Educational Philosophy and Theory* 31, no. 1 (1999): 63–76.

Hall, S. "Cultural Identity and Diaspora." In *The Third Space,* edited by J. Rutherford, 222-237. London: Lawrence and Wishart Limited, 1998

Hayles, N. The Materiality of Informatics, *Configurations* 1, no 1 (1992): 147–170.

Kamalkhani, Z. "Recently Arrived Muslim Refugee Women Coping with Settlement." In *Muslim Communities in Australia*, edited by A. Saeed and S. Akbarzadeh. Sydney: UNSW Press, 2001.

Lankshear, C. *Changing Literacies*. Philadelphia: Open University Press, 1997.

Luke, A., and C. Luke. "A Situated Perspective on Cultural Globalization." In *Globalization and Education: Critical Perspectives*, edited by N. Burbules and A. Torres. New York: Routledge, 2000.

McCarthy, C., and Dimitriades, G. "Governmentality and the Sociology of Education: Media, Education Policy and the Politics of Resentment." *British Journal of Sociology of Education* 21, no. 2 (2000): 186–205

McKay, S., and S. Wong. "Multiple Discourses, Multiple Identities: Investment and Agency in Second Language Learning among Chinese Adolescent Immigrant Students." *Harvard Educational Review* 66, no. 3 (1996): 577–608.

McLaren, P. "Schooling the Postmodern Body: Critical Pedagogy and the Politics of Enfleshment." *Journal of Education Policy* 170, no. 3 (1988): 53–71.

McWilliam, E., and Palmer, P. "Pedagogues, Tech (No)Bods: Re-Inventing Postgraduate Pedagogy." In *Pedagogy, Technology and the Body*, edited by E. McWilliam and P. Taylor. New York: Peter Lang, 1996.

Morris, G., and D. Beckett. "Performing Identities: A New Focus on Embodied Adult Learning." In *Adult Education @ 21st Century*, edited by P. Kell, S. Shore, and M. Singh. New York: Peter Lang, 2003.

O'Loughlin, M. "Paying Attention to Bodies in Education: Theoretical Resources and Practical Suggestions." *Educational Philosophy and Theory* 30, no. 3 (1998): 275–98.

Peirce, B. "Social Identity, Investment and Language Learning." *TESOL Quarterly* 29, no. 1 (1995): 9–29.

Pennycook, A. *Critical Applied Linguistics: A Critical Introduction*. Mahwah, NJ: Lawrence Erlbaum Associates, 2001.

———. *English and the Discourse of Colonialism*. London: Routledge, 1998.

Schatzki, T. "Practiced Bodies: Subjects, Genders and Minds". In *The Social and Political body*. edited by T. Schatzki and W. Natter. New York: The Guilford Press. 1996.

Singh, M., P. Kell, and A. Pandian. *Appropriating English: Innovation in the Global Business of English Language Teaching*. New York: Peter Lang, 2002.

Swirsky, R. "Migration and Dislocation: Echoes of Loss in Jewish Women's Narratives." In *Thinking Identities: Ethnicity, Racism and Culture,* edited by A. Brah, M. Hickman and M Ghaill. Basingstoke, Macmillan, 1999.

Thesen, L. "Voices, Discourses and Transition: In Search of New Identities in EAP." *TESOL Quarterly* 31, no. 3 (1997): 487–511.

# Chapter 9

## Developing Local Teachers' Skills for Addressing Ethno-Specific Drug Issues of Global Proportions

Scott K. Phillips

### Introduction

The changing ethnocultural and linguistic diversity in Minority World nations is a product of contemporary shifts in globalization and is giving rise to renewed contestation over the development of global/local curricula. This chapter describes a pedagogical orientation and strategies adopted in producing a professional development (PD) program for enhancing teachers' abilities to deliver drug education in ethnoculturally and linguistically diverse school communities. The aims are to make problematic and critically reflect on the pedagogical approach adopted in this training program, showing how it addresses and is influenced by the multicultural dimensions of globalization. These are associated with the way that "the global now" has been constituted through the interrelated globalization of mass media and mass migrations (Appadurai, 1996: 2–9). The central argument of this chapter is that while the abuse of legal and illegal drugs is a global problem affecting young people, any educational response needs to be situated historically in terms of the specific ethnocultural as well as global contexts in which young people live (see Ziguras, this volume).

The PD program and conceptual framework described here are based on the recognition that the use and abuse of drugs by young people are not universally the same but are historically, politically, economically, and culturally situated. Consequently, educational programs aimed at engaging with this situation have to be constructed on a similar basis. Such an approach acknowledges that the globalized contexts in which young people live

> are not objectively given relations that look the same from every angle of vision but, rather…are deeply perspectival constructs, inflected by the historical, linguistic and political situatedness of different sorts of actors: nation-states, multinationals, diasporic communities, as well as sub national groupings and movements (whether religious, political or economic), and even intimate face-to-face groups, such as villages, neighbourhoods and families. (Appadurai, 1996: 33)

The global/local flows of drugs and people, as well as media images of contemporary life, intersect on the subjectivity of young people and their understandings of drugs and drug issues. This engenders different perspectives within transnational diasporic families and their communities toward drug use and drug education. The chapter indicates how teachers, students, families, and community workers may collaboratively create relevant drug education curriculum *from below*. This is facilitated by teaching/learning strategies and curriculum materials that ground public health promotion in the needs and dispositions of specific interethnic communities.

## Situating a Professional Development Program

Drug abuse is a global issue. The *World Drug Report 2000* makes its dimensions very clear. Trafficking in illicit drugs now affects some 170 countries and territories worldwide. As well, illicit drug abuse is a global phenomenon, with some 134 countries reporting it as a current problem (United Nations Office for Drug Control and Crime Prevention, 2000). However, drug abuse involves more than the trafficking and abuse of illicit drugs. It also encompasses problematic use of alcohol and tobacco. These substances have a worldwide distribution and are responsible for many more illnesses and fatalities than those linked with illicit drugs. For example, in Australia, there are 18,200 deaths attributable to tobacco in any year, 3,700 to alcohol, and only 800 to illegal drugs (Victorian Drug Policy Expert Committee, 2000: 3).

The global dimensions of the abuse of both legal and illegal drugs among young people are well documented. Tobacco, whether as cigarettes or in smokeless forms, is regarded as a highly addictive substance that produces severe and often fatal consequences for habitual users. According to World Health Organization estimates, 50 million children in China and 330 million children and youths in Europe face premature death from tobacco-related causes, unless tobacco use is checked (Blum, 1991).

As regards alcohol and illicit drugs, abuse of these substances commonly begins before the age of 20 in the United States and other similar countries. In Egypt, alcohol use begins at 15 to 20 years, barbiturate use at 15 to 17 years, and cannabis use at 16 to 18 years (Kandel and Logan, 1984). A related global trend is that as youths migrate from rural to urban areas, the availability of alcohol and other drugs increases. Consequently, traditional social controls on alcohol and illicit drug use have been weakened, and urbanizing Minority World as well as urbanized Majority World nations alike are increasingly challenged by problems of juvenile substance abuse (Blum, 1991).

While the production and distribution of alcohol and tobacco products are susceptible to international and national regulatory regimes, illicit drugs pose a more difficult challenge. The gap between the production and seizures of illegal drugs is widening, despite the increased efforts and resources being invested by national and international criminal justice systems. Parallel to this development is the highly organized structuring of the global/local drug markets. These markets are distinguished by high profits, high levels of investment in security and transport, and sophisticated marketing and production methods (Victorian Drug Policy Expert Committee, 2000: 3).

Illicit drug trafficking is bound up with transnational crime, which in turn is associated with the larger context of economic globalization. Global trading and financial systems, as well as advances in transport and communications, "have created enormous new opportunities for organized crime" (Geldenhuys, 2002). By the end of the previous decade, transnational crime was estimated to have cost Majority World countries around 2 percent of their annual gross national product (Canadian Security Intelligence Service, 1998). The Group of 8 (G8) states in 1998 described this kind of crime as "a global threat which can undermine the democratic and economic basis of societies through the investment of illegal money by international cartels, corruption, a weakening of institutions and a loss of confidence in the rule of law" (*Birmingham Summit Final Communiqué*, 1998)

There is a vast array of international agencies brought to bear on the global trade in illicit drugs. The United Nations (UN) Office for Drug

Control and Crime Prevention (established in 1997) includes the UN International Drug Control Program and the UN Center for International Crime Prevention. The Drug Control Program is directed toward bolstering multilateral efforts against the production and trafficking of narcotics. The Center for International Crime Prevention focuses on crime prevention and reform of the criminal justice systems of member states. As well, the UN's Commission on Narcotic Drugs formulates UN policy on drug-related issues, while the International Narcotics Control Board monitors implementation of UN drug conventions (Geldenhuys, 2002).

This "drug problem" is also manifest in the flows of cultural commodities and people. For instance, globally mediated images—via films, music videos, billboards, television programs, and popular song lyrics—portray the exchange, consumption, and abuse of drugs as part of postmodern life, or the escape from it by those experiencing alienation and disaffection. Fashion styles such as "heroin chic" are contrived to imitate the emaciated body resulting from prolonged consumption of heroin. Films like *Trainspotting*, *Traffic*, and *Buffalo Soldiers* dramatize the illicit drug industry and the experiences of users and traffickers. The global/local flow of people—tourists, soldiers, and students—brings individuals and drugs into contact across borders and cultures.

Similarly, strategies to address drug issues are part and parcel of worldwide efforts in criminal justice, social work, and education. Practitioners in these fields have cooperated on a range of international initiatives, including the development of a "risk factor prevention paradigm." The assumptions of this approach are hinted at in one criminologist's observations: "The basic idea of this paradigm is very simple: Identify the key risk factors for offending and implement prevention methods to counteract them" (Farrington, 2000: 801). The most influential ideas about drug abuse prevention have emanated from North America, where the greatest abuse of all types of drugs actually occurs. The *Communities That Care* model developed in the United States has informed much policy work elsewhere in the world with regard to preventing and/or reducing the harms associated with drugs (Hawkins, Catalano, et al., 1992; Phillips, 2000).

In response to drug abuse among young people, many nation-states have formulated policies informed by the risk factor prevention paradigm. For instance, Australia's National Drug Strategy is built on the belief that a balance is required between the three aspects of "harm minimization," namely, reduction of supply by deploying the criminal justice system, reduction of demand through educational means, and reduction of serious harm to drug users through various treatment and service delivery options. To achieve this balance, the policy emphasizes the value of partnerships between law enforcement, health, and education agencies, on the one hand, and drug users, people affected by drug abuse, community-based organizations, and industry, on the other. The aim is to bring community groups and workers more squarely into the equation of planning and providing community-based, responsive information and treatment services.

Public schools are important local-level partners, as they can link young people, families, and community organizations with drug education professionals and information. School-focused programs have therefore been developed to facilitate community-based approaches to drug education (Phillips, 2000; Phillips and Khoo, 2003). While drug education materials continue to be produced for schools, these give relatively little attention to issues of multicultural and linguistic diversity. This is despite the evidence that the tailoring of educational strategies to meet the needs of local students and their families is well established, especially in the case of those from multicultural and linguistically diverse communities (Paglia and Room, 1998; Davison, Ferraro, Wales, and Robins, 2000). The PD program described below was given shape and substance through working with government education agencies to develop drug education strategies for ethno-specific communities. This included developing tools for culturally inclusive drug education and providing advice on culturally inclusive service delivery.

## Developing a Collaborative Understanding of Drug Education for Ethnoculturally and Linguistically Diverse School Communities

Each PD program begins by foregrounding its interactive pedagogy. The basic framework of activities is adjusted depending on the (planned and unplanned) issues that emerge as discussions evolve and evaluation feedback is collected. The presenters recognize the professional expertise of the teachers, placing emphasis on learning taking place through dialogue and sharing. This is not an unusual approach; Walker and Surman (2002), for example, report a similar teaching and learning philosophy in a training program they have conducted with parents and teachers to enhance children's literacy.

During the first half of the PD program, the course presenters initiate dialogue by inviting each participant to explain how they understand the term "diversity." This exercise has prompted revealing discussions of the multiple dimensions of ethnocultural diversity, with issues canvassed including ethnicity, economic circumstances, class, communication styles, religious beliefs, and sexuality. The participants' attitudes to immigration and diversity have been explored through a "Defend the Statement" activity. The statements used are designed to trigger a range of positive and negative attitudes and feelings to these issues, thereby generating less personalized data for open discussion (Singh, 1996). Participants are required to defend a range of value statements for and against immigration and cultural diversity. Video clips on interethnic cosmopolitanism also are used to portray and prompt attitudinal responses to linguistic and multicultural difference.

For the purpose of this exercise, participants are divided into randomly selected groups of about six people. Each group is asked to write down arguments in support of their statement, irrespective of whether they personally agree or disagree with it, and to draw examples from the video material, where appropriate. Participants are then asked to consider how their attitudes and values about immigration and the sustainability of multicultural diversity would affect the ways they develop culturally and linguistically specific drug education strategies. The trigger statements that participants are asked to defend are as follows.

(A) The differences among our students and their parents mean that we have to consider everything we do, from the way we work as teachers to the way we relate to our students and their families. This will benefit our school and our communities. It is an approach that reflects the way the world is.

(B) The differences among our students and their parents are pretty harmless, such as their different countries of origin and their cultures. They make the school a more interesting, colorful place, just like the streets of our city.

(C) It's okay to have students and parents from different countries and cultures together, so long as they are "fast tracked" into the national way of doing things. It's fine to have a diverse school population if we can help them to get the hang of the school's way of doing things. After all, that is what this country is all about—helping people feel at home with our wonderful way of life.

(D) You basically cannot have students from vastly different cultural backgrounds working closely together. It just doesn't work. Have a look at the bitter racial, religious, and cultural differences in the other parts of the world. Different groups of students are best kept apart.

In the discussion that follows this activity, participants are asked to characterize the underlying policy viewpoint that each statement represents with respect to immigration and sustaining multicultural diversity. statement D has been described as the policy of segregation; statement C as integration or assimilation; statement B as tokenistic multiculturalism, and statement A as positive interethnic multiculturalism. The presenters then suggest that these statements are less a scale of the most enlightened (A) to least enlightened (D) but rather offer a contradictory range of attitudes and values, each of which could have instances of "best practice" as well as "worst practice." The presenters also demonstrate that statement A encompasses some attitudes associated with B, C, and D.

With regard to statement (D), best practice may be ethno-specific services while worst practice is the exclusion associated with intranational and international apartheid.

For statement (C), best practice involves showing immigrants the local "rules" for survival as well as how and when to subvert these markers of power and privilege; and worst practice is assimilation effected through projects aimed to breed out of existence racial differences and to enforce English-only politics and pedagogies.

For statement (B), best practice may involve an initial response to ethnocultural diversity by introducing the food, dance, and songs of different cultures; worst practice would entrench this cosmetic, superficial approach, reinforcing the consumption of ethnocultural folk-life.

In the case of statement (A), best practice might be ethnocultural niche marketing and making ethnocultural diversity productive by harnessing its economic and social benefits; worst practice involves tying this approach exclusively to an economic reductionist agenda. Such an approach reduces diversity to considerations of customer service rather than considering citizens' rights to equity of access to public services. It means that services would be tailored exclusively to the needs of those niche communities/customers able to pay for them.

The presenters suggest how these best practice/worst practice scenarios for responding to ethnocultural and linguistic diversity may inform the design and delivery of drug education interventions in specific interethnic communities. Noting the way that people's experiences of social life are inflected by their social association and historical-cultural background, the presenters propose pedagogical strategies that take account of these global/local inflections.

With regard to statement (D), the ethno-specific approach, best practice could mean tailoring messages and information to meet the needs of particular ethnic groups, for instance by grouping student sessions along specific language levels, length of residence in the country, or specific identity groups. In terms of worst practice, the focus is too heavily or exclusively on drug issues associated with one particular ethnic group.

With respect to statement (C), the integrationist approach, best practice may involve showing people the rules for minimizing or avoiding the harms of drug abuse and how and when to adapt drug education strategies for particular groups. Worst practice claims that there is only one "best practice" for drug education, leading to the requirement that everyone use that approach to the exclusion of all others. While some groups may be open to the approach of harm minimization as a realistic way of dealing with drug use by young people, others—especially families from backgrounds that favor highly protective parenting practices—may prefer to have teachers deliver more prohibition-oriented messages to their children. These differences and preferences need to be understood and respected by teachers when tailoring drug education sessions for diverse audiences.

As regards statement (B), or the tokenistic approach to multiculturalism, best practice may entail, as an initial "safe" or "nonthreatening" response, the introduction of drug education materials through the different festivals and organizations of multicultural communities. In contrast, worst practice would entrench and standardize a cosmetic, superficial approach to ethnocultural and multilingual diversity, such as providing drug education solely through folkloric media, or worse still as an add-on component of the program.

The positive interethnic multiculturalism approach, statement (A), holds that best practice involves ethno-specific niche marketing and productive diversity. The culturally and linguistically diverse skills of teachers, students themselves (as peer educators) and community leaders are harnessed to craft messages for delivery in school settings and community-based parent education programs. This stands in marked contrast to the worst practice, where ethno-specific drug education is tied to an economic reductionist agenda, provided only on a user-pays basis.

Discussion and written evaluation following these PD programs indicated that participants found this framework helpful and revealing. In particular, it helped teachers to bring to the surface of their thinking the difficulties of addressing negative attitudes toward ethnocultural diversity when trying to deal with drug abuse in such communities. They reported that it enabled them to better conceptualize how to negotiate linguistic and multicultural diversity and to relate this to the design of culturally inclusive drug education strategies. Finally, the framework helped them to tie their pedagogy strongly to global/local community needs.

In this respect, such an emphasis is akin to recent thinking about a New Basics curriculum that would link school-based curriculum development to funds of community knowledge. For instance, Bean and Readence (2002: 203–25) argue that in a community with significant health needs, a *knowledge producing curriculum* could "center on content area activities and readings aimed at helping adolescents and the community address these problems." Similarly, in an ethnically and linguistically diverse school concerned about the prevention of drug abuse, it would be appropriate that drug education strategies engaged students in producing knowledge about the needs, experiences, and initiatives already underway within and across different diasporic communities.

In designing culturally relevant drug education, it is important to develop teachers' understandings of the fluidity, diversity, and multiple dimensions of students' "ethnoscapes," that is, "the landscape of persons who constitute the shifting world in which we live" (Appadurai, 1996: 297). This landscape of persons includes tourists, immigrants, refugees, exiles, guest workers, and other mobile groups and individuals who constitute or otherwise affect the transnational politics and policies governing drugs and drug education. So, while many of today's students continue living in relatively stable communities and social networks, their life trajectory is affected by constant human motion, and it is this diversity and fluidity that innovative education programs are addressing.

The cultural dimensions of globalization affect the social spheres of students' local communities, their neighborhoods, and their schools, through the global/local flows of diverse peoples and their selected traditions. Innovative educational strategies, including PD programs, attempt to take account of and make a productive advantage of this diversity. The ethnocultural and linguistic diversity of multicultural Australia provides an analytical framework for making sense of, and responding in educationally novel ways to, such diversity. In the second half of this PD program, attitudes toward the sociocultural diversity of youth and their drug use are considered in detail. This part of the program relates understandings of youth culture and patterns of drug use to the history and global patterns of multicultural change.

## Understanding Global/Local Youth Culture and Drug Use

This session helps teachers to unpack the global/local cultural formation of youth culture, drug use, and policy thinking as it evolved, especially during the twentieth century. A summary of the material covered in this session follows.

## 1900 to 1950

A dual representation of youth emerged in the first half of the twentieth century; youth were at once seen as a threat or inherently bad and as a focus of hope and optimism. Educationalists and psychologists concentrated on assisting adolescents to develop from an uncontrollable phase of "storm and stress" into respectable adults disciplined by education and social convention (Wyn and Whyte, 1997: 18–19). In the 1940s, the word "teenager" came into use in Australia, associated with the "bobbysoxers" in the United States. Following World War II, there was an increase in leisure and income; young Australians started to feign the accents of American service personnel. Youth culture of the "bodgies" also adapted the dress and greased hairstyles of American youths. Youth culture developed around drive-ins, television and car ownership, jazz music, and then rock 'n' roll. Films like *Rebel without a Cause* and *The Wild One* portrayed youths as "delinquents." Alcohol and tobacco were the main recreational substances associated with youth culture (Bucksten, 1995: 4). Drug use was associated with popular music and dance during this period. Alcohol (particularly whisky) in the 1920s, and later cannabis in the 1930s were the drugs associated with jazz culture. Jazz musicians like Charlie Parker began to use heroin and cocaine during the 1940s and 1950s (Plant, 1999: 163).

In the first half of the twentieth century the Australian government adopted prohibitionist responses to drug use (Pennington, 1999: 26; Wodak and Moore, 2002: 12). This was an essentially morally grounded approach born out of the American and British temperance movement's concern with total abstinence from "the demon drink" (Bucksten, 1995: 4; Rumbold and Hamilton, 1998: 131). Such a policy stance, associated with the neoliberal approach and represented as a "war on drugs," was the result of international pressure. The Geneva Convention of 1926 extended its clauses on the prohibition of opium derivatives to include cocaine and cannabis. It was amended in the mid-1930s to include heroin, and this was subsequently folded into the UN Single Convention on Narcotic Drugs in 1961. But at the time when Australia enacted laws prohibiting the use of cannabis (in 1926) and later heroin (1953), the use of these drugs was relatively insignificant (Pennington, 1999: 26; Wodak and Moore, 2002: 12–15).

The evolution of Australia's policy approach to drug use at this time, therefore, can be understood only in the context of Australia's enmeshment in global alliances with dominant imperial powers. As Wodak and Moore (2002: 14) note:

Compliance with international conventions…became the main force driving the development of domestic drug policy in Australia. Initially through blind association with Great Britain's participation in international treaties, later by alignment with the United States, Australia intensified application of the criminal justice system to particular substances.

If drug use was relatively insignificant during the first half of the twentieth century in Australia, it was to become more problematic during the second half.

## 1950 to 2000

Pop music, film, theater, and magazine culture, especially in the 1960s, promoted greater sexual freedom, protest, diversity of experience, psychedelia, and drug use linked with individual searching for knowledge and insight (Fuller, 2002: 97–101; Pennington, 1999: 27). Use of cannabis and heroin grew substantially, when large numbers of U.S. soldiers visited Australia on leave from the American war against Vietnam (Pennington, 1999: 27). American soldiers also are credited with introducing "the practice of drug injecting to a widening circle of young Australians" (Wodak and Moore, 2002: 16)

The 1970s were a time of social and musical diversity. Gay liberation and women's liberation challenged patriarchal concepts of family life, promoting debate about the culture and acceptance of dominating patriarchal relationships (see Franzway, this volume). Political turmoil in the United States, imaginings of the waning influence of America following its defeat by the Vietnamese people, and the effect of oil shocks on the international economy created an atmosphere of change and uncertainty (Bucksten, 1995: 8). The young became more globally aware regarding issues of pollution, population growth, oil crises, uranium mining, and nuclear war (Fuller, 2002: 101–5). The number of young Australians starting to inject drugs grew during this decade. As Wodak and Moore (2002: 4) observe: "One recent estimate concluded that the number of injecting drug users has been doubling since the 1960s, reaching 100,000 regular injectors and an additional 175,000 occasional injectors by 1977." This number grew even more spectacularly during the remaining decades of the century, indicating the failure of "war on drugs" policies to reduce usage, decrease the price of illicit drugs, or reduce the number of deaths caused by drugs (Wodak and Moore, 2002: 4).

During the 1960s and 1970s policies regarding drug use shifted away from the moralistic prohibitionist approach. Drug taking increasingly came to be conceptualized in terms of medical ideas about illness and treatment. In the United States and in Australia, treatment aimed at addressing issues of physical and psychological dependency was seen as an alternative to criminal justice solutions (Bucksten, 1995: 9; Rumbold and Hamilton, 1998: 131).

In the 1980s, the spread of AIDS caused a backlash against challenges to patriarchal relationships, although during this decade the Gay and Lesbian Mardi Gras and the Sleaze Ball became truly mass events. Dance parties grew in popularity. "Skunk weed"—an enhanced form of marijuana—became widely available, as did cocaine, a "yuppie" drug (Bucksten, 1995: 9; Fuller, 2002: 106–10).

By the 1990s many young people under 19 had direct experience of a culture other than Australia. Nearly 9 percent of this age group was born overseas, and 37.4 percent had at least one parent who was born overseas. Teenagers of the 1990s faced increasing diversity, options, information sources, and technologies. The 1990s saw a continuation of domination of the world's youth culture by American sources—basketball, videos, and films. At this time a substantial shift occurred in the types of drugs being used by young people. Skunk weed became more popular, despite its damaging effects. Inhalants and drugs like ecstasy and amyl nitrate were increasingly used in rave and nightclub scenes, which by then were all-night affairs. Heroin reemerged, but as a cheap way to get high, with low-price "smack packs" being readily available. Alcohol was repackaged for the youth market by multinational corporations, which blurred the boundary between alcohol and soft drinks through alcoholic lemonades. Chroming, or the inhalation of aerosol paints, became popular among alienated young people (Fuller, 2002: 110–12; Wyn and White, 1997: 20).

Over the eighties and nineties policy thinking shifted toward a public health approach. The principal concern was expressed in terms of harm minimization. This model recognizes that licit and illicit drugs are part of the community, and people need to be educated as to how they can be used safely. As Rumbold and Hamilton (1998: 131) observe:

> The past twenty years have seen a shift away from "seeking" and "treating" those with the pathology or disease (the addicts), toward a public health approach that focuses on the overall patterns of drug use in the community: our drinking, smoking, self-medicating, and our search for chemical pleasure. Under the public health model, drug use is seen as a continuum in the community, with those who abstain at one end and those who use very heavily at the other....The public health approach moves the focus away from "alcoholics" and "addicts" toward the *discourse* of alcohol- and drug-related problems.

The development of drug education and information campaigns has been undertaken largely in the context of this harm minimization policy context.

Finally, during the last two decades variations in young people's experiences of drugs have been considered in terms of gender differences. There is a growing body of research on the differing drug use patterns of men and women (Ezard, 1998; Taylor, 1993). Contemporary Australian studies reveal, for instance, that men are more likely to use alcohol than women. Furthermore, a gender-sensitive framework is being used to examine the harm related to drug use by women (Ezard, 1998: 99).

This sweep across the last century of the globalization of youth culture, drug taking, and policy responses reveals fluidity and diversity in the conceptualization of "youth," "drugs," and what constitutes an appropriate policy approach to drug use. "Youth" is not a single, fixed, or unitary concept (Wyn and Whyte, 1997: 10–25). Just as cultural, linguistic, and gender diversity influence a person's values and behaviors, including those associated with drug use, so people form their identity in part through belonging to various age-related subcultures and groupings. And this has an impact on their orientations toward drugs. For example, some (but not all) young people go to rave parties. And not every rave party-goer will consume Ecstasy pills. Some will; most will not.

Similarly, young people from certain ethnoreligious communities have been reported as possibly being more protected from involvement in drug taking because of the "high care and high protection" parenting practices (New South Wales Department of Education and Training, 2001: 5). On the other hand, some bilingual parents have reported difficulties in communicating with their children about drugs and have only limited knowledge about drug services or how to access them (New South Wales Department of Education and Training, 2001: 6). The extent to which a young person's ethnocultural and family backgrounds may constitute a "risk" or protective factor relative to drug use requires further research to enable the design of better drug information and education strategies.

A key conclusion drawn for this PD program on global/local youth culture and drug use is that, in crafting drug education messages, it is important to appreciate the situatedness of young people themselves as well as their diverse cultural and family backgrounds. This may help in avoid the pitfalls of stereotyping or otherwise universalizing young people's identities and drug use practices.

Following this session on the diversity of youth and their experiences with drugs, participants in the PD program spend time with a panel of community workers from the areas in which their schools are located. This enables participants to consider the diverse ways in which young people's experiences with drugs are imbricated with their migration, class, and ethnic identities. A panel of three or four community workers gives presentations on the developmental issues that affect the ethnic communities to which they belong. For example, a Pacific Islander worker might describe the social structures and experiences of Samoan and Tongan communities; a Middle Eastern worker could cover Lebanese, Iranian, and suchlike communities; and Indo-Chinese workers can describe the lives of people associated with Vietnamese and Cambodian communities.

Consistency of coverage is assisted by the PD facilitators briefing the presenters before the course is run about intended outcomes and the sorts of issues it would be helpful for them to speak about. Some of the areas panel presenters can be asked to cover include:

1. *Community profile*, e.g., population size, language groupings, average length of residency in Australia, and occupational groupings.
2. *Cultural beliefs* about child rearing, discipline, respect, schooling as well as attitudes toward smoking, alcohol, illicit drugs, significant cultural or religious beliefs, and so on.
3. *Communications with students.* What teachers should consider when discussing drug education with primary and secondary students.

4. *Communications with parents.* What teachers should be aware of when talking with parents about drug education. This might include strategies for consultation with parents and the community.
5. *Examples of successful and unsuccessful drug education strategies* in their particular cultural community, and some explanation as to why they worked or failed.
6. *Community organizations and resources* that teachers can use when doing drug education work with a particular ethnic community.

Evaluation feedback from participants indicates that teachers find this sort of session very revealing and helpful. It allows them to establish contact with community workers who can help them tap into rich veins of local knowledge and cultural understandings. As well, it extends their network of support agencies and partners who provide drug information and services in ways that are meaningful for parents and students who belong to particular ethnic communities.

Dialogue with community workers helps teachers to reflect on the debates around whether it is possible to construct a generic prevention curriculum on drug issues or if it is of more value to ground drug education curriculum in the specific issues and disadvantages facing particular communities in their localities (Botvin, 1995; Rizvi, 1991). Research evidence from the United States suggests that culturally focused programs, which entail interactive educational strategies and which use examples appropriate to the cultural groups involved, have a greater impact than generic skills prevention programs in delaying drug uptake by young people (New South Wales Department of Education and Training, 2001: 6). The PD approach reported here similarly helps to provide Australian teachers with ideas and strategies for this sort of program.

## Designing Strategies for Culturally Inclusive Drug Education

The final session of the PD program involves participants in applying their understandings on global/local ethnocultural diversity about youth, as well as their insights gained from contact with the panel of local community workers, to the design of strategies for engaging and educating parents and young people about drugs in interethnic multicultural schools. This involves program participants in developing plans for use in their own schools for involving and informing parents and the community more generally about drugs. Participants brainstorm useful strategies and initiatives and then share their ideas for engaging and communicating with interethnic communities. Several questions were proposed for teachers to consider when thinking, talking, and writing about how schools might work with their particular community:

- What *processes* do we have for knowing what parents need and expect?
- What are the *main lines of communication* that we use, and what alternatives are possible or desirable?
- How can existing *relationships* be further developed?
- How can *parents* be supported in their role?
- What different, ethno-specific *messages* might be employed?
- How might community workers or ethnic community leaders be involved in providing information to particular linguistic constituencies?

Participants work in their school groups to complete an action plan, including a timeline for implementation. The plan ultimately is taken back to the school's executive council for approval. After this, the action plan provides the basis for monitoring progress toward proposed goals as well as communicating with the state education authorities about resource needs for identified areas of support.

At the end of this PD program each school group briefly reports on the plan they have developed. These reports reveal how the teachers have begun to rethink not only their pedagogies but also schooling. In some cases the processes for understanding parents' expectations are reconsidered beyond the usual parent-teacher evening format. There has been a recognition that some recently arrived immigrants may feel intimidated by such evenings, daunted by the prospect of having to communicate in English only, or have work commitments important to the family's sustenance. Home visits and the use of interpreters were proposed in response to these considerations.

The teachers consider how they might adjust their ways of communicating with young people and parents. Peer education strategies and the incorporation of community elders in classroom sessions offer ways to produce, craft, and deliver relevant messages about drugs. The use of relevant multilingual media like television, radio, and press are employed more fully than previously. Participants have reported that the PD program provided them with a useful, theoretically informed framework to assist in planning interactive strategies for use in their schools and class-rooms, and suggested ways to enhance the dialogue between the school and bilingual parents. In these ways, schools contribute to developing the "resilience" of students and families—that is, their ability to negotiate the challenges they encounter in dealing with drug use and abuse (Bryan and Batch, 2002; Currie, Hurrelmann, Settertobulte, Smith, and Todd, in Bryan and Batch, 2002; Fuller, McGraw, and Goodyear, 2001).

## Conclusion

Many public schools provide a supportive environment for promoting the health and well-being of young people from ethnically and linguistically diverse backgrounds. But schools are not the only or main resource in enabling young people to develop problem-solving skills that help them deal effectively with the adversity and challenges posed by illicit (and legal) drugs. Family connectedness, spiritual or religious affiliation, and belief in social norms also help to engender such resilience among young people. However, public schools can play an important role in creating the sense of connectedness and belonging that enhances their resilience. With respect to addressing the global/local issue of substance abuse in inter-ethnic communities, drug education may not reduce young people's experimentation with illicit or legal drugs, but it may increase their awareness of the likely health disorders stemming from substance misuse and prevent them from engaging in this sort of activity.

To contribute to the promotion of resilience in young people, schools in interethnic communities require understandings and strategies that help parents, students, and teachers to make productive use of their ethnocultural diversity and varied parenting practices as resources for designing effective drug education experiences. Not all young people are involved in activities that entail drug use. The more that teachers deepen their understanding of the globalization of ethnocultural diversity and about the global trade in drugs, the more they are able to gauge when a "harm minimization" or "abstinence" message is appropriate. The teachers who participated in the PD program reported here acknowledged the importance of adjusting their messages for interethnic, multilingual audiences, if they are to establish and maintain open communication about drug issues.

By working with parents and students in a culturally sensitive way, teachers open up the possibilities for dialogues that contribute to enhancing young people's resilience in their proximal and extended communities. The PD approach outlined in this chapter may have wider application for teachers beyond Australia, although it would have to be modified. At the very least, the trigger statements would be changed to reflect the relevant social history of each country or regions within countries. Similarly, the global/local history of youth culture would need to be adapted to the particular circumstances of each country. Suitably modified for local circumstances, however, the approach described here could provide a framework for helping parents, community workers, students, and teachers to develop the resilience that young people need so they can handle issues associated with drug use in their everyday lives.

## References

Appadurai, A. *Modernity at Large: Cultural Dimensions of Globalisation*. Minneapolis: University of Minnesota Press, 1996.

Bean, T., and J. Readence. "Adolescent Literacy: Charting a Course for Successful Futures as Lifelong Learners." *Reading Research and Instruction* 41, no. 3 (2002): 203–10.

*Birmingham Summit Final Communiqué* 1998 [cited September 26, 2003]. Available from www.cnn.com/WORLD/europe/9805/17/g8.text/.

Blum, R. "Global Trends in Adolescent Health." *Journal of the American Medical Association* 265, no. 20 (1991): 271–91.

Botvin, G. "Drug Abuse Prevention in School Settings." In *Drug Abuse Prevention with Multiethnic Youth*, edited by G. Botvin, S. Schinke, and M. Orlandi, 169–92. Thousand Oaks, CA: Sage Publications, 1995.

Bryan, B., and J. Batch. "The Complexities of Ethnic Adolescent Health: An Australian Perspective." *Youth Studies Australia* 21, no. 1 (2002): 24–33.

Bucksten, O. *Adolescent Substance Abuse: Assessment, Prevention and Treatment*. New York: John Wiley and Sons, 1995.

Canadian Security Intelligence Service. *Transnational Criminal Activity* 1998 [cited September 26, 2003]. Available from www.globalpolicy.org/globaliz/law/orcrime.htm.

Cope, B. "Tools for Culturally Inclusive Drug Education." In *Taking It On: Conference Papers*, edited by Department of Education Employment and Training, Canberra: Australia, 11–19, 2001.

Davison, T., L. Ferraro, R. Wales, and G. Robins. "Review of the Antecedents of Illicit Drug Use with Particular Reference to Adolescents." Paper presented at Prevention: Developing the Framework, RE Ross Trust, Melbourne, July 26–27, 2000.

Ezard, N. "Hannah's Story: Perspectives on Women's Drug Use." In *Drug Use in Australia: A Harm Minimisation Approach*, edited by M. Hamilton, A. Kellehear, and G. Rumbold, 98–110. Melbourne: Oxford University Press, 1998.

Farrington, D. "Explaining and Preventing Crime: The Globalization of Knowledge." *Criminology* 38, no. 1 (2000): 801–24.

Fuller, A. *Raising Real People: Creating a Resilient Family*. Melbourne: ACER Press, 2002.

Fuller, A., K. McGraw, and M. Goodyear. "Resilience—the Mind of Youth." In *Taking It On: Conference Papers*, edited by Department of Education Employment and Training, Canberra: Australia, 2001.

Geldenhuys, D. *Non-State Deviants in World Affairs* Strategic Review for Southern Africa, 2002 [cited September 26, 2003]. Available from http:// web3. infotrac. gale group.com/itw/infomark/974/395/66384526w3/purl=rc1_EAIM_0_A95355502&dyn=4 !xrn_12_0_A95355502?sw_aep=rmit.

Hawkins, J., R. Catalano, et al.. *Communities That Care: Action for Drug Abuse Prevention*. San Francisco: Jossey-Bass Publishers, 1992.

Kandel, D., and J. Logan. "Patterns of Drug Use from Adolescence to Young Adulthood." *American Journal of Public Health*, no. 74 (1984): 660–67.

Kell, P., ed. *Ways of Learning: The Revolution in Teaching and Learning*. Seaholme, Australia: Common Ground, 2002.

New South Wales Department of Education and Training. *Drug Education in a Culturally Diverse Society*. Sydney: New South Wales Department of Education and Training, 2001.

Paglia, A., and R. Room. *Preventing Substance Abuse among Youth: A Literature Review and Recommendations*. Toronto: Addiction Research Foundation, 1998.

Pennington, D. "An International Perspective on Drug Use in Australia." In *Heroin Crisis: Key Commentators Discuss the Issues and Debate Solutions to Heroin Abuse in Australia*, edited by B. Jones. Melbourne: Bookman Press, 1999.

Phillips, S. "Community-Based Approaches to Drug Abuse Issues: Some Lessons Learned and Future Implications." *Youth Studies Australia* 19, no. 3 (2000): 39–43.

Phillips, S., and C. Khoo. "Culturally Inclusive Drug Education: Developing and Delivering Grounded Training for Teachers in Australia." Paper presented at the New Learning: Cultures, Technologies, Literacies, Persons. Learning Conference, Beijing, China, July 16–20, 2003.

Plant, S. *Writing on Drugs*. London: Faber and Faber, 1999.

Rizvi, F. "The Idea of Ethnicity and the Politics of Multicultural Education." In *Power and Politics in Education*, edited by D. Dawkins, 161–96. London: Falmer Press, 1991.

Rumbold, G, and M. Hamilton. "Addressing Drug Problems: The Case for Harm Minimisation." In *Drug Use in Australia: A Harm Minimisation Approach*, edited by M. Hamilton, A. Kellehear, and G. Rumbold. Melbourne: Oxford University Press, 1998.

Singh, M. "Teaching against Racisms: Developing Multicultural Perspectives." In *Teaching Society and Environment*, edited by R. Gilbert. Sydney: Macmillan, 1996.

Taylor, A. *Women Drug Users: An Ethnography of a Female Injecting Community*. Oxford: Clarendon Press, 1993.

United Nations Office for Drug Control and Crime Prevention. *World Drug Report* 2000 [cited September 26, 2003]. Available from www.undcp.org/wdr_executive_ summary_2000.html.

Victorian Drug Policy Expert Committee. *Stage Two Report—Drugs: Meeting the Challenge* 2000 [cited September 26, 2003]. Available from www.dhs.vic. gov.au/phd/ dpec/downloads /stagetwo/execsumm.pdf.

Walker, I., and L. Surman. "Learning Together: A Co-Operative Parent and Teacher Training Program to Enhance Children's Literacy." In *Ways of Learning: The Revolution in*

*Teaching and Learning*, edited by P. Kell, 69–81. Seaholme, Australia: Common Ground, 2002.

Wyn, J., and R. White. *Rethinking Youth*. Sydney: Longman, 1997.

Wodak, A., and T. Moore. *Modernising Australia's Drug Policy*. Sydney: University of New South Wales Press, 2002.

## Acknowledgments

Thanks to Dr. Bill Cope and Mr. Charles Khoo, with whom I worked in designing and delivering the professional development projects reported here. This chapter draws on intellectual material we developed together. Any inaccuracies or errors in this paper, however, are my sole responsibility.

# Chapter 10

# Virtual Spaces for Innovative Pedagogical Actions: Education, Technology, and Globalization

Lynton Brown

## Introduction

In postindustrial societies, the media and formal education represent two key mechanisms defining the meaning and the relationship between the patterns of world events and their consequences for local communities. In the twenty-first century, both the media and education are converging in cyberspace, providing resources for developing a global reflexive consciousness among students, with the information "superhighway" stimulating needs, threats, and opportunities by expediting data flows and programming possible responses. There are significant educational implications for individual and group identities and relationships, for the state and to civil society, for communities and their cultures, and for the work of teachers.

Governments around the world claim that education is especially significant in a world where digital technological competence requires a new "literacy" that is an asset in international competition, and where the demand for skilled labor opens borders. Higher education has become a potential point of admission to the world of cosmopolitan advancement, albeit often by default, as academics struggle against the excesses of corporate managerialism. These changes are provoking adjustments in the perceived purposes and organization of higher education. This chapter considers the relationship between globalization and higher education at the level of curriculum and pedagogy. The struggles that constitute these changes have important consequences for efforts by academics to bring forward the tradition of using pedagogies for knowledge production, the future professional work of teachers, and the possibilities for producing critical, creative learners. This chapter presents a case study of an educational response to—and expression of the transitions in global/local relations that are manifest in the changes and continuities in—the technologization of curriculum and pedagogy.

To do justice to the meanings embedded in this story, the case study is located within the ongoing historical development and contestation over technology, power, educational values, and organization. By doing so, it highlights critical shifts in pedagogies of knowledge production; the scope for and constitution of practical educational innovations, and key education policy decisions governing technology that are shaping the education of the rising generation of global/local citizens, transnational workers, and cosmopolitan learners. This case study constitutes a moment in a number of ongoing and overlapping narratives, most of which can only be hinted at in this chapter, but do include:

- the long-evolving, mutually constructive relationship among humans, their technologies, and constructed environments
- the historic struggles between management and labor
- global/local economic geopolitics and national responses
- governance, government policies, and institutional responses
- leadership and organizational management, change management processes, the engineering of organizational culture, and systems compliance
- ongoing ideological contests over the purposes to be served by education
- changes in educational practices affecting curriculum innovation and pedagogies of knowledge production

As the following section indicates, globalization is the most recent in a long string of evocative metaphors used to characterize distinct eras in human history.

## Globalization and Technology

What is currently known as "globalization" has been known by such metaphors as the "industrial and technological revolutions," "modernity," the emergence of a "global village" (McLuhan, 1964), and the "information age" (Castells, 1996). Such terms have been used at different times to create a new language through which to understand the changes and continuities in global/local interconnectedness that impact on and given expression to educational innovations.

Since antiquity, the historical processes of migration, economic integration, technological development and transfer, and cultural exchange that together have intensified during the contemporary era of globalization have been turning the world into a single unified place. Now, more than ever, these developments are producing people throughout the world who are increasingly consciousness of these convergences. These processes have been building in scale and accelerating since the sixteenth-century expansion of Western European empires. Cumulatively they go a long way toward accounting for the unequal distribution of goods, resources, and opportunities around the planet and for the current flows of information, people, finance, goods, and cultural practices that Euro-American imperialism have stimulated. Technological development, the by-product of the reflexive (power) relations inherent in human problem solving through the appropriation and reorganization of elements of the environment, has been used to effect changes in the political economy of education. The material basis of higher education has shifted from being part of the public economy created by the state to build a nation with the aid of ever-advancing technologies creating and destabilizing institutions, power relationships, and worldviews. The quantum leap in contemporary developments in digital technologies is attended by interrelated sociopolitical disruptions and continuities that are having global/local consequences for higher education. The mechanization of mass production via the production line, the manufacture of overconsumption, and now the proliferation of telecommunications and information technologies are having global and local consequences on higher education, effecting and being used to effect techno-political changes.

James Burke (1978: 7) argued that technological development is auto-catalytic, with every innovation acting as a trigger of change and having multiple flow-on effects, not all of which are or can be anticipated. As new technological knowledge and competence become assimilated in educational practices, they add to the knowledge-base of the curriculum and the technical capacity of students to solve real-world problems, as well as modifying definitions of education. At the same time technological changes create new perceptions of educational priorities, needs, and possibilities. In this process unrelated and uneven developments in education create new potentialities that are realized through technological, economic, and sociopolitical convergence. If one applies the processes and techniques developed for the purposes of managerial control, it is possible for innovative educators to exploit these points of techno-political convergence. The instigation of technological innovation in and through education sets loose a new set of divergent possibilities that sees them applied to an array of counter-hegemonic purposes. In turn, this creates new possibilities, creates new problems, and calls forth new technological solutions, which in the process elicit new ways of working, living, teaching, and learning.

Just as the production line made the consumables accessible to the working class who created them, they are now the market for the mass-cultural products of the postindustrial economy. On the production side, mechanization involved a shift in knowledge from workers to factory managers. This was done by disaggregating workers' skills and then re-incorporating their knowledge into management control systems for governing production. The whole production system became a technology producing institutions, knowledge, practices, experiences, relationships, identities, and cultures in addition to material products. The resulting centralization of knowledge control and the loss of worker autonomy was a feature of mechanized production and industrial education, which is now being reproduced through struggles over the technologization of higher education.

## Education as Technology

Technologies of power do not always take material forms. The industrial education systems conceived in the nineteenth century were created as mechanisms responding to the dual needs of nation building in an age of empires and serving the emergent needs of industry for technically skilled labor. In the Minority, overdeveloped World the popular endorsement for mass industrial education that underpinned the constitutional commitment to "free, compulsory and secular" education had a strong egalitarian component. This reflected and gave legitimacy to a popular belief that access

to education would create a new informed democracy where the links between wealth, knowledge, and privilege, on the one hand, and poverty,
ignorance, and exploitation, on the other, would be broken. However,
state secondary education was organized into parallel systems of technical
and academic education; the former for students exiting to industrial employment (or unemployment) and the latter providing for those continuing
onto higher education and white-collar employment. The stratification
effected through industrial education supported the growth of the bureaucratic and administrative classes.

When major inquiries in the 1970s (Karmel, 1973) and '80s (Blackburn, 1985) confirmed that state education in Australia (as elsewhere) was
operating to reproduce socioeconomic inequities, governments intervened
through a series of programs to reform education. These programs were
ostensibly intended to be instruments of redistributive socioeconomic policy, mechanisms for achieving "social justice" in the face of the legacies
and rising threats of neoconservative politics. These education reforms
represented an extension of the federal government's role in shaping and
reshaping the character of public education. These federal programs provided grants directly to schools for the achievement of specific objectives.
This not only invited and incited schools to redirect their priorities, but
also interrupted and reduced the influence of local education authorities.
Instead, the federal government became a strategic provider of funding for
education reforms.

## Shifting Ground

The incoming neoconservative, neoliberal coalition that formed the federal government in the late 1990s retained the mechanism of direct funding to school, but for purposes contrary to the goals of combating social
injustices. Since 1996, this government has pursued its own localized ver-
sions of neoconservative and neoliberal globalism by supporting elite private schools through policies that are directed at the commodification,
consumerism, and marketization of education. The election of this overtly
neoconservative, neoliberal government saw the extension of its predeces-
sors' efforts to extend centralized control over the "nationalized" curriculum, with the public education system being disaggregated under a policy
of self-managing schools designed to promote a consumerist culture in
education. In response to the changing world economy of the 1990s, governments claiming to represent labor reoriented their policy agenda to engage with and promote neoliberal globalism by bargaining with workers

for the restructuring and destructuring of their industries, working conditions, and modes of labor representation. No one marked the date, but the conditions that the state had created to sustain the nation through public education could no longer be taken for granted. The state had now been captured by neoliberal ideologues to serve the interests of globalization from above, and no longer served the purposes of underwriting the socioeconomic conditions required by its citizens or small businesses.

The state's focus on acting as an ally and agent of international political and economic interests was done on the promise of maintaining the relative living standards of Australians. Over twenty years, this has now created a new political economy for higher education institutions, as the state's commitment to the public good has been rolled back. Responding to a growing trade deficit in the mid-eighties, the government reviewed potential sources of export earnings and concluded that a significant demand existed for tertiary education (Smart and Ang, 1993). Since then, Australian higher education has been increasingly exposed to global/local market forces through policies directed to the production of human capital and the commodification of education (see Ziguras, this volume). As the leader of one government explained:

> Australia's great comparative advantage in the Asia Pacific is its education system—there is no country in Asia with an education system as strong as ours. And selling innovative products, elaborately transformed goods, internally traded services are all things that Australia can do if we can open these markets up, but then we have to follow through, and of course, we will follow through if we have a trained and skilled workforce. Again all roads lead back to vocational education. (Keating, 1994)

The demand for skilled labor increased the focus on the vocational outcomes of all levels of education. Increasingly the supply and demand for labor had created a global trade in skills, with education being repositioned as a private investment rather than a public good by governments ready to disinvest themselves of responsibility for underwriting their citizens' social and economic security. On every front local expressions of this agenda of neoliberal globalism have accelerated since 1996. In the case of postcompulsory education, this occurred by incremental administrative restructurings and destructurings that have now made the sector largely unrecognizable. The government repositioned itself as a consumer of services, no longer responsible for assuring its citizens against socioeconomic risks through public education; it would "purchase" a declining number of training places, paying less and less, while demanding more "compliance" and more "productivity." Increasingly institutions of higher education have been expected to fund their operations from commercial earnings. The result has been what Marginson and Seddon (2001: 203) have characterized as a "crisis trifecta." The "resource crisis" has been created by the state's reduced commitment to the education of its citizens. An "identity crisis" has resulted from the corporatization of public education systems and cultures. A "strategy crisis" has resulted from the need for senior management in these institutions to make their own way in the increasingly complex, contradictory, and uncertain conditions of globalization.

## Responses

Universities' responses to and expressions of this "crisis trifecta" have had a number of profound consequences. Declining state investment in public education has led to demands for senior management to be responsible for what are effectively privatized institutions in an increasingly uncertain market after having spawned a corporatist style of management committed to entrepreneurialism. The "crisis trifecta" has been devolved via program budgeting that has been employed to re-engineer academic culture, which had been habituated to recurrent funding as a public good. The state manufactured public concerns about "quality" and "accountability" to justify the proliferation of bureaucratic technologies of appraisal, based on models of control developed for military and commercial circumstances, for example "management by crisis" and "change by disorganization." The corporate desire for image management added impetus to the misleadingly named "quality assurance" systems that have been used to direct an increasing amount of academics' time, which might otherwise have been devoted to a critique of the system, into "administrivia." These demands now extend far beyond the requirements of a normal workweek, creating a 24/7 command-and-response system. Academic work is absorbed in bureaucratic compliance rather than in actual teaching, research, pastoral care, or making requisite curriculum improvements. Moreover, this has shifted the focus of academics away from practices of professional judgment and away from peers to the agents of corporate management and private enterprise advisors (e.g. Ashenden and Milligan, 2000).

Reorganization has long been a key strategy used by senior managers in universities (and elsewhere) seeking to destabilize established cultures, interests, and alliances. It allows for the exercise of executive power in the definition of boundaries through the creation of new departments, centers, and "research concentrations," or allowing for the development of hybrid programs involving elements from a variety of disciplines while undermining the conditions that created distinctive disciplinary cultures. Restructuring also creates an ideological test of loyalty between the management's agendas and the traditions and communal values of academics. This advantages opportunists who, unbound by professional ethics or expertise, are ready to align with the agenda of authority, while marking those who are loyal to established cultures as "part of the problem" supposedly threatening the long-term survival of universities.

It is against this background that universities have increasingly looked to the potentials proffered by advancing technologies, especially the Internet and the World Wide Web. The use of such technology was sold to senior managers with the promise of cutting costs by reinventing the teacher-proof curricula of the 1960s under the name of "reusable learning objects." Naively, the idea was to extend market reach without increasing the load on existing "bricks and mortar" facilities by implementing centrally controlled systems for the appropriation and management of academics' knowledge and the "delivery" of education. The consequences for teaching, learning, and the pedagogies for knowledge production constitute the focus of the case study that follows.

## Case Study

This case study is taken from the Bachelor of Arts (International Studies) program in which I teach. Designed and created in 1998 by Michael Singh (see this volume), it was conceived of as a meditation and mitigation of the changing conditions of higher education created by government-orchestrated practices of global/local restructuring and destructuring. Rather than repackaging a regional or area studies program, and rather than simplistically rebadging a suite of existing subjects in the field of multicultural education, the new program was purposely designed by Singh to engage and push against the limitations of neoliberal globalism. The program structure was designed with a core sequence inspired by Arjun Appadurai's (1996) critique of cultural globalization to engage the rise in postindustrial ventures trading in the movement of peoples, the production of technologies, and the enterprises involved in media, finance, and knowledge, as well as risks. Associated with these studies of the "new" economy are opportunities for students to undertake field studies and internships in these fields. The study of a language, including the option to study "English as a global language" (Singh, Kell, and Pandian, 2002), was a third mandatory element of the program. Despite persistent opposition from those keen to build strong boundaries around the program, the remaining quarter of courses of this three-year program enabled students to select and study a vocational specialism from any field across the university. While allowing students to pursue their interests in specific vocational skills, the program was designed to promote deep learning, to provide broad cosmopolitan knowledge and engender sophisticated capabilities suited to the transnational knowledge workers of the twenty-first century. The program was also designed by Singh to incubate and spin off new courses and programs as the need arose, in areas such as English language studies, global/local governance, ecocultural sustainability, and dual language education. The knowledge-producing pedagogy Singh promoted in the program explores a "sociocultural, community connectionist" theory of learning, which was inspired by models of socially critical education promoting participatory action research developed in government-funded education reforms of the 1980s (Kemmis, 1983, 1987; Minister of Education, 1983; Participation and Equity Program Committee, 1984).

From the first, the use of new technologies was an integral aspect of program development. An electronic mailing list was created for each new cohort of students. Personal e-mail addresses were used rather than those automatically created by the university at enrollment, with the aim of making electronic communications about the program part of students' everyday lives rather than a "pigeonhole" to be visited occasionally. With both staff and students as members of these electronic mailing lists, this symmetrical communication channel helped to give substance to the view of the program as a scholarly community interested in extending possibilities for deep learning, sharing the knowledge they produced, and creating symbols of inclusion.

Many assessment tasks involve applied, work-related projects requiring teamwork, problem solving, and knowledge production. These projects create the conditions for the dynamic reflexive interplay of theory and practice. Such projects provide platforms for students' investigations, analyses, and culturally responsive communications and are premised on the view that students can learn to be producers of useful knowledge. One course dedicated to the study of human mobility as part of globalization provides an example of the productive use of this technology. Necessarily, the prescribed text for the course provides an account of migration history up to its year of publication (Castles and Miller, 1993). The need to update this text, itself a "reusable learning object," created an opportunity for student investigations that drew on the collective resources of the whole class, including the fund of knowledge that they were able to access through their proximal and extended transnational communities. In a collaborative project involving two phases, each student researched and reported on recent developments in a country selected for its potential to provide insights into global human migration. In the second phase, these individual reports were pooled, creating a communal resource to be analyzed by students for patterns and trends. In the absence of university support, hotmail e-mail accounts were created specifically for the purpose of sharing files. Mailing their own reports to a common point, students were able to download material from the rest of the group. The electronic texts that they were able to accumulate could then be searched, transferred to a database, or reproduced by "copy and paste," thereby saving rekeying when using quotations.

Requests for a website to support the work of this pedagogy for knowledge production took second place to the university's agenda of appropriating and managing knowledge through its centralized authority structures using reproductive pedagogies. The situation was experienced as an instance wherein the use of new technology by corporate managerialists served to control, contain, and co-opt the possibilities for teacher-initiated innovations in technologically integrated practice-based curriculum development. This experience highlighted the way in which new technologies are used by corporate managers to frame the pedagogical options available to academics.

Their franchizing of teaching creates a culture of dependency that requires teachers to rely on tools that require the intervention of technological experts if any pedagogical changes are to be made. This reduces the scope of teachers for using their professional expertise in the pursuit of curriculum innovations.

Corporate managers have introduced ICT specialists as a "third force" shaping the landscape and the tools for teaching and learning, being directly accountable to management. If the processes of pedagogy and curriculum innovation are to remain dynamic and grounded in practice, academics may need to create an alliance or collaborate with ICT specialists.

## Critical Decisions

In 1999, the university established a Distributed Learning System (DLS). This is a commercially packaged web-based software system. The flow-on effects from these software choices have had negative consequences for teacher-based curriculum innovation and for attempts by academics to use this software to support a collaborative, knowledge-producing approach to teaching and learning. The limits to the functionality of this on-line learning system constrain pedagogy. The DLS had been based on software using a reproductive transmission model of teaching and learning with a focus on "fixing" content. It embodied what Michael Lewis (2001) has described as the cornerstones of the new Silicon Valley "religion"—automation, speed and access to volumes of resources, and the creation of provider/client relationships. This Fordist industrial system of software, hardware, and social organization is based on the commodification of knowledge and the centralization of control over intellectual capital through forming reusable learning objects.

This industrial system provided generic "course shells" with a series of standard templates equipped with a basic array of tools. The range of pedagogical choices available to academics about how to teach is now largely defined and constrained by the design of the software product and the limitations of the imagination of the institution's senior management. As Michael Apple (1982: 142) explained, the use of such technological systems invoke the conditions for de-skilling:

> It usually has involved taking relatively complex jobs... and breaking them down into specified actions with specified results so that less skilled and costly personnel can be used, or that control of the workplace and outcome is enhanced.

The primary choices shaping curriculum and pedagogy are increasingly defined through technological consumption, with corporate managers rather than academics exercising key choices from a relatively limited number of "bundled products." The moment of purchasing these pedagogical tools creates a significant chain of dependence. Academics become dependent on ICT staff, who are in turn dependent on the supplier. The result for academics threatens their capacity to pursue continuing innovations on the basis of reflective practice. The implications of this shift in power over pedagogy for innovative teaching practice are profound. Pedagogy is regressively coming to mean the use and "advertorial" promotion of commercial ICT products and services. The improvement of teaching and learning is increasingly reduced to a technical problem to be addressed by product improvement and consumer selection. Educational innovation has been corporatized, commodified, and technologized in the slow, unrelenting colonization of academics and their work by technology and technologists working to service neoliberal globalism. Procedures at my university require that courses be "quality assured" before being "delivered" online, meaning that they are constituted as a fixed body of digital information waiting to be downloaded rather than a virtual "space" in which to conduct collaborative projects of inquiry and knowledge production.

The DLS made no provision for building connections between courses to give coherence to programs. Contrary to managerial rhetoric about "blurring boundaries," the system threatens to destructure programs, effectively creating hard-edged boundaries between areas of knowledge and disrupting the community-forming processes of enculturation embodied in the B.A. (I.S.) program. The DLS constrained the pedagogical options available to academics. It concentrated on those for advancing managerial control by capturing a palette of disaggregated courses upon which marketers could draw to create hybrid programs for online delivery to emerging market niches.

## Reconfiguring for Collaboration

Since the first year of the B.A. (International Studies) program, staff had been requesting the construction of a website to support the program's knowledge producing pedagogy and to respond to and engage the needs of a "distributed learning community." Students were often apart as a result of the need to undertake international internships and offshore field studies. In a program where the study of globalization/localization incorporated the study of technology and its part in the compression of time/space relations, it is pedagogically important to explore the possibilities for teaching and learning in cyberspace. Apart from serving students at a distance, a website could provide a point of focus for all students irrespective of their location. Physical spaces on the city campus are multi-use and in high demand, denying the program any dedicated physical space. A website offered the prospect of creating a continuing space for knowledge production and the expression of community to complement the face-to-face activities of the program. The website offered an opportunity to develop collaborative projects and to treat it as a "home" base. The type of website envisaged would support a community of authors, sharing news, producing ideas, creating resources, providing useful contacts, and acting as audience for each other's work. It would provide a university showcase for student publications, be a medium for celebrating their intellectual achievements, and eventually build into an archive recording their collective history making efforts. We could not implement this vision without university resources and technical assistance. Nevertheless, inspired by Apple (1982) we continued the ongoing search to find spaces for innovative pedagogical actions. This case suggests that such spaces may be created through a partnership involving ICT specialists and academics.

The university's timetable for putting courses online required faculties to nominate courses for "renewal." A momentous opportunity came in 2002 when the faculty proposed all six core courses of the B.A. (International Studies) for renewal in a response to a submission from Michael Singh. The critical mass that this created allowed for the deployment of sufficient resources to test the possibilities for developing knowledge-producing pedagogies using new technologies.

Within universities both corporatization and new technologies have created opportunities for academics to make the transition into management or technology. Ironically, this provides a cultural basis for academics developing a shared understanding with those who are still interested in knowledge-producing pedagogies. Delivering on this initiative served the interests of management and the faculty in course renewal. DLS and faculty ICT staff agreed to collaborate to create a secure "portal" for the exclusive use of staff and students in the program. Creating this site provided the opportunity to explore the potential of the university's software and to create a pedagogical model that could demonstrate the unrealized flexibility of ever-advancing technologies.

The focus was on creating a space for shared knowledge production and functionalities that would develop reciprocal relationships. The design involved a student-administered publishing system organized around three types of space: private, project, and public. Students' peers were the primary audience. The public space was restricted to the program community. Project spaces allowed teams to share documents. Collaborative reports were drafted and edited in the team's private space.

Experience revealed the extent of the taken-for-granted acceptance of centrally controlled pedagogical technologies based on proprietary software. The politics and pedagogical assumptions driving the appropriation, control, and management of academics' knowledge has become deeply ingrained throughout the university. The standardized and standardizing

DLS software is premised on a reproductive pedagogy and a transmission model of industrial education that does not support collaborative learning and knowledge production proposed in the B.A. (International Studies). The short-term resolution involved the creation of a "hybrid" site, integrating two of the university's existing software systems. The resulting compromize did not deliver all the requested functions, but it did allow for the creation of a learning environment that reflected the program's orientation to curriculum innovation and knowledge-producing pedagogies. The effort this required highlighted the constraints on innovation imposed by the consequences of the "bundling functions" in software packages, convergence of corporate managerialism, and the use of technological systems to intensify academics' work and to reduce their control over their work, while sapping their own self-exploitative desires and capacities

## Techno-Social Pedagogies: The Socialization of Technology and the Technologization of Society

The historically embedded uptake of information technology not only requires planning but also frames future options. Pragmatic decisions have to be made in real time. They are influenced by a constellation of factors including institutional policies (in all their incoherence and inconsistencies), the characteristics of the technology itself, the competing objectives of stakeholders, the disposition of the powerful to desire the control of resources, and the context where the new technology is applied. These choices have unintended and unanticipated consequences, as Winner (1988: 42) observes:

> By far the greatest latitude of choice exists the very first time a particular instrument, system or technique is introduced. Because choices tend to become strongly fixed in material equipment, economic investment, and social habit, the original flexibility vanishes for all practical purposes once the initial commitments are made. In that sense technological innovations are similar to legislative acts or political foundings that establish a framework for public order that will endure over many generations.

The critical location of postindustrial education in pedagogies of knowledge formation and cultural production means that these decisions have serious implications, most unrecognized by corporate mangers wedded to industrial education. The relationship between humans and their information technologies is mutually constitutive; both the tool and the user "program" each other. Teaching students to use information technology requires the assimilation of terms, symbols, and routines to interact or "interface" with the technology. To use Donna Harraway's (1997) term, students become "cyborgs" or an extension of the system through the use of its conventions. The technology becomes just another part of the sociopolitical environment, shaping experience, influencing students' identities and their perceptions of the world.

The political decision by university corporate managers to implement online learning represents an investment in people as well as technological infrastructure that shapes but does not absolutely or decisively determine the trajectory of future pedagogical developments. Nevertheless, implementation is a reductive process in which prior decisions frame present options and create new dependencies, new hierarchical relations of power. As complex as they necessarily are, decisions about educational technology and its not-so-"hidden curriculum" are of critical importance for the mechanisms reproducing managerial control of both academics and knowledge. The critical question is whether the corporately inscribed potential of software for effecting the commodification of knowledge and the standardization of pedagogical practice will win out against academic struggles to appropriate technology by extending the possibilities for organically grounded pedagogies and ongoing curriculum innovations. While technological convergence allows software "options" to proliferate, their bundling together in commercial "software products" operates to savagely reduce pedagogical choices. Nevertheless, technological innovation creates opportunities for those able to make a strategic advantage of changing conditions by forging new alliances to appropriate new technologies to serve knowledge-producing, rather than reproductive, pedagogies.

## Issues for Making the Future

In analyzing local consequences of practices of globalizing higher education, this chapter has ascribed a key role to the development of ICT. The consequences of the contraction of time and space have reverberated throughout the world, being mediated and mitigated by governments and responded to and engaged with by university corporate managers, creating the conditions that frame the micro-processes of technological uptake and the development of knowledge-producing pedagogies. The spread of new technologies has been used by university corporate managers to redefine power over knowledge as well as to reduce the status of academics by enhancing the influence of those who control technology. Technology is both a strategy and an environment in which this contest is being played out. The systemic uses of information technology in higher education are being politicized by their:

- potential to exacerbate hierarchical power relationships and centralize control;
- constraining of equitable access to education for all by reinforcing its contribution to stratification and the creation of sociopolitical elites based in part on educational experience;
- impact on the character, control, and organization of work, and
- pedagogical assumptions and their subliminally encoded messages about consumption, knowledge, power, and social relations and the appropriate roles of teacher and learner.

Centralized ICT systems constitute a sociopolitical extension of the bureaucratic technologies already used to maintain and extend the control of senior management. Power and privilege are key stakes in their interests. The costs of development, implementation, and training associated with the structural use of centrally controlled systems of information technology and curriculum standardization all tend toward concentrating managerial power. Corporate managers use the introduction of new technology to effect the refocusing of educational innovations, misrepresenting them as technical problems whose solutions are located at a considerable distance from teacher/student interactions. This approach effectively seeks to reduce the agency of academics. Despite the questionable claims that online education will be cheap and enable the extension of educational opportunities to those who currently cannot afford higher education, working in conjunction with neoliberal, neoconservative governments, it is being used to extend the gap between costs and quality. Extending socioeconomic stratification by using markets is a key agenda.

The ways new technologies are implemented in the university are shaped by sociopolitical decisions. In contrast, postindustrial struggles to use the democratic and empowering potential of new technologies create a basis for imagining new forms of knowledge-producing pedagogy. For an international studies program it provides the prospect of creating a "distributed learning community" involving transnational partnerships that enable participants to travel educational trails that track around the world. The program portal provides a point of contact and an arena for sharing, facilitating collaboration and the ongoing exchange of information, and the provoking of critical reflection. Students' research projects achieve an added global/local dimension because they are able to collect and compare translocal and transnational data.

Undoubtedly, information technology is providing profound and enriching educational experiences for some tertiary students. However, the lack of willingness of senior management to commit resources to the human component in education plays a large part in shaping its effects. In this instance, it constrains possibilities to enrich educational experiences by engineering acceptance, compliance, and consumption, or what Herman and Chomsky (1988) call the manufacturing of consent. Corporate managers are determined to reinforce the fixed, reductionist view of knowledge as a commodifiable object and to make the university a site for the mass distribution of an information-based service as competing players in the world of mediated infotainment.

## Conclusion

We are left to consider the world of the corporate managerialist agenda embedded in software functions being used to "renew" curriculum and pedagogy. Certainly the tools currently available to academics are inscribed with pedagogical politics that are creating hierarchically differentiated roles that privilege technological experts and compliance operatives over and above academics. The market-driven flow of technological refinements is not extending the menu of pedagogical choices to enable academics to create the technological tools to support a democratic, student-centered, collaborative, critically empowering pedagogy. Increasingly, commercially produced software is reinforcing client relationships framed by capitalist modes of production and consumption.

In the meantime, academics are attempting to appropriate politically inscribed projects for the technologization of pedagogy and to re-engineer these to serve progressive ends and to produce alternative cultural meanings. In the process, we are learning the huge cost of corporate managerial incompetence and the failings of centralized systems to sustain worthwhile education. When Michael Apple (1982) described technological control and its de-skilling tendencies, he highlighted the possibility of locating opportunities for counter-hegemonic action in the spaces created by the tensions arising from corporate managerial incompetence and the contradictions of structural and technological change. The technology of commodified "learning packages" with their graduated exercises was appropriated and adapted by teachers:

> Internal contradictions need not preclude teachers from making these commodified forms their own, to generate their own creative responses to dominant ideologies in a manner similar to what countercultural groups...have done to commodified culture. These groups transformed and reinterpreted the products they brought and used so that they became tools for creating alternative pockets of resistance. (Apple, 1982: 156)

Advancing technologies may offer similar possibilities. However, the collaboration of technologists is now required to reconfigure the spaces necessary for productive pedagogical action. This means creating avenues for mutually informing symmetrical dialogues and practical partnerships between academics and information technologists. This is a strategic priority to further the technologization of education in way that extends rather than constrains the reflexive processes linking practice-based curriculum innovation, knowledge production, and cultural formation.

# References

Appadurai, A. *Modernity at Large: Cultural Dimensions of Globalisation*. Minneapolis: University of Minnesota Press, 1996.

Apple, M. *Education and Power*. London: Routledge and Kegan Paul, 1982.

Ashenden, D., and S. Milligan. *The Good Universities Guide: Universities, TAFE, Private Colleges*. Subiaco, Australia: Hobsons Australia, 2000.

Blackburn, J. *Ministerial Review of Postcompulsory Schooling*. Melbourne: Victorian Government Printer, 1985.

Burke, J. *Connections*. London: Macmillan, 1978.

Castells, M. *The Rise of the Network Society. The Information Age: Economy, Society and Culture*. Vol. 1. Oxford: Blackwell, 1996.

Castles, S., and M. Miller. *The Age of Migration: International Population Movement in the Modern Worlds*. 2nd ed. London: Macmillan, 1993.

Harraway, D. *Modest_Witness@Second_Millemium.FemaleMan_Meets_OncoMouse*. New York, Routledge, 1997.

Herman, E., and N. Chomsky. *Manufacturing Consent: The Political Economy of the Mass Media*. London: Vintage, 1988.

Karmel, P. and Interim Committee for the Australian Schools Commission. *Schools in Australia: Report of the Interim Committee for the Australian Schools Commission, May 1973*. Canberra: Australian Government. Printing Service, 1973.

Keating, P. *Australian Training: Vol. 1, Issue 3*. Brisbane: Australian National Training Authority, 1994.

Kemmis, S. *Orientations to Curriculum and Transition: Towards the Socially-Critical School*. Melbourne: Victorian Institute of Secondary Education, 1983.

————. *Dilemmas of Reform: The Participation and Equity Program in Victorian Schools*. Geelong, Australia: Deakin Institute for Studies in Education, 1987.

Lewis, M. *The Future Just Happened*. London: A&E Network Co-production, 2001.

Marginson, S., and T. Seddon. "The Crisis Trifecta: Education." In *Globalisation: The Australian Impacts*, edited by C. Shiel. Sydney: University of New South Wales Press, 2001.

McLuhan, M. *Understanding Media: The Extension of Man*. London: Sphere Books, 1964.

Minister of Education. *Ministerial Paper No 2: The School Improvement Plan*. Melbourne, Australia: Government Printer, 1983.

Participation and Equity Program Committee. *Participation and Equity Program Guide*. Melbourne, Australia: Ministry of Education, Equal Educational Opportunities Branch, 1984.

Singh, M., P. Kell and A. Pandian. *Appropriating English: Innovation in the Global Business of English Language Teaching*. New York: Peter Lang, 2002.

Smart, D., and G. Ang. "The Origins and Evolution of the Commonwealth Full-Fee Paying Overseas Student Policy 1975–1992." In *Case Studies in Public Policy*, edited by A. Peachment and J. Williamson. Perth, Australia: Public-sector Research Unit, Curtain University, 1993.

Winner, L. "Do Artifacts Have Politics?" In *Technology and Politics*, edited by M. Kraft and M. Vig. Durham: Duke University Press, 1988.

# Chapter 11

# Living in Liminal Times: Early Childhood Education and Young Children in the Global/Local Information Society

Susan Grieshaber and Nicola Yelland

## Introduction

Computers, the Internet, electronic mail, and instantaneous communication around the globe are features of life for many in the Minority World, including (and excluding) vast numbers of young children. While computers and Internet access are available in many kindergartens, preschools, and child care centers, political and economic processes of globalization make teaching and learning to use these resources problematic in the early childhood years. Globalization has meant access to information and communication technologies (ICT), but at the same time it has been accompanied by policies generated by politicians that focus on "accountability," "standardization," and the upholding of these in exploitative relationships of doing much more with much less (see Raduntz, this volume). For early childhood education, creating new pedagogies that use ICT for effective teaching and learning is compounded by its reluctant acceptance by early childhood educators (Clements, 1999; Yelland, 1999). Part of this reluctance is due to concerns that childhood is being lost through children being denied their right to be children. Far from being lost, we argue that dominant ideas about children as innocent, vulnerable, dependent, cute, and needing control (Cannella, 2002) are under threat as childhood is reinvented in ways not seen previously. Further, lamenting the loss of childhood is occurring because of the perceived vulnerability of children to "new forms of exploitation, particularly to an intense commercialization with children as consumers of technical goods, toys and leisure services" (Foley, Roche, and Tucker, 2001: 1). Continuing with this theme, Kenway and Bullen (2001) have shown that traditional barriers among education, entertainment, and advertising are crumbling, with children consuming technological goods and services both in and out of school contexts.

In this chapter, we foreground the lives of young children in the twenty-first century and highlight the ways in which their lives are changing assumptions about childhood and educational contexts involving technologies. We provide examples of young children engaged in activities that illustrate a sophisticated understanding of concepts and a high level of competence with new technologies. We begin with a discussion of globalization and its relevance to early childhood education to make the point that despite the globalization of the world through ICT and the production of consumer culture and its associated subjectivities, many of the curriculum policies used in the field focus on content and approaches that are commensurate with rational and industrial methods. We discuss the changes in global/local societies to make an argument for the use of new pedagogies and new technologies. Against this, we highlight some of the tensions produced when constructions of children as technologically competent compete with dominant constructions of children as innocent and naïve. Following that, we demonstrate the abilities of some young children to use technologies in their classrooms as part of daily learning. We conclude that young children's abilities with technologies need to form an integral part of the curriculum-in-practice in ways that are not currently evident in many early childhood classrooms.

We live in liminal, postindustrial times in which new structures are struggling to emerge, supplementing the old industrial forms and ways of doing things that certainly have not yet disappeared. For example, in the field of early childhood education, after an initial rejection of the use of computers by teachers of young children (Clements, 1999), there has been a reluctant recognition that ICT are a significant and important part of children's lives and that there is a role for them in the educational experiences of young children (National Association for the Education of Young Children [NAEYC], 1996). Yet in the main, early childhood programs remain anchored to structures that privilege a developmental paradigm and incorporate experiential learning activities that are relics of a conservative, industrial educational heritage (Grieshaber, 2000b). More recently, there have been innovations in early childhood curricula and pedagogies that have recognized the potential of ICT. We highlight some of the creative approaches of using ICT with young children as well as some of the struggles involved in integrating ICT into early childhood classrooms. These methods might transform not only the ways in which young children may experience ideas and representations, but also provide opportunities for them to communicate their ideas in new and dynamic ways. However, when considering computer use in schools, priority is often given to older children, especially when resources are limited and professional development scarce.

Significant progress is being made throughout the nations of the Minority World toward achieving the goal of providing reasonable computer access; for example, one state government report planned to have in public schools "one computer per five students for children in Years 3 to 7 [children aged 8 to 12] by 2004" (Queensland Government, 2002: 5). However, this target has already been met for students aged 13 to 17, and there is no mention of children aged 6 to 8 years, or of children aged 4 and 5 attending preschool programs provided by the state being supplied with computers in similar proportion. This is despite the same report stating that:

> Research shows ICTs innovation has a positive effect on student achievement in all major subject areas—from pre-school through to higher education—for "mainstream" [see Shore, this volume] and special needs students, urban and remote students. We know that computer use has positive effects on student attitudes toward learning, motivation to learn and increases in self-confidence and self-esteem. (Queensland Government, 2002: 4)

While economic factors may be at the basis of this decision, we question the "othering" of young children that has occurred by ignoring the issue of supplying computers to those children in the public education system who are between the ages of 4 and 8 years. This inequitable approach is characteristic of pedagogical debates that are embedded in issues of gender and social justice and adds the concept of age to current deliberations.

There is evidence concerning the reluctance of some early childhood teachers to include technologies in their classrooms (Clements, 1999). This resistance exists in spite of confirmation that young children use and operate a variety of technological devices in their everyday lives. They are used to interacting competently with and experiencing a range of media, including television, remote-controlled cars, Game Boy, Nintendo, Play Station, videocassette recorders, and compact disc players. This competence was shown in a study by the Kaiser Family Foundation (1999), which reported that children aged 2 to 7 years spend an average of 3.34 hours a day using media, while older children (8 to 18 years) used media for 6.43 hours a day. Further, one-third (32 percent) of 2- to 7-year-old children had a television in their bedroom and the majority of these children had a computer in their home. The study reported that "on an average day, sixteen percent of two to seven year olds play video games and twenty-six percent use computers" (Kaiser Family Foundation, 1999: 3). Those who play computer games spend about 50 minutes a day at the controls and when using computers spend about 40 minutes a day at the keyboard, which suggests that there are times when they use both media with others, as an instructional or collaborative experience. In terms of choosing their favorite media, 29 percent of young children (aged 2 to 7 years) named television ahead of computers (23 percent). Thirty-three percent of older children (8 to 18 years of age) said that they would want a computer with Internet access if stranded on a desert island.

This presents an interesting image about older children's conceptualizations of what life might be like if they were to become stranded and the assumption that they would have electricity and cable to facilitate this happening. The Kaiser Family Foundation's (1999) report highlights the role of media in students' daily lives. The experiences they encounter in school are often focused on traditional materials (e.g., pencils/pens) and processes (writing, presentations without media) associated with industrial education.

The relevance of these findings for educators is considerable. Some children are not gaining access and not developing skills in the use of ICT for learning tasks. Instead, they are mainly using computers for fun, often in out-of-school contexts. This situation occurs at a time when there would seem to be "a consensus among business leaders, educators, policymakers and parents that our traditional, industrial practices are not delivering the skills our students need to thrive in the 21st century" (CEO Forum, 1999: 6). It is evident that traditional industrial education is not appropriate for preparing students to function in today's postindustrial society or to be productive in the postindustrial workplaces of the twenty-first century. Very little seems to have changed since late last century, when Becker (1992: 1) reported that "although most elementary school students use computers, that use has mainly been occasional and for purposes of lending variety and 'enrichment' to the school day, rather than as a central component of teachers' instructional programs."

## Globalization and Early Childhood Education

While globalization is a multifaceted concept and a hugely debated practice, our interpretation of it here is in terms of "the emergence of new global cultural forms, media, and technologies of communication, all of which shape the relations of affiliation, identity, and interaction within and across local cultural settings" (Burbules and Torres, 2000: 2). When combined with changes in the global/local economy, changes in the form and functions of families, the cultural and ethnic composition of Minority World societies, and changes in the workplace, it becomes apparent that new postindustrial approaches are needed for many aspects of daily life. In the twenty-first century, attributes such as problem-solving skills, critical analysis, adaptability, flexibility, interpersonal skills, and competence and confidence in the use of ICT are highly valued. The significance of these skills is no less important for young children and early childhood educators than others involved in different sectors of public education.

Changes to public education in many Minority World nations have been shaped mostly by the ideologies and politics of neoliberal globalism (Lingard, 2000). Neoliberal globalism translates into an agenda for public education "that privileges, if not directly imposes, particular policies for evaluation, financing, assessment, standards, teacher training, curriculum, instruction and testing" (Burbules and Torres, 2000: 15). The dominating neoliberal globalism norm, according to Apple (2000), expressed in its key tenets, which include "efficiency and 'ethic' of cost benefit analysis" (p.38). In Australia, these dominating norms find expression in early childhood education through nationalized literacy and numeracy tests for children age 8; a state-initiated Diagnostic Net for children age 7, and the Quality Improvement and Accreditation System (QIAS) of assessment for all long-day-care centers (National Childcare Accreditation Council, 2001). The QIAS, for example, is an externally imposed assessment of curriculum, staff, and the general operation of long-day-care centers that regulates and standardizes their performance and productivity in accordance with federal government requirements. These state and national measures of accountability are the result of the imposition of neoliberal policies requiring national data for making international comparisons of efficiency, productivity, and cost effectiveness in educational endeavors.

The rhetoric around these neoliberal imperatives focuses on two main issues. The first pertains to accountability of educators' productivity, which is generally measured using test scores of children's successes or lack of it and, secondly, around discussions of "adding value," which entail justifying reduced expenditure for improved performance. Both imperatives have ramifications for the use of ICT in schools, especially insofar as they reinforce resistance among early childhood educators. The content of tests tends to be related to traditional subject areas and, because of the sheer numbers of children involved, are usually multiple choice in format so that they can be marked electronically; all of which reinforces the prevailing industrial model of education. There is no room for lateral thinking or the incorporation of tasks based on the capacity of new technologies to aid students in information and knowledge production. Further, while governments allocate large amounts of funding to place computers and associated peripherals in school, there are limited funds for the professional development of teachers to ensure that they can learn how to best incorporate the machines into the teaching/learning process; this adds further to understanding resistance among early childhood educators. Additionally, the curriculum that they are required to enact is often devoid of applications of computer tasks, thereby denying early childhood educators necessary guidance. It is left to teachers to make the connection between current offerings of software on the market and the content of their programs, while they prepare their students to meet the requirements of state tests. In this way the use of technologies in schools veers toward being an add-on to existing experiences, if they are used at all.

Early childhood curriculum policies are strongly influenced by theories of child development as well as instrumental, overly rationalistic approaches to education (Grieshaber, 2000a, 2000b). This means that many early childhood curriculum policies do not reflect or give expression to the current social conditions of society, and in particular their meditation and mitigation of the globalization of technologies. There exist significant sociocultural contrasts between the uses of industrial curriculum in early childhood settings and some private preschools and child care centers where parents are able to view snapshots of what their children are doing via the Internet while at home or at work. While multiliteracies and ICT are changing teaching and learning, the importance of social justice within the Minority World, and between it and the Majority World, is rarely mentioned in early childhood curriculum policies. This is in contrast to the effects of globalization, which include the instantaneous movement of ideas and messages around the world and the migration of people from the Majority World to the Minority World, creating new transnational cultural dimensions for early childhood settings, and societies generally.

The knowledge now needed by young children growing up in the postindustrial societies of the twenty-first century differs markedly from times past, when the industrial economy ruled the world. The major function of school is not simply to prepare young children for their unknown and unknowable future as workers, but to enable them to use new technologies to facilitate information production and knowledge creation. Although there are early childhood educators already engaged in doing this in ways that we are still trying to understand, young children need opportunities to use a variety of ICT in early childhood settings. While young children already use new and ever-advancing technologies as integral parts of their daily lives, they are only gradually being offered similar opportunities in early childhood settings. Quite apart from the cognitive and social skills young children can develop through the use of ICT (Clements, 1994), they want to be able to "use the tools of their time in their daily learning. Just as slate and chalk were indispensable to learning 40 years ago, computers and computer skills are essential for success today" (Queensland Government, 2002: 4). While computers and computer skills are essential for success today, making ICT integral parts of our early childhood pedagogies, curricula, and assessment, sooner rather than later remains a significant challenge.

Given the disinclination of some early childhood teachers, and the state-driven disincentives for many to use computers in their classrooms, professional development of early childhood educators in relation to ICT (not just computers) remains an unrealized priority for public education systems. Increasingly, early childhood teachers find they are being required to use ICT in all aspects of their work, "from curriculum plans to assessment, for literacy and numeracy and in all subjects" (Queensland Government, 2002: 5).

In the early 1990s, Clements, Nastasi and Swaminathan (1993) suggested that we were at a crossroads in terms of computer use in the classroom. They highlighted three options in which computers were used at that point in time:

- As *drill and practice* or a *bribe* when children finished their regular work in the class and were allowed to play on the computer.

- Incorporating pieces of computer software as an *integral* part of classroom activity. This included the use of software such as *The Logical Journey of the Zoombinis* that could be incorporated in social studies of settlements and journeys, in language arts as a stimulus for creative story writing, and in mathematical problem solving. Additionally, activities within a software package have been used to provide opportunities to practice specific skills. For example, the *jellybean* game in *Trudy's Time and Place House* has proven a useful way to use coordinates, as has the *hide and seek* game in *Snootz*. Furthermore, the electronic sandbox in *Trudy's Time and Place House* affords opportunities not only for making links between real-world experiences in building with sand, but also for making connections between two-dimensional map symbols of landforms and buildings with three-dimensional representations in the sand.

- As an *artifact of innovation,* wherein the use of the computer fundamentally changes what children (and teachers) do in classrooms by incorporating the effective and appropriate use of the computer as they deem necessary.

The focus in the next sections is the latter two options, where we provide examples of innovative ways in which new technologies are being used in early childhood classrooms.

## New Pedagogies

In this postindustrial information age, children interact and communicate with others in sophisticated ways in virtual spaces. In contrast, some early childhood educators limit their use of new media to trivial and mechanistic tasks that have little relevance or connection to the lives of children outside school (Yelland, 2002). The push to have all teachers use ICT in pedagogically sanctioned ways has produced many counter-discourses, causing teachers to ignore new media, switch it off when too noisy, and locate it in another room where they are not forced to look at it (Simpson, 2003). Policies requiring all teachers to be skilled to certain levels in specified time frames (e.g., Simpson, 2003) are invocations of modernist regulatory mechanisms mediated by the assumption that the provision of ICT will seduce teachers into pedagogical compliance, the ultimate goal of which is skilling young people for employment not only in the state sector (Queensland Government, 2002), but also in the global marketplace.

These neoliberal strategies for producing economically competitive schools and citizens belie the disaffection experienced by many teachers and the ways they resist and contest integrating ICT into their teaching repertoires (see for example Simpson, 2003). The literature is replete with other examples of the failure of teachers to enthuse about and embrace ICT and to enact the advice of experts (e.g., Bigum et al., 1987; Cuban, 2001; Lankshear et al., 1997). The effects of the new ICT discourses are dynamic and illustrate not only that the processes of educational governance are very messy (Simpson, 2003), but also that the outcomes expected from such educational governance are very particular forms of knowledge. Despite this, new postindustrial pedagogies are being developed to engage and enchant children with their schooling (see Kenway, this volume). We now discuss approaches that have been used in early childhood classrooms as examples of the changing political economy of early childhood curriculum and pedagogies.

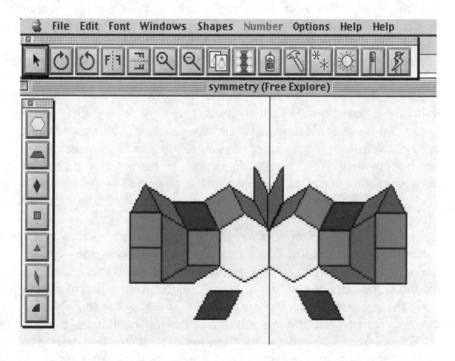

Figure 11.1: *Shapes* software for exploring symmetry

These new pedagogies illustrate the different cultural knowledge that is required of both children and teachers in a global economy. A number of studies based around a curriculum called *Investigations in Number, Data and Space* have investigated mathematical understandings and how young children learn when technology is embedded in their mathematics curriculum (Clements, 1994; Yelland, 1998). The curriculum was designed to encourage active exploration of mathematical concepts through tasks that incorporate the use of computers as well as activities in the local environments. In the curriculum, computer tasks are both integrated and integral to the conceptual development of each topic. For example, software called *Shapes* and *Geo Logo* are included in a number of the teaching/learning modules pertaining to the concepts of measurement and geometry.

The *Shapes* software is a two-dimensional representation of three-dimensional pattern blocks that users can play with on the computer screen. Children are able to create shapes and make pictures using the on-screen blocks in similar ways to their play with traditional pattern blocks. However, the blocks can also provide experiences that are not possible in the "real world." For example, there is a "gluing" tool that allows children to stick pattern blocks together, and mirror functions that allow for the exploration of symmetry in new and dynamic ways (see Figure11. 1). Clements (1999) argues that such software provides manipulative experiences that are very different to those engaged in when using "concrete" materials and are considered essential for early learning. Although the software is based on 3D pattern blocks there are several differences between the on-screen version and the wooden blocks. For example, children can create as many copies of each shape that they want; the shapes can be combined, glued, frozen, duplicated, and arranged to make pictures on screen; and the shapes can be saved and/or printed to make a hard copy of designs. Clements (1999) has outlined several benefits associated with these uses.

There are *pedagogical benefits* whereby the blocks are experienced in a medium that can be stored and retrieved, as well as allowing children to make constructions that are not possible with physical manipulatives. For example, they enable children to build triangles from different classes beyond the equilateral ones that are provided as part of the set. The children can make nonequilateral triangles by covering equilateral triangles to varying degrees with other shapes and in doing so create a myriad of triangle types. Further, the printing and storage aspect allows for revisiting and discussing the designs, as well as taking home or storing in portfolios.

There are *mathematical and psychological advantages* that include the on-screen blocks enabling the children to bring mathematical ideas and processes to a different level of conscious awareness; changing the concept of what is meant by a manipulative from being solely three-dimensionally based; allowing for the composition and decomposition of shapes and the patterns created with them, as well as facilitating the connection of spatial awareness and number learning with on-screen "base ten" blocks.

This evidence supports the notion that the *Shapes* software can play an important role in children's construction of meaningful ideas in mathematics (Clements, 1999). However, it is apparent that children cannot do this if they are not embedded in a context that supports the integration of ideas. It is not the advantages that come with computers that cause doubt and concern for teachers. Rather, it is the changes that are required in how teachers teach and how they use the ICT resources that are reasons for apprehension. Teachers are required to reinvent themselves, to create new pedagogical identities that go well beyond the techniques and strategies that they have used in the past, but at the same time operate in the neoliberal climate of child assessment and testing and teacher accountability.

Similarly the use of *Geo Logo* is particularly effective when supported by appropriate scaffolding and opportunities to share strategies with others. It is a computer environment in which children direct a turtle using a number of basic commands. For example, the turtle can move forward and back with an input number and make turns left or right as specified by the number of degrees. As with *Shapes*, there are on-screen devices that can assist in creations and specifications for moving across distances to any given point. Explorations with *Geo Logo* tasks have been shown to provide contexts in which young children can engage with powerful ideas (Yelland, 2002). Furthermore, *Geo Logo* tasks have enabled such children to experience concepts well beyond those normally expected for their age or experience. In one instance, children as young as 8 years of age worked on activities that included the use of negative numbers to 250; quadrants; and the development of procedures for action incorporating the abstract notion of variables, including the design of projects that integrated their use (Yelland, 2002). An example of one project completed by two boys age 7 is shown in Figure 11.2. The planning and development for this work incorporated a number of phases as well as the use of higher-order thinking skills that are meta-strategic, and it afforded ample opportunities for collaborative problem solving and negotiated meaning making (Davidson and Sternberg, 1984).

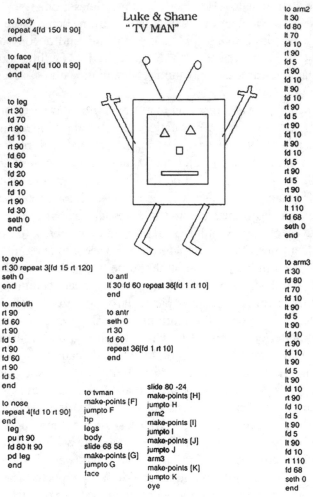

Luke & Shane
" TV MAN"

to body
repeat 4[fd 150 lt 90]
end

to face
repeat 4[fd 100 lt 90]
end

to leg
rt 30
fd 70
rt 90
fd 10
rt 90
fd 60
lt 90
fd 20
rt 90
fd 10
rt 90
fd 30
seth 0
end

to eye
rt 30 repeat 3[fd 15 rt 120]
seth 0
end

to mouth
rt 90
fd 60
rt 90
fd 5
rt 90
fd 60
rt 90
fd 5
end

to nose
repeat 4[fd 10 rt 90]
end
  leg
  pu rt 90
  fd 80 lt 90
  pd leg
end

to antl
lt 30 fd 60 repeat 36[fd 1 rt 10]
end

to antr
seth 0
rt 30
fd 60
repeat 36[fd 1 rt 10]
end

to tvman
make-points [F]
jumpto F
hp
legs
body
slide 68 58
make-points [G]
jumpto G
face

slide 80 -24
make-points [H]
jumpto H
arm2
make-points [I]
jumpto I
make-points [J]
jumpto J
arm3
make-points [K]
jumpto K
eye

to arm2
lt 30
fd 80
lt 70
fd 10
rt 90
fd 5
rt 90
fd 10
lt 90
fd 10
fd 10
rt 90
fd 5
rt 90
fd 10
lt 90
fd 10
fd 5
rt 90
fd 5
rt 90
fd 10
lt 110
fd 68
seth 0
end

to arm3
rt 30
fd 80
rt 70
fd 10
lt 90
fd 5
lt 90
fd 10
rt 90
fd 10
lt 90
fd 5
lt 90
fd 10
rt 90
fd 10
lt 90
fd 5
lt 90
fd 5
lt 90
fd 10
rt 110
fd 68
seth 0
end

Figure 11.2: TV man

Such activities and concepts are not generally introduced until the second year of high school, when students are age 14. It is not contended here that the children in the study understood such concepts at the same level as their older counterparts but rather that early exploration with these ideas is likely to change the ways in which they think and experience them later and that this will impact on the curriculum. If that is not the case, then the curriculum that they experience is likely to be inappropriate and to have the effect of alienating students from the subject, which they will deem as disenchanting.

The *Shapes* and *Geo Logo* software embedded in the *Investigations* curriculum demonstrate new ways of teaching and learning with computer technologies in the mathematics curriculum that challenge traditional industrial education, its content, and sequences of subject matter. Research associated with the curriculum modules has not only shown, as previously mentioned, high levels of cognitive activity and the use of higher-order thinking skills, but has also provided case studies of children engaged with learning mathematical concepts in collaborative partnerships characterized by persistence and interest in the tasks (Clements, 1999; Yelland, 2002). What is more important is that such research has also suggested that the role of the teacher, government funding, professional development, and new curriculum policies are critical for the *deep learning* of mathematical concepts. Scaffolding by the teacher, together with class discussions about strategies for problem solving, promote deep learning and the successful completion of tasks. In this way the computer activity is viewed as an integral aspect of mathematical learning and understanding and not an add-on.

By creating contexts for ICT learning that are fully integrative across the traditional subject areas offered under the industrial education model, we come a step closer to providing challenging experiences for children who will be the workers, citizens, and learners of the postindustrial information age. The incorporation of ICT skills in literacy and numeracy education afford opportunities to engage young children with concepts from all curriculum areas in ways that make the intersections between subjects/knowledge evident. In some cases, a topic or theme may be a catalyst for an investigation that requires children to identify a problem or issue, research it, collect and present information, and communicate their findings to their peers.

A class of children age 7 and 8 years studied Mini-beasts (small animals) as part of their science curriculum. One of the integrative tasks involved the children in making a "mini-beast" of their choice. They researched information about their particular animal, synthesizing it into a multimedia production that included an animated sequence of the mini-beast, coupled with a summary of important information about its characteristics and habitat. When the children had made the mini-beast, they created a backdrop and foreground that represented the habitat of the animals. Thus, if their mini-beast was a ladybird, they created a collage that resembled the undergrowth, complete with leaves, twigs, and discarded bark. The children set up a digital camera on a tripod and took a large number of shots of the ladybird in a sequence of moves that was co-ordinated using the Imovie software program on the *imac* Finally, they incorporated the movie with their information in a hyper-studio stack so that it became an interactive package that could not only be presented to the class as a summary of their investigation, but could also be accessed by others when required. In completing these tasks in groups of four to six, the children were engaged with processes and content in science, social studies, literacy, and numeracy.

Similar projects have been completed with young children using different media such as *Kid Pix Studio*. Because the children were 5 years of age and emergent writers, using an oral medium for the presentation of their "story" was more appropriate, and the use of the slide show in *Kid Pix Studio* suited this need. The point here is that new technologies enabled the children to produce and represent information in diverse ways that would not have been possible without these technologies. The final products were of a quality that exceeded the possibilities present in the best of traditional materials. In all of these examples, the sources of information were derived from shared readings of books and audiovisual material from the library and not so-called "reusable learning objects."

These examples display what is possible with the use of ICT in early childhood classrooms. Knowing what is possible and being aware of the outcomes of previous research that exemplifies the difficulties of integrating ICT into classrooms delimits present and future action. However, such action comes at the cost of compromises, such as when young children's equity of access to ICT is ignored in policy documents (see Queensland Government, 2002). This, combined with a multiplicity of other factors (see Simpson, 2003) that operate in the current neoliberal climate, emphasize the folly of thinking that simplistic solutions such as providing access to ICT will solve complex pedagogical problems.

## Conclusion

As an integral part of globalization, the ever-advancing information and communication technologies have received a mixed reception in many early childhood contexts, due in no small part to the effects and impact of neoliberal globalism. This is particularly evident in the pressures manufactured by mechanisms for effecting accountability and standardization, especially in relation to expectations of teachers to meet especially in relation to expectations of teachers to meet the demands of literacy and numeracy testing. This chapter has illustrated ways in which computer-based, knowledge- and information-producing activities may enhance teaching/learning contexts for young children, and has discussed the ramifications for curriculum design. It has been suggested here that the state needs to be engaged to reinvent curriculum policies so that computer activity and the use of new media are thoroughly embedded in curricula, to create teaching/learning opportunities that cross the traditional subject boundaries constructed for the era of industrial education, and emphasize the use of ICT as part of investigative, knowledge-producing pedagogies. Additionally, the use of ICT may enhance the ways in which young children share their findings with their peers or community members, with forms for presenting ideas being significantly broadened.

This begs a discussion of the role of activities that are part of the industrial tradition of education (e.g., handwriting) and the time that is currently spent on them. The use of technologies in schools will not solve all the problems that we face in education today, and in some instances they have already compounded the intensification of teachers' work. However, there are early childhood educators who are making opportunities to deepen and extend their repertoire of teaching/learning practices with ICT. The examples of exciting teaching/learning opportunities for young children hinted at in this chapter illustrate new ways for engaging and enchanting young children's learning in public schools.

Given professional development opportunities to reflect on the ways in which early childhood educators help organize schools for the twenty-first century should bring recognition of the need to abandon some of the old ways associated with industrial education while incorporating and creating a postindustrial education for these liminal times. These are challenging and exciting times, and early childhood educators are among those embracing change rather than perpetuating and propping up tired practices and theories of education that were an expression of and response to the industrial era. Much from the era of industrial education is now way past its "use by" date. This fact is potently symbolized in the old technology of the "qwerty" keyboard, which is still a feature of nearly every computer, but which was designed for mechanical typing so as not to jam the "hammers" together.

# References

Apple, M. "Between Neo-Liberalism and Neo-Conservatism: Education and Conservatism in a Global Context." In *Globalization and Education: Critical Perspectives*, edited by N. Burbules and A. Torres. New York: Routledge, 2000.

Becker, H. "Computer Based Integrated Learning Systems in the Elementary and Middle Grades: A Critical Review and Synthesis of Evaluation Reports." *Journal of Educational Computer Research* 8, no. 8 (1992): 1–41.

Bigum, C., S. Bonser, P. Evans, S. Groundwater-Smith, S. Grundy, S. Kemmis, D. McKenzie, D. McKinnon, M. O'Connor, R. Straton, and S. Willis. *Coming to Terms with Computers in Schools. Report to the Commonwealth Schools Commission.* Geelong, Australia: Deakin Institute for Studies in Education, Deakin University, 1987.

Burbules, N., and C. Torres. "Globalization and Education: An Introduction." In *Globalization and Education: Critical Perspectives*, edited by N. Burbules and C. Torres, 1–26. New York: Routledge, 2000.

Cannella, G. "Global Perspectives, Cultural Studies and the Construction of a Postmodern Childhood." In *Kidworld: Childhood Studies, Global Perspectives, and Education*, edited by G. Cannella and J. Kincheloe, 3–18. New York: Peter Lang, 2002.

CEO Forum. *The Power of Digital Learning: Integrating Digital Content*: CEO Forum on Education and Technology, 1999.

Clements, D. "The Uniqueness of the Computer as a Learning Tool: Insights from Research and Practice." In *Young Children: Active Learners in a Technological Age*, edited by J. Wright and D. Shade, 31–50. Washington, DC: National Association for the Education of Young Children, 1994.

———. "The Future of Educational Computing Research: The Case of Computer Programming." *Information Technology in Childhood Education Annual* 1 (1999): 147–79.

Clements, D., B. Nastasi, and S. Swaminathan. "Young Children and Computers: Crossroads and Directions from Research." *Young Children* 48, no. 2 (1993): 56–64.

Cuban, L. *Oversold and Underused: Computers in Classrooms.* Cambridge: Harvard University Press, 2001.

Davidson, J., and R. Sternberg. "Competence and Performance in Intellectual Development." In *Moderators of Competence*, edited by E. E. Niemark, R. Delisi, and J. Newman, 43–76. Hillsdale, NJ: Lawrence Erlbaum, 1984.

Foley, P., J. Roche., and S. Tucker. "Children in Society: Contemporary Theory, Policy and Practice." In *Children in Society: Contemporary Theory, Policy and Practice*, edited by P. Foley, J. Roche, and S. Tucker, 1–6. Basingstoke, UK: Palgrave, 2001.

Grieshaber, S. "Regulating the Early Childhood Field." *Australian Journal of Early Childhood* 25, no. 2 (2000a): 1–6.

———. "The State Re-Inventing the Preschool Child." *Discourse: Studies in the Cultural Politics of Education* 21, no. 3 (2000b): 269–81.

Kaiser Family Foundation. *Kids and Media and the New Millennium*. The Kaiser Family Foundation, 1999. Available from www.kff/content/ 1999/1535/.

Kenway, J., and E. Bullen. *Consuming Children: Education—Entertainment—Advertising.* Buckingham, UK: Open University Press, 2001.

Lankshear, C., C. Bigum, C. Durrant, B. Green, W. Morgan, J. Murray, I. Snyder, and M. Wild. *Digital Rhetorics: Literacies and Technologies in Education—Current Prac-*

*tices and Future Directions. Project Report: Children's Literacy National Projects.* Brisbane, Australia: Queensland University of Technology/Department of Employment, Education, Training and Youth Affairs, 1997.

Lingard, B. "It Is and It Isn't: Vernacular Globalization, Educational Policy, and Restructuring." In *Globalization and Education: Critical Perspectives*, edited by N. Burbules and C. Torres, 79–108. New York: Routledge, 2000.

National Association for Education of Young Children (NAEYC). *Position Statement: Technology and Young Children.* 1996. Available from www.naeyc.org/resources/ position_statements/ pstech98.htm 1996.

National Childcare Accreditation Council. *Putting Children First: Quality Improvement and Accreditation System Handbook.* 2nd ed. Canberra, Australia: Author, 2001.

Queensland Government. *Queensland the Smart State: Education and Training Reforms for the Future.* Brisbane, Australia: The State of Queensland, Department of the Premier and Cabinet, 2002.

Simpson, N. "The Limits of Computers in Schools: An Actor-Network Analysis." Unpublished Ph.D. thesis, Central Queensland University, 2003.

Yelland, N. "Empowerment and Control with Technology for Young Children." *Educational Theory and Practice* 20, no. 2 (1998): 45–55.

———. "Reconceptualising Schooling with Technology for the 21st. Century: Images and Reflections." In *Information Technology in Childhood Education Annual*, edited by D. Shade, 39–59. Norfolk, Virginia: AACE, 1999.

———. "Shades of Gray: Creating a Vision of Girls and Computers." In *Ghosts in the Machine: Women's Voices in Research with Technology*, edited by N. Yelland and A. Rubin. New York: Peter Lang, 2002.

# Chapter 12

# Are Markets in Education Democratic? Neoliberal Globalism, Vouchers, and the Politics of Choice

Michael W. Apple

## Understanding Conservative Modernization

This is both a good and bad time in the world of educational policy. On the one hand, there have been very few periods when education has taken such a central place in public debates about our present and future. On the other hand, an increasingly limited range of ideological and discursive resources dominates the conceptual and political forms in which these debates are carried out. They are occurring on an uneven playing field, one in which what were formerly seen as rightist policies have now become "commonsense" (Apple, 2000, 2001). Yet such conservative policies have a different kind of cachet today. There is a sense that these are not only things that will protect a romantic past; these policies are now often seen as "radical" but necessary solutions to an educational system that is out of control and is no longer responsive to the needs of "the people."

Thus, a new kind of conservatism has evolved and has taken center stage in many nations, one that is best seen as "conservative moderniza-tion" (Dale, 1989, 1990; Apple, 2001). Although parts of these positions may have originated within the New Right, they are now not limited to what has traditionally been called the Right. They have been taken up by a much larger segment of government and policy makers and have even been appropriated by groups that one would least expect to do so. How are we to understand this development? In answering this question, while my focus here shall largely be on the United States, the tendencies I describe are evident well beyond this one nation.

The concepts we use to try to understand and act on the world in which we live do not by themselves determine the answers we may find. Answers are determined not by words but by the power relations that impose their interpretations of these concepts. Yet there are key words that continually surface in the debates over education. These key words have complicated histories; histories that are connected to the social movements out of which they arose and in which they are struggled over today. These words have their own histories, but they are increasingly interrelated. The concepts are simple to list: markets, standards, accountability, tradition, God, along with a number of others. Behind each of these topics is an assemblage of other words that have an emotional valence and that provide support for the ways in which differential power works in our daily lives. These concepts include democracy, freedom, choice, morality, family, culture, as well as other key concepts. And each of these in turn is intertextual. Each and every one of them is connected to an entire set of assumptions about "appropriate" institutions, values, social relationships, and policies.

Think of this situation as something of a road map. Using one key word—markets—sends you onto a highway that is going in one direction and that has exits in some places but not others. If you are on a highway labeled market, your general direction is toward a section of the country named the economy. You take the exit named individualism that goes by way of another road called consumer choice. Exits with words such as unions, collective freedom, the common good, politics, public control, and similar destinations are to be avoided if they are on the map at all. The first road is a simple route with one goal—deciding where one wants to go without a lot of time-wasting discussion and getting there by the fastest and cheapest method possible. There is a second route, however, and this one involves a good deal of collective deliberation about where we might want to go. It assumes that there may be some continuing deliberation about not only the goal, but also even the route itself. Its exits are the ones that were avoided on the first route.

There are powerful interests that have made the road map and the roads. Some want only the road labeled market because this supposedly leads to individual choice. Others will go down that road, but only if the exits are those that have a long history of "real culture" and "real knowledge." Still others will take the market road because for them God has said that this is "His" road. And finally, another group will sign on to this tour because they have skills in map making and in determining how far we are from our goal. There's some discussion and some compromise—and perhaps even some lingering tension—among these various groups about which exits will ultimately be stopped at, but by and large they all head off in that direction.

In important ways, this exercise in storytelling maps onto reality. The first group is what is appropriately called neoliberals. They are deeply committed to markets and to freedom as "individual choice." The second group, neoconservatives, has a vision of an Edenic and romanticized past and wants a return to discipline and traditional knowledge. The third, one that is increasingly powerful in the United States and elsewhere, is what I call authoritarian populists—religious fundamentalists and conservative evangelicals who want a return to (their) God in all of our institutions. And finally, the mapmakers and experts on whether we got there are members of a particular fraction of the managerial and professional new middle class.

In a number of recent books, I have critically analyzed why and how this situation has occurred. Along with Whitty, Power, and Halpin (1997) as well as Gillborn and Youdell (2000), I have examined a range of proposals for educational "reform" such as marketization, standards, national/statewide curricula, and national/statewide testing. Together we have demonstrated that even with the good intentions of the proponents of many of these kinds of proposals, in the long run they may actually exacerbate inequalities, especially around class and race. Furthermore, they may paradoxically cause us both to misrecognize what actually causes difficult social and educational problems and to miss some important democratic alternatives that may offer more hope in the long run (Apple, et al., 2003; Apple, 1996, 2000, 2001; Apple and Beane, 1995).

It is helpful to think of this current political conjuncture as having been accomplished through the use of a vast socio-pedagogic project, a project that has actively—and in large part successfully—sought to transform our very ideas about democracy. Democracy is no longer a political concept; rather, it is wholly an economic concept in which unattached individuals—supposedly making rational choices in an unfettered market—will ultimately lead to a better society. As Foner (1998) reminds us, it has taken decades of creative ideological work to change our commonsense ideas about democracy. Not only does this change fly in the face of a very long tradition of collective understandings of democracy in the United States, but it has also led to the destruction of many communities, jobs, health care, and so many other institutions not only in the United States but also throughout the world (Greider, 1997; Katz, 2001). Hidden assumptions about class and a considerable element of the politics of whiteness may make it hard for us to face this honestly since it is almost impossible to understand U.S. educational policies unless one also understands the intricate politics of race (Apple, 2001).

What is the picture of reality that conservative modernization has constructed that has necessitated these new maps?

For its varied proponents, our educational institutions are seen as failures. High drop-out rates, a decline in "functional literacy," a loss of standards and discipline, the failure to teach "real knowledge" and economically useful skills, poor scores on standardized tests, and more—all of these are charges leveled at schools. And all of these, we are told, have led to declining economic productivity, unemployment, poverty, a loss of international competitiveness, and so on. Return to a "common culture"; make schools more efficient, more responsive to the private sector. Do this and our problems will be solved.

Behind all of this is an attack on egalitarian norms and values. Though hidden in the rhetorical flourishes of the critics, in essence "too much democracy"—culturally and politically—is seen as one of the major causes of "our" declining economy and culture. Similar tendencies are quite visible in other countries as well. The extent of the reaction is captured in the words of Kenneth Baker, former British secretary of education and science in the Thatcher government, who evaluated nearly a decade of rightist efforts in education by saying, "The age of egalitarianism is over" (Arnot, 1990). He was speaking decidedly positively, not negatively.

The threats to egalitarian ideals that these attacks represent is not usually made quite this explicitly, since they are often couched in the discourse of "improving" competitiveness, jobs, standards, responsiveness, and quality in an educational system that is seen as in total crisis. This discourse is clearly present today in "New Labor" in the United Kingdom and in similar policies in the United States. In all too many ways, both nations' educational policies continue trends established under earlier conservative governments.

It would be simplistic, however, to interpret what is happening as only the result of efforts by dominant economic elites to impose their will on education. Many of these attacks do represent attempts to reintegrate education into an economic agenda. Yet they cannot be fully reduced to that; nor can they be reduced to being only about the economy (see Nixon in this volume). Cultural and institutional struggles and struggles over race and gender coincide with class alliances and class power.

Education is a site of struggle and compromise. It serves as a proxy as well for larger battles over what our institutions should do, whom they should serve, and who should make these decisions. And yet, by itself education is one of the major arenas in which resources, power, and ideology specific to policy, finance, curriculum, pedagogy, and evaluation in education are worked through. Thus, education is both cause and effect, determining and determined. Because of this, no one paper could hope to give a complete picture of this complexity. What I hope to do instead here is to provide an outline of some of the major tensions surrounding education in the United States as it moves in conservative directions, especially in terms of marketization and voucher plans. A key word here is *directions*. The plural is crucial to my arguments, since as I showed there are multiple, and, at times, contradictory tendencies within the rightist turn.

While my focus will largely be internal, it is impossible to understand current educational policy in the United States without placing it in its international context. Thus, behind the stress on higher standards, more rigorous testing, education for employment, and a much closer relationship between education and the economy in general, was the incitation of racialized fears about losing jobs and money in international competition with Japan, the "Asian Tiger" economies, Mexico, and elsewhere; although this was mediated by the economic upheavals and SARS health crisis experienced in Asia (Greider, 1997). In the same way, the equally evident pressure in the United States to reinstall a (selective) vision of a common culture, to place more emphasis on the "Western tradition," on religion, on the English language, and similar emphases are deeply connected to the inciting of racialized fears about Latin America, Africa, and Asia. This context provides a backdrop for my discussion.

The rightward turn has been the result of the successful struggle by the Right to form a broad-based alliance. This new alliance has been so successful in part because it has been able to win the battle over common sense (Apple, 1996, 2000). That is, it has creatively stitched together different social tendencies and commitments and has organized them under its own general leadership in issues dealing with social welfare, culture, the economy, and education. Its aim in educational and social policy is what I earlier called "conservative modernization" (Apple, 2001; Dale,

1989). There are four major elements within this alliance: neoliberals, neoconservatives, authoritarian populists, and a particular fraction of the upwardly mobile professional and managerial new middle class. Each has its own relatively autonomous history and dynamics, but each has also been sutured into the more general conservative movement. I shall pay particular attention to the first of these groups here, since neoliberals are currently in leadership in this alliance to "reform" education and this is the dominant group behind the pressure to institute voucher and similar "choice" plans. However, in no way do I want to dismiss the power of these latter three groups, and I have discussed them in much greater depth elsewhere (Apple et al., 2003; Apple 2001).

## Neoliberal Globalism

As I mentioned above, neoliberals are the most powerful element within the alliance supporting conservative modernization. They are guided by a vision of the weak state. Thus, what is private is necessarily good and what is public is necessarily bad. Public (that is, state-funded) institutions such as schools are "black holes" into which money is poured—and then seemingly disappears—but which do not provide anywhere near adequate results. For neoliberals, there is one form of rationality that is more powerful than any other—economic rationality. Efficiency and an "ethic" of cost-benefit analysis are the dominant norms. All people are to act in ways that maximize their own personal benefits. Indeed, behind this position is an empirical claim that this is how *all* rational actors act. Yet rather than being a neutral description of the world of social motivation, this is actually a construction of the world around the valuative characteristics of an efficiently acquisitive class type (Apple, 1996; Honderich, 1990).

Underpinning this position is a vision of students as human capital. The world is intensely competitive economically, and students—as future workers—must be given the requisite skills and dispositions to compete efficiently and effectively. Given the current emphasis on this vision by neoliberals, it may be the case that while Bowles and Gintis's (1976) book, *Schooling in Capitalist America,* which explored the relationship between education and capitalism and was reductive, economistic, and essentializing when it first appeared, oddly it may be more accurate today (for criticisms of their position, see Apple, 1988, 1995; Cole, 1988). Further, any money spent on schools that is not directly related to these economic goals is suspect. In fact, as "black holes," schools and other public services as they are currently organized and controlled supposedly constitute a "waste" of public economic resources that should go into subsidizing the welfare of private enterprise.

The idea of the paying "consumer" is crucial here. For neoliberals, the world in essence is a vast supermarket. "Consumer choice" is the guarantor of (market) democracy. In effect, education is seen as simply one more product like bread, cars, and television (Apple, 1990). By turning it over to the market through voucher and choice plans, it will be largely self-regulating. Thus, democracy is turned into consumption practices. In these plans, the ideal of the citizen is that of the purchaser. Yet the ideological effects of this are momentous. Rather than democracy being a *political* concept, it is transformed into a wholly *economic* concept. The message of such policies is what might best be called "arithmetical particularism," in which the unattached individual—as a consumer—is de-raced, de-classed, and degendered (Apple, 1996; Ball, 1994).

The entire project of neoliberalism is connected to a larger process of exporting the blame for the decisions of dominant groups onto the state and onto poor people. After all, it is claimed that the government did not make the decisions to engage in capital flight and to move factories to those nations that have weak or no unions, fewer environmental regulations, and repressive governments. And it was not working-class and poor communities that chose to lose those jobs and factories, with the loss of hope and with schools and communities in crisis that were among the results of these decisions. And it was neither of them who chose to lay off millions of workers—many of whom had done rather well in school—due to mergers and leveraged buyouts.

With their emphasis on the (paying) consumer rather than the (knowledge) producer, neoliberal policies need also to be seen as part of a more extensive attack on government employees. In education in particular, these politics constitute an offensive against teacher unions, who are seen to be much too powerful and much too costly. While perhaps not conscious, this offensive needs to be interpreted as part of a longer history of attacks on women's labor, since the vast majority of teachers in so many other nations are women (Acker, 1995; Apple, 1988: 31–78). A number of the larger gender implications of neoliberal globalism in education and the economy can be seen in Brine (1992) and Arnot, David, and Weiner (1999).

There are varied policy initiatives that have emerged from the neoliberal segments of the new hegemonic alliance. Most changes have centered on either creating closer linkages between education and the economy or placing schools themselves into the market. The former is represented by widespread proposals for "school to work," "education for employment," and "work-related education" programs (see Morris, this volume), and by vigorous cost-cutting attacks in areas where the state has been responsible for underwriting its citizens' social and economic security: health, education, employment, childcare, and aged-care. The latter has spread worldwide and is becoming increasingly powerful. It is represented by both national and state-by-state proposals for voucher and choice programs (Chubb and Moe, 1990; House, 1998). These include providing public money for private and religious schools (although these are highly contested proposals). Behind this is a plan to subject schools to the discipline of market competition. Such "quasi-market solutions" are among the most divisive and hotly debated policy issues in many nations (Carnoy and Rothstein, in press; Fuller, Burr, Huerta, Puryear, and Wexler, 1999; Henig, 1994; Smith and Meier, 1995; Wells, 1993), with important court cases concerning funding for private and/or religious schools through voucher mechanisms having been decided or now being closely watched, something I shall discuss below.

Some proponents of "choice" argue that only enhanced parental "voice" and choice will provide a chance for "educational salvation" for minority parents and children (Chubb and Moe, 1990; Whitty, 1997). For instance, Moe (cited in Whitty, 1997: 17) claims that the best hope for the poor to gain the right "to leave bad schools and seek out good ones" is through an "unorthodox alliance." Only by allying themselves with Republicans and business—the most powerful groups supposedly willing to transform the system—can the poor succeed. As I have shown in great detail in *Educating the "Right" Way* (Apple, 2001), there is growing empirical evidence internationally that the development of "quasi-markets" in education has often led to the exacerbation of existing social divisions surrounding class and race (see also Lauder and Hughes, 1999; Whitty, Power, and Halpin, 1997).

In order to understand the larger movement out of which voucher and choice plans have arisen, it is important to recognize that there is a second variant of neoliberalism. This one *is* willing to spend more state and/or private money on schools, if and only if schools meet the needs expressed by various dominant fractions of capital. Thus, resources are made available for "reforms" and policies that further connect the education system to the project of making our economy more competitive (see Nixon, this volume). The attractiveness of conservative policies in education rests in large part on major shifts in our common sense—about what democracy is, about whether we see ourselves as possessive individuals ("paying consumers"), and ultimately about how we see the market working. Underlying neoliberal policies in education and their social policies in general is an unquestioning faith in the essential fairness and justice of markets. Supposedly, markets will ultimately, some day, distribute resources efficiently and fairly according to effort. It is claimed that ultimately they will create jobs for all who want them. The ideological and political promise is that the marketization of education supposedly offers the best possible mechanism to ensure a better future for all citizens (paying consumers).

Neoliberals argue that making the market the ultimate arbiter of social worthiness will eliminate politics and its accompanying irrationality from our educational and social decisions. Cost-efficiency and cost-benefit analysis will be the engines of social and educational transformation, the drivers of never-ending change. Yet among the ultimate effects of such "economizing" and "depoliticizing" strategies is actually to make it ever harder to interrupt the growing inequalities in resources and power that so deeply characterize many societies. Nancy Fraser (1989: 168) illuminates the process in the following way:

> In male dominated capitalist societies, what is "political" is normally defined contrastively against what is "economic" and what is "domestic" or "personal." Here, then, we can identify two principal sets of institutions that depoliticize social discourses: they are, first, domestic institutions, especially the normative domestic form, namely the modern restricted male-headed nuclear family; and, second, official economic capitalist system institutions, especially paid workplaces, markets, credit mechanisms, and "private" enterprises and corporations. Domestic institutions depoliticize certain matters by personalizing and/or familializing them; they cast these as private-domestic or personal-familial matters in contradistinction to public, political matters. Official economic capitalist system institutions, on the other hand, depoliticize certain matters by economizing them; the issues in question here are cast as impersonal market imperatives, or as "private" ownership prerogatives, or as technical problems for managers and planners, all in contradistinction to political matters. In both cases, the result is a foreshortening of chains of interpretation in-order-to relations for interpreting people's needs; interpretive chains are truncated and prevented from spilling across the boundaries separating the "domestic" and the "economic" from the political.

These very processes of depoliticization make it very difficult for the needs of those with less economic, political, and cultural power to be accurately heard and acted upon in ways that deal with the true depth of the problem (see Franzway, this volume). This is because of what happens when "needs discourses" get retranslated into both market talk and "privately" driven policies.

For our purposes here, we can talk about two major kinds of needs discourses. There are first *oppositional* forms of needs talk. They arise when needs are politicized *from below* and they are part of the crystallization of new oppositional identities on the part of subordinated social groups. What was once seen as largely a "private" matter is now placed into the larger political arena. Sexual harassment, race and sex segregation in paid labor, and affirmative action policies in educational and economic institutions provide examples of "private" issues that have now spilled over and can no longer be confined to the "domestic" sphere (Fraser, 1989: 172; see also Apple, 1988; Bowles and Gintis, 1986; Opdycke, 1999).

A second kind of neoliberal political discourse is what might be called the *reprivatization* of needs discourses. They emerge as a response to the newly emergent oppositional forms and try to press these forms back into the private or the domestic arena. They are often aimed at dismantling or cutting back social services, deregulating private enterprise, or stopping what are fabricated as "runaway needs." Thus, reprivatizers may attempt to keep issues such as, say, domestic violence from spilling over into overt political discourse and will seek to define it as purely a family matter. Or they will argue that the closing of a factory or the shifting of public funds from working-class schools and universities to those of the elite are not political questions but instead they are falsely misrepresented as an unassailable imperative of an impersonal market mechanism or an unimpeachable prerogative of private ownership (Fraser, 1989: 172). In each of these cases, the task for neoliberals is to contest both the possible breakout of runaway needs and to depoliticize the issues.

A distinction that is useful in understanding what is happening in current instances of change (and continuity) in public education is that between "value" and "sense" legitimation (Dale, 1989). Each signifies a different strategy by which privileged groups or nation-states legitimate their power and authority. In the first (value) strategy, legitimation is accomplished by actually giving people what may have been promised. Thus, the social democratic state may provide social services for the population in return for continued support. That the state will do this is often the result of oppositional discourses gaining more power in the social arena with more power to redefine the border between public and private.

In the second (sense) strategy, rather than providing people with policies that meet the needs they have expressed, states and/or dominant groups attempt to *change the very meaning* of the sense of social need into something that is very different. Thus, if less powerful people call for "more democracy" and for a more responsive state, the task is not to give "value" that meets this demand, especially when it may lead to runaway needs. Rather, the task is to change what actually *counts* as democracy. In the case of neoliberal policies, democracy is now redefined as guaranteeing choice in an unfettered market. In essence, the state withdraws. The extent of acceptance of such transformations of needs and needs discourses shows the success of the reprivatizers in redefining the borders between public and private again and demonstrates how a people's common sense can be shifted in conservative directions during a time of economic and ideological crisis. The discourse of vouchers and its increasing acceptance and use offers a prime example of the effectiveness of strategies based on sense legitimation.

## The Politics of Choice

In the previous sections of this chapter, I critically analyzed many of the political and conceptual assumptions that stand behind the growth of marketized models of educational policy. I need now to give an overview of what is happening "on the ground" in terms of the legal status of vouchers and similar proposals and where they stand in neoliberal processes of restructuring (and destructuring) public schools.

The empirical situation surrounding voucher plans is unsettled. There have been contradictory court decisions. In the United States, the Supreme Court of the state of Wisconsin has ruled that voucher plans—*limited to low-income residents of Milwaukee*—are constitutional. The Supreme Court of the United States ruled that Cleveland's voucher plan (also rather limited in terms of which people may use it) is also constitutional. However, a federal court in the United States has ruled that Florida's voucher plan is unconstitutional, since it allows for public funding to be used to support religious schools and does not have sufficient accountability on the use of public funds by private and religious schools. There will be other court cases, given the disputed nature of the issues surrounding vouchers. However, while no one can be certain, since many of the federal courts in the United States as elsewhere are currently dominated by very conservative judges, it is likely that some form of voucher plan will ultimately spread throughout the nation and internationally. Most of the empirical research on voucher plans has been limited to the issue of whether such choice plans increase the measured achievement of students who have transferred from public schools to schools supported by vouchers and/or whether there is greater parental satisfaction with voucher schools compared to public schools. The evidence on achievement scores is hotly debated, but by and large it is inconclusive. While there does seem to be somewhat more parental satisfaction with voucher schools, here too the evidence is not robust enough to generalize to every situation and locality (Witte, 2000).

Recent polls have shown interesting responses to the question of public acceptance of vouchers. One of the largest polls found that a majority of respondents were in favor of increased school choice, including voucher plans. However, when the same group was asked if they would support voucher plans if it meant that *less money* went to public schools, the support dropped precipitously, with nearly two-thirds now opposed to voucher plans.

It is crucial to recognize that voucher plans are not the only choice program on the largely conservative and neoliberal agenda. In the United States, a group that is again largely made up of conservative Republicans has proposed a controversial set of policies. A primary component of these policies would be a system of tax credits, in which parents could deduct the costs of private and/or religious schooling for their children from their taxes. This, of course, privileges middle-class and affluent groups much more than those who are poor, since one must *have* sufficient money to pay for the fees of such schools in order to get the tax deduction. In the long run, passage of tax credit legislation may do more (to realize the goal) to damage the already difficult financial status of public schools than vouchers.

Voucher and tax credit plans do not stand alone. Charter schools have been growing as well. For a number of people on both the left and the right, charter schools have been seen as a compromise that can satisfy some of the demands of each group. Here, though, I would urge even more caution. Much of the discussion of these schools has been more than a little romantic. It has accepted the rhetoric of "de-bureaucratization," experimentation, and diversity as the reality. Yet as Wells, Lopez, Scoot, and Holme (1999) have demonstrated, charter schools can and do often serve less meritorious ends. They can be manipulated to provide public funding for ideologically and educationally problematic programs, with little public accountability. Beneath the statistics of the racial equality they supposedly produce, they too can exacerbate white flight and be captured by groups who actually have little interest in the culture and futures of those who they assume are the "Other." They are used as the "constitutive outside" in attacks on public schooling for the majority of children, by deflecting attention away from what must be done there. Thus, they often can and do act to deflect attention from our lack of commitment to provide sufficient resources and support for public schools in urban and rural areas. And in a number of ways they threaten to become an opening wedge for voucher plans (Wells, Lopez, Scoot, and Holme, 1999). Recent research on the ways charter schools and "reforms" surrounding school finance have functioned in Arizona, for instance, should make us extremely wary of the connections between rhetoric and reality (Moses, 2000; Wilson, 2000).

Having said this, however, I do not believe that charter schools will go away. Indeed, during the many periods of time when I have lectured and engaged in educational and political work in countries in, say, Latin America and Asia, it has become ever more clear to me that there is considerable interest in the charter school movement. This is especially the case in those nations that have a history of strong states and strong central control over the curriculum, teaching, and evaluation and where the state has been inflexible, highly bureaucratic, and unresponsive. Given this situation, it is absolutely crucial that the terrain of charter schools not be occupied by the forces within the conservative alliance. If charter schools become, as they threaten to, primarily a site where their function is to deflect attention from the needs of public schools where the vast majority of students go, if they are allowed to be used as vouchers incognito, if they serve to legitimate concerted attacks on public school teachers and other educators, then the effects will not be limited to the United States. This will be a worldwide tragedy.

For these very reasons, it is crucial that some of our empirical, educational, and political energy goes into guaranteeing that charter schools are a much more progressively inclined set of possibilities than they are today. We need to work so that the elements of good sense in the movement are not lost by it being integrated under the umbrella of conservative modernization. While Schorr (2000) advances some interesting arguments that deserve to be taken seriously and should not be rejected out of hand, I am still not convinced that this support for the progressive possibilities of charter schools can overcome the conservative context in which charter schools are actually situated.

## Vouchers and Race

Many of the strongest proponents of vouchers and similar plans may claim that their positions are based on a belief in the efficiency of markets, on the fear of a secularization of the sacred, or on the dangers of losing the values and beliefs that give meaning to their lives. However, historically, neither the economic nor the moral elements of this critique can be totally set apart from their partial genesis in the struggles over racial segregation, in the struggles over busing to achieve integration, and in the loss of a federal tax exemption by conservative—and usually white only—religious academies. In short, inciting fears about the "racial other" plays a significant role in this discursive construction of the "problem of the public school" (Apple, 2001).

Having said this, however, there is also increasing support for voucher and similar choice plans among minority groups. While "progressive" traditions are not free of racializing and racist logics (Selden, 1999), so much of the conservative tradition was explicitly shaped by racist and racializing discourses and practices as well as by a strongly anti-immigrant heritage and so many of the current neoliberal and neoconservative attacks on the public sphere have had disproportionate effects on the gains of poor communities and on communities of color that the existence and growth of support among some members of dispossessed groups is more than a little striking. That, say, a number of African American groups, ones that are making alliances with distinctly conservative movements, exist and are growing says something very important about the fascination with identity politics among many progressive scholars and activists in education and elsewhere. Too often writing on identity (wrongly) assumes that identity politics is a "good thing," that people inexorably move in progressive directions as they pursue what Nancy Fraser (1997) would call the politics of recognition. Yet any serious study of rightist movements demonstrates that identity politics is just as apt to take, say, angry and retrogressive forms—anti-gay, racist nativism, anti-women. For many such people, "we" are the new oppressed, with that "we" not including most people of color, feminists, "sexual deviants," immigrants, and so on. Yet as I noted earlier, even people within these "despised" groups themselves may take on such retrogressive identities.

A complex process of discursive and positional disarticulation and rearticulation is going on here, as dominant groups attempt to pull dispossessed collectivities under their own leadership and dispossessed groups themselves attempt to employ the social, economic, and cultural capital usually possessed by dominant groups to gain collective power for themselves. As we shall see, the label "conservative" cannot be employed easily in understanding the actions of all of the dispossessed groups who do ally themselves with conservative causes, without at the same time reducing the complexity of the particular social fields of power on which they operate.

Perhaps the most interesting example of the processes of discursive and social disarticulation and rearticulation that one could find today involves the growing African American (at least among some elements of the African American community) support for neoliberal policies such as voucher plans (Moe, 2001). A key instance is the Black Alliance for Educational Options (BAEO), a group of African American parents and activists that is chaired by Howard Fuller, the former superintendent of Milwaukee public schools, one of the most racially segregated school systems in the United States. BAEO provides vocal support for voucher plans and similar neoliberal proposals. It has generated considerable support within black communities throughout the nation, particularly within poor inner-city areas. A sense of the language that underpins the commitment of the Black Alliance for Educational Options can be seen in the following quote:

> Our children are our most precious resource. It is our responsibility to love them, nurture them and protect them. It is also our responsibility to ensure that they are properly educated. Without a good education, they will [not] have a real chance to engage in the practice of freedom: the process of engaging in the fight to transform their world. (BAEO website: http://www.baeo.org/home/index.php)

BAEO's mission is clear:

> The Black Alliance for Educational Options is a national, nonpartisan member organization whose mission is to actively support parental choice to empower families and increase educational options for Black children. (BAEO websit. http://www. baeo.org/home/index.php)

The tactical use of language here is striking. The language of neoliberalism (choice, parental empowerment, accountability, individual freedom) is reappropriated and sutured together with ideas of collective black freedom and a deep concern for the community's children. This creates something of a "hybrid" discourse that blends together meanings from multiple political sources and agendas. In some ways, it is similar to the long history of critical cultural analyses that demonstrate that people form bricolages in their daily lives and can employ language and commodities in ways undreamed of by the original producers of the language and products (Willis, 1990).

While this process of rearticulation and use is important to note, it is equally essential to recognize something that makes the creative bricolage in which BAEO is engaged somewhat more problematic. A very large portion of the group's funding comes directly from conservative sources such as the Bradley Foundation. The Bradley Foundation, a well-known sponsor of conservative causes, has not only been in the forefront of providing support for vouchers and privatization initiatives, but also is one of the groups that provided significant support for Herrnstein and Murray's book *The Bell Curve* (1994), a volume that argued that African Americans were on average less intelligent than whites and that this was genetic in nature.

Thus, it would be important to ask about the nature and effects of the connections being made between rightist ideological and financial sources and BAEO itself. It is not inconsequential that neoliberal and neo conservative foundations provide not only funding but media visibility for "minority" groups who support—even critically—their agendas. The genesis of such funding is not inconsequential. Are groups such as BAEO simply being manipulated by neoliberal and neoconservative foundations and movements? An answer to this question is not easy, but even with my cautions stated above it is certainly not a simple "yes."

In public forums and in discussions that Tom Pedroni and I have had with some of the leaders of BAEO, they have argued that they will use any funding sources available so that they can follow their own specific program of action. They would accept money from more liberal sources; but Bradley and other conservative foundations have come forward much more readily. In this regard, Tom Pedroni's (in progress) ongoing research on BAEO is of considerable importance. In the minds of the leaders of BAEO, the African American activists are in control, not the conservative foundations. Thus, BAEO sees itself as strategically positioning itself in order to get funding from conservative sources. What it does with this funding, such as its strong (and well-advertised in the media) support for voucher plans (although this support too is contingent and sometimes depends on local power relations), is wholly its decision. For BAEO, the space provided by educational markets can be re-occupied for black cultural and/or nationalist politics and can be employed to stop what seems to them (more than a little accurately in my judgment) to be a *war on black children.*

However, while I have a good deal of respect for a number of the leaders of BAEO, it is important to remember that they are not the only ones strategically organizing on this social field of power. Groups affiliated with, say, the Bradley Foundation know *exactly* what they are doing and know very well how to employ the agendas of BAEO for their own purposes, purposes that in the long term often may run directly counter to the interests of the majority of those with less power at both the national and regional levels. Is it really in the long-term interests of people of color to be affiliated with the same groups who provided funding and support for books such as *The Bell Curve*? I think not, although once again we need to recognize the complexities involved here.

I am certain that this kind of question is constantly raised about the conservative stances taken by the people of color who have made alliances with, say, neoliberals and neoconservatives—and by the activists within BAEO itself. When members of groups who are consistently "othered" in society strategically take on identities that support dominant groups, such questioning is natural and I believe essential. However, it is also crucial to remember that members of historically oppressed and marginalized groups have always had to act on a terrain that is not of their choosing, have always had to act strategically and creatively to gain some measure of support from dominant groups to advance their causes (Lewis, 1993, 2000). It is also the case that, more recently, national and local leaders of the Democratic Party in the United States have too often assumed that black support is simply *there,* that it doesn't need to be worked for. Because of this, we may see the further development of "unusual alliances" over specific issues such as educational policies. When this is coupled with some of the tacit and/or overt support within some communities of color not only for voucher plans but for anti-gay, anti-abortion, pro-school prayer, and similar initiatives, the suturing together of some black groups with larger conservative movements on particular issues is not totally surprising (Dillard, 2001).

The existence and growing power of committed movements such as BAEO, though, does point out that we need to be careful about stereotyping groups who may publicly support neoliberal and neoconservative policies. Their perspectives need to be examined carefully and taken seriously, not simply dismissed as totally misguided, as people who have been duped into unthinking acceptance of a harmful set of ideologies.

There are complicated strategic moves being made on an equally complex social field of power. I may, and do, strongly disagree with a number of the positions that groups such as BAEO take. However, to assume that they are simply puppets of conservative forces is not only to be too dismissive of their own attempts at social maneuvering, I believe that it may be tacitly racist as well.

Saying this does not mean that we need to weaken our arguments against marketization and privatization of schooling. Voucher and tax credit plans (as I noted, the latter ultimately may actually be more dangerous) will still have some extremely problematic effects in the long term. One of the most important effects could be a *demobilization* of social (justice) movements within communities of color. Schools have played central roles in the creation of movements for justice. In essence, rather than being peripheral reflections of larger battles and dynamics, struggles over schooling—over what should be taught, over the relationship between schools and local communities, over the very ends and means of the institution itself—have provided a crucible for the *formation* of larger social movements toward equality (Hogan, 1982; Wong and Apple, in press). These collective movements have transformed our definitions of rights, of who should have them, and of the role of the government in guaranteeing these rights. Without organized, communitywide mobilizations, these transformations would not have occurred.

This is under threat currently. I argued earlier that definitions of democracy based on possessive individualism, on the citizen as only a "consumer," are inherently grounded in a process of de-racing, de-classing, and degendering (Ball, 1994). These are the very groups who have employed struggles over educational access and outcomes to form themselves as self-conscious education and community policy actors. If it is the case, as I strongly believe, that it is the organized efforts of social movements that ultimately have led to the transformation of our educational system in more democratic directions (Apple et al., 2003; Apple, 2000), the long-term effects of neoliberal definitions of democracy may be truly tragic for communities of color (and working-class groups), not only in increasing inequalities in schools (Apple, 2001; Gillborn and Youdell, 2000; McNeil, 2000), but in leading to a very real loss of the impetus for *collective* solutions to pressing social problems. If all problems are simply "solved" by individual choices in a market, then collective mobilizations tend to wither and perhaps even disappear.

## Conclusion

In this chapter, I have raised a number of critical questions about the economic, social, and ideological tendencies that often stand behind significant parts of the neoliberal agenda in educational policy. In the process, I have situated it within larger social movements that I and many others believe can have quite negative effects on our sense of community, on the health of the public sphere, and on our commitment to building societies that are less economically and racially stratified. I have suggested that issues need to be raised about the effects of its commitment to marketized "choice" programs, its attack on the state, and its partial acceptance by some segments of oppressed communities.

Yet I also want to indicate that we should not ignore the fact that there are clear elements of *good sense* in its criticisms of the bureaucratic nature of all too many of our institutions, in its worries about the managerial state, and in its devotion to being active in the education of our children.

In my mind, the task is to disentangle the elements of good sense evident in these concerns from the selfish and anti-public agenda that has been pushing concerned parents and community members into the arms of the conservative restoration. The task of public schools is to listen much more carefully to the complaints of parents and activists and to rebuild our institutions in much more responsive ways. As I have demonstrated in *Cultural Politics and Education* (Apple, 1996), all too often public schools push concerned parents who are not originally part of neoliberal and neoconservative cultural and political movements into the arms of such alliances by their defensiveness and lack of responsiveness and by their silencing of democratic discussion and criticism. Of course, sometimes these criticisms are unjustified or are politically motivated by undemocratic agendas. However, this must not serve as an excuse for a failure to open the doors of our schools to the intense public debate that makes public education a living and vital part of our democracy (Apple, 1996, 1999).

We have models for doing exactly that (Apple and Beane, 1995). There *are* models of curricula and teaching that are related to community sentiment, that are committed to social justice and fairness, and that are based in schools where both teachers and students want to be (Apple et al., 2003). If public schools do not do this, there may be all too many parents who are pushed in the direction of anti–public–school sentiment. This would be a tragedy both for the public school system and for our already withered sense of community that is increasingly under threat. Even though state-supported schools have often served as arenas through which powerful social divisions are partly reproduced, such schools have also served as powerful sites for the mobilization of collective action and for the preservation of the very possibility of democratic struggle (Apple et al., 2003; Hogan, 1982; Reese, 1986). Struggles over the school, as one of the few remaining institutions that *is* still public, are crucial. This is obviously a tightrope we need to negotiate. How do we uphold the vision of a truly public institution at the same time as we rigorously criticize its functioning (see further Reid, this volume)?

In the United States of America this is one of the tasks that the critical educators involved in *Democratic Schools* and the National Coalition of Education Activists have set for themselves. One of the best places to turn for an understanding of the more progressive movements surrounding education and social justice in public schools in the United States is the fast-growing newspaper *Rethinking Schools* (1001 E. Keefe Avenue, Milwaukee, WI 53212, USA or at *www.rethinkingschools.org).* Along with the British journal *Education and Social Justice,* it represents one of the most articulate outlets for critical discussions of educational policy and practice in the country and brings together multiple activist voices: teachers, community activists, parents, academics, students, and others. They have recognized that schools have both contradictory impulses and pressures on them, especially in a time of conservative modernization. It is not romantic to actively work on and through those contradictions so that the collective memory of earlier and partly successful struggles is not lost. Nor is it romantic to engage in what I have called elsewhere "non-reformist reforms," reforms whose aim is to expand the space of counter-hegemonic action in public institutions (Apple, 1995). Yet in order to do this, it is necessary to defend the *public* nature of public spaces such as public schools.

Raymond Williams may have expressed it best when—positioning himself as an optimist without any illusions—he reminded us of the importance of the *mutual* determination of the meanings and values that should guide our social life. In expressing his commitment toward "the long revolution," his words are worth remembering: "We must speak for hope, as long as it doesn't mean suppressing the nature of the danger" (Williams, 1989: 322). There are identifiable dangers to identifiable groups of people in public schooling as we know it. But the privatizing alternatives may be much worse. This tension between realism and hope is inescapable, but that is a tension that we must live with in a time when the very idea of public and democratic schooling is under threat.

# References

Acker, S. "Gender and Teachers Work." In *Review of Research in Education, Vol. 21*. Edited by M. Apple. Washington, DC: American Educational Research Association, 1995.

Apple, M. W. *Teachers and Texts*. New York: Routledge, 1988.

———. *Ideology and Curriculum*. 2nd ed. New York: Routledge, 1990.

———. *Education and Power*. New York: Routledge, 1995.

———. *Cultural Politics and Education*. New York: Teachers College Press, 1996.

———. *Official Knowledge*. 2nd ed. New York: Routledge, 2000.

———. *Educating the "Right" Way: Markets, Standards, God and Inequality*. New York: Routledge Falmer, 2001.

Apple, M., P. Aasen, M. Cho, L. Gandin, A. Oliver, Y. Sung, H. Tavares, and T.-H. Wong. *The State and the Politics of Knowledge*. New York: Routledge, 2003.

Apple, M., and J. Beane, eds. *Democratic Schools*. Alexandria, VA: Association for Supervision and Curriculum Development, 1995.

Arnot, M. "Schooling for Social Justice." Unpublished paper, Department of Education, University of Cambridge, 1990.

Arnot, M., M. David, and G. Weiner. *Closing the Gender Gap*. Cambridge, UK: Polity Press, 1999.

Ball, S. *Education Reform: A Critical and Post-Structural Approach*. Buckingham, UK: Open University Press, 1994.

Bowles, S., and H. Gintis. *Schooling in Capitalist America*. New York: Basic Books, 1976.

———. *Democracy and Capitalism*. New York: Basic Books, 1986.

Brine, J. *Under-Educating Women, Globalizing Inequality*. Philadelphia: Open University Press, 1992.

Carnoy, M., and R. Rothstein. *All Else Equal*. New York: Routledge, in press.

Chubb, J., and T. Moe. *Politics, Markets, and American Schools*. Washington, DC: Brookings Institution, 1990.

Cole, M., ed. *Bowles and Gintis Revisited*. New York: Falmer Press, 1988.

Dale, R. *The State and Education Policy*. Philadelphia: Open University Press, 1989.

———. "The Thatcherite Project in Education." *Critical Social Policy* 9, no. 1 (1989, 1990): 4–19.

Dillard, A. *Guess Who's Coming to Dinner: Multicultural Conservatism in America*. New York: New York University Press, 2001.

Foner, E. *The Story of American Freedom*. New York: Norton, 1998.

Fraser, N. *Unruly Practices*. Minneapolis: University of Minnesota Press, 1989.

———. *Justice Interruptus*. New York: Routledge, 1997.

Fuller, B., E. Burr, L. Huerta, S. Puryear, and E. Wexler. *School Choice: Abundant Hopes, Scarce Evidence*. Berkeley and Stanford: Policy Analysis for California Education: University of California at Berkeley and Stanford University, 1999.

Gillborn, D., and D. Youdell. *Rationing Education*. Philadelphia: Open University Press, 2000.

Greider, W. *One World, Ready or Not*. New York: Simon and Schuster, 1997.

Henig, J. *Rethinking School Choice*. Princeton, NJ: Princeton University Press, 1994.

Herrnstein, R., and C. Murray. *The Bell Curve*. New York: Free Press, 1994.

Hogan, D. "Education and Class Formation." In *Cultural and Economic Reproduction in Education*, edited by M. Apple. Boston: Routledge and Kegan Paul, 1982.

Honderich, T. *Conservatism*. Boulder, CO: Westview, 1990.

House, E. *School for Sale*. New York: Teachers College Press, 1998.

Katz, M. *The Price of Citizenship*. New York: Metropolitan Books, 2001.

Lauder, H., and D. Hughes. *Trading in Futures*. Philadelphia: Open University Press, 1999.

Lewis, D. *W. E. B. Dubois: Biography of a Race, 1868–1919*. New York: Henry Holt, 1993.

———. *W. E. B. Dubois: The Fight for Equality and the American Century, 1919–1963*. New York: Henry Holt, 2000.

McNeil, L. *Contradictions of School Reform*. New York: Routledge, 2000.

Moe, T. *Schools, Vouchers, and the American Public*. Washington, DC: Brookings Institution, 2001.

Moses, M. "The Arizona Tax Credit, Hidden Considerations of Justice." Paper presented at the American Educational Research Association Annual Meeting, New Orleans, LA, 2000.

Opdycke, S. *No One Was Turned Away*. New York: Oxford University Press, 1999.

Pedroni, T. "Strange Bedfellows: African American Participation in the Milwaukee School Choice Coalition." Unpublished PhD thesis, University of Wisconsin, Madison, in progress.

Reese, W. *Power and the Promise of School Reform*. Boston: Routledge and Kegan Paul, 1986.

Schorr, J. "Giving Charter Schools a Chance." *The Nation*, June 5, 2000, 19–23.

Selden, S. *Inheriting Shame*. New York: Teachers College Press, 1999.

Smith, K., and K. Meier, eds. *The Case against School Choice*. Armonk, NY: M. E. Sharpe, 1995.

Wells, A. *Time to Choose*. New York: Hill and Wang, 1993.

Wells, A., A. Lopez, J. Scoot, and J. Holme. "Charter Schools as Postmodern Paradox." *Harvard Educational Review* 69 (1999): 172–204.

Whitty, G., S. Power, and D. Halpin. *Devolution and Choice in Education: The School, the State and the Market*. Buckingham, UK: Open University Press, 1997.

Williams, R. *Resources for Hope*. New York: Verso, 1989.

Willis, P. *Common Culture*. Boulder, CO: Westview Press., 1990.

Wilson, G. "Effects on Funding Equity of Arizona Tax Law." Paper presented at the American Educational Research Association Annual Meeting, New Orleans, LA, 2000.

Witte, J. *The Market Approach to Education*. Princeton, NJ: Princeton University Press, 2000.

Wong, T., and M. Apple. "Rethinking the Education/State Formation Connection." *Comparative Education Review,* in press.

# Chapter 13

## The Marketization of Education within the Global Capitalist Economy

Helen Raduntz

### Introduction

In this chapter I propose to address the issue of education's marketization within the global capitalist economy under three interrelated questions. The first, what has driven the restructuring of education systems in conformity with capitalist market requirements? The second, what is it about the marketization process and its penetration into the domain of education that fills concerned educators with apprehension? Third, what are the likely implications of this departure from the promise of affordable, accessible, quality education for everyone who wants it, within a communal and collaborative setting dedicated to the free exchange of ideas, to understanding the world, and to transmitting and thinking critically about the received wisdom of participants' cultures (Noble, 2002a: xii)?

These questions highlight the importance of marketization in shaping contemporary education systems, which demands critical investigation as a basis for informed democratic action.

While critical education theorists, such as Ball (1994); Gewirtz, Ball, and Bowe (1995); Kenway, Bigum, Fitzclarence, and Collier (1993); Lauder and Hughes (1999); Marginson (1997); and Smyth, Dow, Hattam, Shacklock, and Reid (1999), have made valuable contributions to understanding the phenomenon of education's marketization, their analyses tend to be descriptive of effects without investigating at an economic level the nature of the marketization process itself. The omission is due in part to an assumption that market exchange is a normative and therefore neutral and benign aspect of any socioeconomic activity, even under capitalism. What many critical educators fail to recognize is that under the impact of capitalism's social conditions, market exchange acquired a pivotal role, which it has not historically enjoyed, in shaping contemporary society and its institutions. As a result, their theories present only a partial picture of the phenomenon.

In order to redress the imbalance so that a more comprehensive account can be formulated, I propose to adopt a Marxian dialectical critique that, first, sets out the socioeconomic conditions shaping education's marketization; second, examines the dynamics of marketization as the driving force underlying not only the global expansion of the capitalist economy but also the reforms of contemporary education; and third, discusses the implications of marketization for the future of quality education provisions. Education here, following Noble (2002a: 2), is characterized by an interpersonal and reciprocal relationship between educators and those who are being educated, and the chief determining factor of its quality is taken to be the establishment and enrichment of that relationship.

The critique rests on Marx's foundational analysis of the capitalist mode of production, informed by the work of Harvey (1982), who has sought within the parameters of historical materialism not only to interpret Marx's analysis but also to extend it. Marx intended to demonstrate that capitalism is not an economically self-perpetuating system, but one that is a result of human productive activity. Hence, capitalism is a historical phenomenon with a necessarily limited "shelf life," possible to transform through democratically informed and strategically targeted action.

On this basis I attempt to show that globalization and the marketization of education are both interrelated contemporary outcomes of capitalism's expansionary tendencies, driven by the need to maintain economic growth based on the accumulation and expansion of private capital wealth. The tendency constantly to expand arises as a means of overcoming the contradiction posed by economic growth because it creates economic instability, which jeopardizes the social stability necessary if economic growth is to be maintained. However, the contradiction is never resolved but is carried over and internalized in the targets of expansion such as education. Thus, through marketization education inherits the contradiction that is expressed in the conflicting demands set up by the introduction of a market-friendly instrumental model into the provision of quality education.

At the risk of oversimplification, the analysis is conducted at a high level of generality in order that the essential dynamics of the subject matter may be grasped more easily without the confusion of detail. This is not to forget, however, that a comprehensive account requires not only the presentation of the "big picture" but also how these dynamics are played out in national and local contexts.

## A Critique of Current Understandings of Globalization

The term "globalization" has come to express the phenomenon of the capitalist market economy's expansion worldwide and its penetration into almost all aspects of social life. The momentum and the changes as a result have caused advocates of neoliberal globalism to interpret globalization in terms of a fundamentally new age in human progress. This is an understandable reaction if observable features of globalization are taken as the basis of qualitative change. It cannot be denied, of course, that there has occurred an exponential growth in almost all sectors of the capitalist market economy, which has given rise to the establishment of global political, economic, and monetary regulatory institutions, such as the United Nations, the World Trade Organization (WTO), and the World Bank. Besides the enormous growth, however, there has been a persistent increase in worldwide poverty, human rights violations, and environmental degradation, and this is cause for increasing global concern (Beck, 2000).

What is missing, however, from the widely differing interpretations of globalization, which tend to adopt a particular perspective—political, cultural, social, or economic—is an account of the dynamics underlying this pattern of growth in order that the imbalance between wealth and poverty may be overcome. As a result, for instance, political analysts propose the supposed reduction in the power and sovereignty of nation-states, even their demise under the influence of globalization, while cultural and social analysts tender the possibility of a standardized world culture. For their part, economic analysts see globalization as constituting the emergence of an integrated global market economy in which production and trade are rationalized across nation-states and rendered "flexible" in order to respond to the rapidly changing economic circumstances aided by the new communications and information technology revolution (Jameson, 2000; Renton, 2001).

Because these views on contemporary globalization tend to exert a practical influence on the shaping of contemporary education, it is useful to identify, in broad outline, the three major paradigms competing to inform the actions of educators, namely the neoliberal, reformist, and Western Marxist. Based on the theories of the classical political economist, Adam Smith, the neoliberal paradigm represents globalization as the realization of its utopian ideology, which espouses an unfettered global capitalist economy regulated only by the market, which governments and workers are supposedly powerless to resist (Harman, 1996). Adopted by business as the new orthodoxy, the ideology of neoliberalism supports individualism, consumerism, competition, and minimal governmental interference, which, it is claimed, will induce self-reliance, initiative, and creativity, attributes a marketized education system would promote. On this account, at a global level it is assumed that transnational corporations pursuing their own self-interest will lead, as if by an "invisible hand," to the collective social good. It follows that the restructuring of education to conform to this utopian market ideal is a necessary corollary.

The reformist paradigm generally accepts capitalism as a normative part of the human condition, but its adherents seek to ameliorate capitalism's worst excesses through legislative regulation based on human rights, ethics, and equality. From the 1970s onward, however, this reform agenda has been reversed and the focus for the reformers is now on endeavoring to ensure that competitive, monopolistic entrepreneurial activity is open, transparent, and accountable, and conducted on a "level playing field." These ideals, of course, are absolutely at odds with the reality of capitalist market conditions.

The Western Marxist paradigm for the most part is noted for a diversity of standpoints, which has tended to weaken its revolutionary resolve as part of the international Marxist movement. Chief among the reasons has been the failure of revolutionary change to materialize in the West in the face of capitalism's phenomenal growth, and the tendency of many of its contemporary exponents to isolate themselves from socialist working-class struggles. One strand of this paradigm claims to be post-Marxist, which submits to a fatalistic view by accepting the inevitability of capitalism's establishment as a single global regime that it is futile to resist except in isolated pockets. The ultimate extension of this line of Western Marxism's evolution is postmodernism, which holds that because capitalism is now so globally all-pervasive, we cannot escape it except by carving out small enclaves of privacy and freedom (Wood, 1997). Therefore, resistance to the marketization of education, if it is even to be contemplated at all, can occur only in particular enclaves or on sectional issues.

In contrast to these trends, there are many critical commentators on the Left, including Marxist educators such as Cole (2003) and Hill, McLaren, Cole, and Rikowski (2002), who regard postmodern theories as a disabling threat to transformative change capabilities. This is because postmodern exponents express little interest in capitalism's dynamics or in the relationship between the economy and education, for instance. They therefore tend unwittingly to support neoliberalism.

There is, however, within the Marxist paradigm a growing recognition of the relevance of Marx's views expressed in the Communist Manifesto that globalization is the predictable outcome of capitalism's expansionary tendencies evident since its emergence as a viable economic system (Rees, 1998; Wood, 1997). The issue has become very topical because, in becoming established as a global system and having penetrated nearly all aspects of social life, capitalism reaches its geographical and social limit. It will therefore have no way of escaping through expansion the destabilizing consequences of its own internal dynamics. Its survival then becomes problematic.

With these observations it is now possible to discuss the conditions that have made the marketization of education a necessity for global capitalism's survival. Here I take marketization as a relation to mean the privatization, commodification, production, and marketing of education goods and services.

## The Conditions Shaping Education's Marketization

In order to discover why marketization has come to dominate social life under capitalism and why of all possible models education is being shaped to conform to market requirements, it is necessary to take account of the conditions that have led to these developments. Unlike any previous modes of production, capitalism is marked by the insertion of *market exchange* into the traditional pattern of production, distribution, and consumption to form a specifically capitalist mode of production directed toward economic growth.

Capitalism's historical appearance as a mode of production incorporating both production and exchange in a reciprocal relationship is attributed to the commodification of labor as well as the means of production, to their availability for sale on the market, and to the existence of a class of capitalists possessing the power of money to purchase these items with the intention of augmenting their investment through the production and exchange of commodities. In this context, money, in its various forms as an exchange medium, as a standard measure of value, and as the embodiment of social wealth that can be accumulated, plays a pivotal role in the conversion of commodity values into capital and the transfer of that capital into the hands of private individuals. It is on the basis of the social division between labor, on the one hand, and capital, on the other, that in the Marxian interpretation distinguishes capitalism and its marketization processes as a unique mode of production.

From the moment capitalism began to exert an influence on social life, it has revealed itself to be a highly dynamic and inevitably expansionary economic system overcoming any barriers to its progress by means of technological change. As Harvey (1982: 156) observes, powered by capital accumulation for its own sake and fueled by the exploitation of labor power, capitalism constitutes a permanently revolutionary force, marked by "roller coaster" cycles of economic "boom and bust" that perpetually reshapes the world in which we live. Counter-intuitively, capitalism's survival depends on these cycles, which tend to disrupt social life but serve to restore the stability of the economy jeopardized by the instability caused by growth.

Because of the importance, at present, to the economy of research and development, and the availability of technically skilled labor, in an age dependent on information and electronics, education is regarded as an important means of resolving the current economic crisis. It is therefore a prime target for "takeover" and marketization. This is a radical departure from past practice, when capitalist enterprises were content to draw their labor and applied scientific requirements from the stock of knowledge and skills socially produced under government supervision by education systems funded out of public revenues.

The conditions favoring the marketization of education have their genesis in the current era characterized by rapidly accelerating accumulation cycles, an intensification of competition, mounting economic crises as reflected in flagging profit margins, and surpluses of capital searching for diminishing investment opportunities. In this climate, powerful business interests have been making intense efforts to establish the market as a universal regulatory mechanism and to exploit every avenue of potential capital growth. From the perspective of these interests, capital circulating through education as revenue represents underdeveloped and underutilized sources of growth and this poses a barrier to ongoing capital accumulation. This is one of the primary reasons why education has been acquiring a growing profile worldwide as a money spinner, especially for advancing technological enterprises (see Apple, this volume).

At the heart of the current drive to marketize education are the problems of sustaining the initial competitive advantage afforded by the introduction of automation and electronic technologies during World War II. By the 1950s, that advantage had been eroded as both technologies became general through industry. Corporations sought salvation in technological change to the extent that pressure to accelerate technological innovation became a permanent feature and an integral part of production. At the same time, automation shifted the locus of surplus value extraction from shop floor labor to the labor of scientists, technicians, and laboratory workers. These trends generated a growing demand not only for scientific knowledge, research, and development, but also for highly skilled intellectual labor power. This helps to explain the explosion in universities worldwide in the 1950s (Mandel, 1975).

As demands for higher education grew, government-funded expansion of education began to occupy a sizeable slice of national budgets, which substantially raised education's potential exchange value if education systems were to be marketized along the lines of private enterprise. However, the marketization of education was not seriously implemented at national levels until the late 1960s, when a severe economic crisis brought about pressures for recovery, thus precipitating corporate pressure for economic reform, which included the privatization of government services. The strategy entailed, first, the restructure of the labor processes and their management, in order (in the new climate of "fast" capitalism) to ensure maximum control over the labor process while at the same time accommodating maximum flexibility to respond almost instantly to the rapidly changing demands of the market place.

Second, it entailed the search for capital expansion into new fields of investment in order to absorb surpluses of capital created by the crisis. The search was accompanied by political pressure on governments, on the one hand, to secure the reassertion of competition in the marketplace and, on the other, to convert state revenues devoted to social services through their privatization into interest-bearing capital (Yates, 2000).

On a global scale and at the political level, these strategies involved the rationalization and restructuring of the capitalist economy on the basis of free trade among competitive nation-states regulated, it was hoped, only by market forces supported and legitimated by a series of international agreements overseen by the World Trade Organization (WTO). Agreements include the General Agreement on Trade in Services (GATS), which also encompasses education (see Ziguras, this volume). In order to realize these objectives there began an all-out assault on workers and their unions followed by the restructuring of the labor process for a "leaner and meaner" mode of production (see Franzway, this volume). As a consequence there has been, almost across the board, an intensification of work through the use of ever-advancing technologies, workforce casualization, labor redundancies, and outsourcing and the creation of work teams with illusory decision-making powers. At the same time, the application of electronic technologies developed at public expense has witnessed not only a reduction in the need for skilled manual workers but also an increase in the ability of managements to monitor, control, and intensify every aspect of the labor process.

Most of these consequences have impacted on education as its marketization has proceeded to subject it to the demands of the global capitalist economy. The question still remains, however: What is it about the dynamics of capitalism's mode of marketization that engenders the effects being recorded in almost all sectors of education?

## The Dynamics of Capitalism's Mode of Marketization

Driven by the need for economic growth, the capitalist mode of production constitutes a web of interwoven factors and relations centering on the exchange of commodities. Understanding the dynamics of marketization as it operates within capitalism is therefore the key to understanding the changes taking place in education and their effects.

In abstract terms market exchange is conceived as a transaction in which buyers and sellers enter freely into a relationship for the purpose of exchanging useful objects of equal value. Underlying this notion of exchange is a set of assumptions. It is assumed, for instance, that the objects as the embodiment of their labor are the property of the parties concerned, so that in the transaction they face each other on the basis of equality. It is also assumed that transactions occur within a mode of production based on use value and consumption and that production is carried out under social conditions characterized by a collaborative division of labor. Under these conditions, producers own or, have access to their means of production and there exist few demarcations between mental and physical labor.

The insertion of market exchange based on money as an integral part of the processes associated with production radically altered the nature of these productive and property relations. It led to the creation of a capitalist mode of production directed toward the production of commodities primarily for exchange, the value of which was to be realized in the exchange transaction and converted into money capital as a form of private property. The formerly collaborative social relations became marked by a division of labor between two opposing but interrelated classes, a class of capitalist enterprises, on the one hand, producing commodities independently of and in competition with each other and a class of laborers who must compete for work in the enterprises in return for a wage. Furthermore, the capitalist form of commodity exchange, rather than social productive activity, became the medium through which these classes interact.

The act of selling is by its very nature an act whereby producers are alienated from the products of their labor. Through the medium of the capitalist form of exchange, however, the web of productive relationships becomes converted into quantifiable, exchangeable objects, even living labor. Thus, what were formerly inalienable, organic relationships surrounding productive activity became alienated and converted into discrete "things" related only incidentally.

Under these circumstances market exchange transactions cannot claim to be freely entered into on the basis of equality between producer-proprietors. The so-called freedom of the former producers, now wage laborers, is illusory because marketization has separated them from their means of production. They therefore have no alternative in order to subsist but to sell their only "property," labor power. Their labor and their means of production, materials and instruments, can be purchased with the power of money now in the hands of a nonproducing capitalist class whose commanding interest and purpose is augmenting and expanding their original capital investment.

These features of marketization set the conditions for a capitalist mode of production characterized by a circular motion of commodity values through two poles, production and exchange, through which the value of labor is converted into expanded capital. The process begins in the sphere of exchange where enterprises purchase labor power and the necessary means of production. In the sphere of production through the labor process, these enterprises extract the surplus value necessary to create a return on their investment by the simple expedient of recouping the costs of labor's wages in less than the contracted time. The surplus value created by labor in the balance of the time is a bonus, and the more labor costs can be reduced through the introduction of technology or the intensification of labor, the more the enterprise can accrue surplus value and convert it into profit if it is able to sell all its commodities on the market, which is not always assured.

The exploitation of labor in this manner is the only source of capital accumulation. However, the incentive to reduce labor costs by technological means, by maximizing labor and management efficiencies and by having on hand a "reserve army" of cheap, unemployed workers, derives not only as a way of surmounting labor's understandable antagonisms inherent in this kind of labor process but also from the competitive relations among members of the capitalist class. If they do not increase their margins of profit beyond their production costs, they face bankruptcy, merger, or takeover. But if they do, it is at the expense of the very labor power that is the source of those margins.

In the realm of exchange, enterprises encounter another set of pressures. They must sell their commodities at a profit, and this depends on the average price prevailing in the marketplace. If commodities were exchanged at the value of the labor time embodied in their production, there would be no problems in their equalization and exchange. However, under capitalist market conditions, because prices of commodities must include a profit above their labor values, a deviation from the average upsets the necessary equalization if commodities are to be exchanged at all.

The phenomenon of prices rising and falling in relation to an average price is an expression of this deviation and is indicative of an over- or underproduction of commodities. They are also a consequence of a production focused on supply outcomes without reference either to consumer demand or the supply output of other enterprises, which, as already noted, all work in competition with and independently of each other. Resolution of the problem of equalizing in exchange the inequalities derived from over- or underproduction is sought by individual enterprises in the labor process by introducing new technology and restructuring the production processes in order to undercut the prices of competitors. Initially, this strategy puts an enterprise ahead of competitors, but eventually the advantage is lost as the technology become generally applied throughout industry. If overproduction becomes generalized the imbalance between supply and demand is corrected by an economic crisis.

The opposing conditions between production and exchange account for capitalism's extraordinary dynamism and for the "roller coaster" pattern characteristic of its historical development, a pattern that is punctuated by periods of destabilizing economic growth followed by the stabilizing influence of canceling out the overabundance of that growth forced by economic crises. Attempts to resolve the tensions thus caused has led to unprecedented technological developments in the forces of production to the extent that the enormous volumes of commodity output cannot be absorbed by consumers who can afford to pay. The problem neatly illustrates one of capitalism's contradictions: in order to produce at a profit, wages must be kept low; however, if the volumes of commodities are to be sold for a profit, wages must be high enough to allow this. This situation cannot be avoided without jeopardizing capitalism's existence altogether, so that enterprises continue to pursue technological change, organizational restructuring, and expansion as a means of overcoming economic instability.

In order to offset the demands for flexibility and speed in responding to the highly volatile, competitive global market while at the same time maintaining fiscal administrative control, one strategy has been the adoption by large corporations of a centralized-decentralized organizational structure, something that is now made feasible by communications technology. This kind of structure combines centralized control with competing decentralized, semi-autonomous divisions. In this way, profit-inducing competition is internalized within a monopoly enterprise. It is a model that appears to be evolving globally in the structuring of relations among nation-states under the hegemony of the United States and one that national education systems, internally and as parts of a global network of education providers, are endeavoring to emulate. While outsourcing might appear to be a contradictory aberration from this model, small enterprises and consultancies, because of their lower overheads and rapid turnaround times, do have some usefulness as satellite service providers.

The ultimate leveler in the face of mounting economic pressures is a major economic crisis. Its advent forces an almost complete renovation of the economy so that surplus goods and capital can be cleared away and inefficient organizational structures dismantled to make way for a new cycle of economic growth. A cycle of "boom and bust" paradoxically therefore is a necessity that keeps capitalism from self-destruction. Chief among the causal factors of economic crises is the overcapacity of productive forces that could, under different social relations, accommodate whole populations in a reasonable standard of living. Rather than dissolve the capitalist social relations, however, the capitalist class resorts to cycles of wasteful destruction of surplus commodity and money values—warfare being the ultimate in destruction—followed by profligate investment speculation. In other words, rather than transform its social relations of production, capitalism indulges in the wholesale destruction of its overabundance.

With this account of the dynamics of capitalism's mode of marketization, we are now in a position not only to understand the rationale for the changes taking place in education as described by critical education theorists, but also to assess the implications for the development of genuine education into the future.

## The Implications of Marketization for the Future of Education

The tensions in everyday life between the demands of maintaining one's existence and the impulse to change and develop socially are also played out in education. Under capitalism, however, the tensions become exacerbated within the confines of marketization, as education is subjugated to the contradictory demands placed on it and to the impersonal regulation of the market. The reason is that the capitalist form of market exchange in its mediating role cannot deal with quality education nor with social, ethical, or equity concerns. It can deal only with quantifiable "things" as commodities.

Thus, in the marketization process educators have been marginalized in favor of trainers and business managers. Learning has become automated through the use of information and communication technologies. The knowledge of educators is commodified and packaged for online learning (Brabazon, 2002; Noble, 2002a), and low-market-value humanities courses are being sidelined as an instrumental model of education takes hold. For Noble (2002b), these trends signify the onset of a truly capitalist mode of education, which is being shaped as capital investors "cherry pick" their way through the most lucrative "bits" of education. Hence, the injection of competition among education institutions and sectors, a growing inequality in the provision of education, and a trend toward increasingly narrow specialization. What is left is a dismembered "body," no longer in a position to generate the critical mass of ideas and creative, skilled labor that capitalism needs.

Universities as idea-generating powerhouses are prime targets for investment, by those knowledge-based industries involved in telecommunications, computers, electronics, and biotechnology. As lucrative sites of investment, their potential has been enhanced by the protection of ideas, as intellectual property generated by research, under copyright and patent laws and global trade agreements (Yates, 2000). These trends in education, however, while promising to resolve current economic crises, nevertheless are not without their contradictions for capitalism.

Because education is not directly involved in the production and exchange of commodities for capital accumulation but rather involved indirectly as a producer of knowledge and labor skills, it can be classified as part of the infrastructure supporting direct accumulation, an infrastructure that besides education includes the production of means of production, such as machinery, as well as transport and energy services.

Investment in the infrastructural sector of the economy can be lucrative but problematic because returns are realized not at the end of a production cycle but recouped only over the period of several cycles or over the lifetime of the machinery or transport systems, or not at all if an economic crisis intervenes. Consequently, while providing a powerful lever for accumulation as well as temporary relief from problems of overaccumulation, investment in this sector becomes imprisoned in methods of doing things and committed to specific lines of production. Thus, capitalism loses its flexibility, and its ability to innovate becomes limited (Harvey, 1982: 220–21). This is why investors favor "cherry-picking" education services, leaving a major portion of education's provision to government funding, with the inevitable reappearance of inequalities of opportunity. In this event, genuine education therefore becomes a privilege and an expensive rarity. At this point, the marketization of education enters the political arena and becomes exposed to democratic agitation for quality and equity in that domain.

The reappearance in new forms of inequity in education as a result of marketization serves to illustrate that inequities are not merely theoretical constructs or something subjectively experienced by individuals. Rather, in this instance, they have their objective basis in the structural relations of the capitalist mode of production, which could not survive or thrive without them. This accounts for inequities not only in terms of class, gender, and ethnicity, but also in terms of the uneven economic relations between producers and consumers, and between developed and under developed countries.

By exploring the conditions from which the need and dynamics for education's marketization has emerged, and the implications for the future of quality education, we now possess a much fuller account on which to base transformative action toward the realization of a genuine education.

## Conclusion

In conclusion, the marketization of education has all the hallmarks of an entrepreneurial takeover executed with blitzkrieg precision backed by the trappings of legality and plausibly justified on the grounds of national economic survival in the face of global competition. Dispossession-based marketization is a strategy that has served capitalism well in its phenomenal growth and expansion. For many educators and concerned citizens, the dispossession of education and the limiting of its goals to profit maximization for the enrichment of the few is a travesty that requires resolute rectification. Accomplishing this democratic project, however, initially demands a critical investigation into the marketization process within the context of a globalizing capitalist economy.

The project calls for a Marxian critique that focuses on analyzing qualitative change processes: the motivating factors, the dynamics involved, and the direction toward which the processes are tending. The critique provided in this chapter has attempted to reveal that the motive for education's marketization lies not within the political or educational arenas but in attempts to revive the capitalist economy in the current period of flagging profits. The likely consequence of the capture of education services by private enterprise is a debased education limited in quality and scope; and this is so despite the dependence of the globalizing capitalist economy on quality education.

The political task then is to work toward capitalism's economic structural transformation from whatever vantage point. The task can be assisted by the realization that while capitalism appears to be all-powerful, it is in fact, as the above analysis has sought to demonstrate, an extremely fragile system. This knowledge places agitation for change on a sound theoretical foundation.

## References

Ball, S. *Education Reform: A Critical and Post-Structural Approach*. Buckingham, UK: Open University Press, 1994.

Beck, U. *What Is Globalization?* Cambridge, UK: Polity Press, 2000.

Brabazon, T. *Digital Hemlock: Internet Education and the Poisoning of Teaching*. Sydney: University of New South Wales, 2002.

Cole, M. "Might It Be in the Practice That It Fails to Succeed? A Marxist Critique of Claims for Postmodernism and Poststructuralism as Forces for Social Change and Social Justice." *British Journal of Sociology of Education* 24, no. 4 (2003): 487–500.

Gewirtz, S., S. Ball, and R. Bowe. *Markets, Choice and Equity in Education*. Buckingham, UK: Open University Press, 1995.

Harman, C. "Globalisation: A Critique of a New Orthodoxy." *International Socialism*, no. 73 (1996). 38–52

Harvey, D. *The Limits to Capital*. Oxford: Basil Blackwell, 1982.

Hill, D., P. McLaren, M. Cole, and G. Rikowski, eds. *Marxism against Postmodernism in Educational Theory*. Lanham, MD: Lexington Books, 2002.

Jameson, F. "Globalization and Political Strategy." *New Left Review* 4 (2000): 49–68.

Kenway, J., C. Bigum, L. Fitzclarence, and J. Collier. "Marketing Education in the 1990s: An Introductory Essay." *Australian Universities Review* 36, no. 2 (1993): 2–6.

Lauder, H., and D. Hughes. *Trading in Futures: Why Markets in Education Don't Work*. Buckingham, UK: Open University Press, 1999.

Mandel, E. *Late Capitalism*. London: NLB, 1975.

Marginson, S. *Markets in Education*. St. Leonards, Australia: Allen and Unwin, 1997.

Noble, D. *Digital Diploma Mills: The Automation of Higher Education*. New York: Monthly Review Press, 2002a.

———. "Technology and the Commodification of Higher Education." *Monthly Review* 53, no. 10 (2002b): 26–40.

Rees, J. "The Return of Marx." *International Socialism*, no. 79 (1998): 3–11.

Renton, D., ed. *Marx on Globalisation*. London: Lawrence and Wishart, 2001.

Smyth, J., A. Dow, R. Hattam, G. Shacklock, and A. Reid. *Teachers' Work in a Globalizing Economy*. London: Falmer Press, 1999.

Wood, E. "Back to Marx." *Monthly Review* 49, no. 2 (1997): 1–8.

Yates, M. "Us versus Them: Laboring in the Academic Factory." *Monthly Review* 51, no. 8 (2000): 40–49.

# Chapter 14

## Teachers' and Public-Sector Workers' Engagement with "Globalization from Above": Resisting Regressive Parochialism in Queensland

Peter Kell

"All politics is local." (Tip O'Neill, Democrat, Speaker of the U.S. House of Representatives)

### Introduction

This chapter examines the local political response of education workers to the cluster of political, economic, and cultural projects associated with globalization from above. It documents a politics (and pedagogy) of engagement that emerged as a reaction to neoliberal globalism. This response, which can be seen as giving form and substance to global/local citizenship, came from a cluster of policies that redefined the purpose of the nation-state in managerial and corporatist terms to enhance competitiveness (Wiseman, 1998). This emphasis on technical and standardized approaches to reform displaced civic values for economic objectives to attain ultimate competitiveness (see Apple, this volume). Under the umbrella rhetoric of "globalization and modernization," this cluster of policies produced a residualization of the public-sector generally, as well as the corporatization and marketization of public education, the implementation of a decentralized industrial relations agenda, and heightened levels of management control through "accountability" regimes for public-sector workers, including teachers. This chapter describes the impact of the integration of the global formulation policy for competitiveness in the context of local political developments in Queensland in the late twentieth century.

Paradoxically, these initiatives emerged in response to demands for more democratic, ethical, and inclusive forms of government after a long period of corrupt neoconservative political domination (Stevens and Wanna, 1993).

With the aim of increasing community and industry participation in the management and direction of public schools, the Labor administration implemented an ambitious "generic" reform package that triggered considerable resistance within the teaching workforce and eventually led to a surprise electoral defeat of this Labor government. These generic reforms are a response to the demands for continuous improvements in economic competitiveness and provided a convenient rationale for the radical introduction of economic rationalism (Considine, 1990; Wiseman, 1998). The differential local impact of these global measures that reduce the capacity of the nation-state to support and maintain aspects of the civic state have the capacity to trigger local responses to neoliberalism to preserve the nation-state and notions of authentic localism that are seen as under threat (Singh, Kell, and Pandian, 2002).

This dual response to "globalization from above" in North Queensland is characterized by the electoral and political battles around the quest for the return to government by the Labor Party, and teachers and education workers occupied a key role. The electoral battle of this era has been reshaped not only by the local/global orientation of public education, but also by claims of legitimacy centered on identity, race, and entitlement that spawn a "regressive parochialism" (Singh, Kell, and Pandian, 2002).

The political conflicts were characterized by a rallying in opposition to populist attacks on public education and teachers that threatened the industrial and intellectual conditions of teachers' work as well as the relationships among the state, the community, and public education. The emerging frontline activism of teachers in resisting the residualization of public education is a universal theme in teacher unionism and now ensures the involvement of teacher unions in Canada, New Zealand, the United States, and Australia in political struggles against the generic aspects of globalization from above (Robertson and Smaller, 1996). Increasingly these struggles have been at the provincial and state government level, as governments seeking to deliver "efficiencies" for global competition squeezing the public systems so that funding cuts and tax reductions are available for citizens.

This chapter documents the rallying points, conflicts, and outcomes of a four-year period of struggle the shifts in left/right politics that suggests that new strategic alliances are emerging around new hybrid class structures where very different from of traditional union and party formations are needed to tap into the anxieties associated with regressive parochialism. Many of these new political affiliations were typified by changes in relations of power among a Labor party forced to confront its racist policy legacy and a demand to connect with a new social democratic movement other than one of white working-class " battler" origins (McMullan, 1992). The struggles around these issues and the temporary success of public education workers contradict orthodox views about their powerlessness and passivity. This includes emergent observations concerning conflict, contestation, accommodation, and consensus.

## Shifting from Agrarian Socialism to Neoliberal Globalism

This case study is situated in a regional Australian city. The North Queensland city of Townsville, which sits on the sixteenth parallel, has a population of over 130,000, a strong public-sector centered on the army, public service, and a major university, as well as a vibrant private sector based on the mining industry, tourism, and sugar production. Townsville is the regional capital of North Queensland, the thirteenth largest city in Australia and the second biggest city in the state of Queensland outside the state capital, Brisbane, which lies 1,500 kilometers to the south.

The region has been labeled as the "deep north," reflecting a deeply entrenched white racist streak in its public culture. The deep north is a term that invokes the parochialism and racism that typifies popular images of the "deep south" in the United States of America. Queensland may be described as an Australian equivalent of the southern state of Alabama. At the time of Australia's federation in 1901, this strong regional identity, with its manifest racism, fed into moves for it to cede from the federation to avoid proposed restrictions on the recruitment of non-white (slave) labor from the South Pacific (La Nauze, 1965). This desire to secede was not an expression of any democratic impulse. Primary industrialists were concerned about threats to its ability to import exploitable black labor for the sugar cane industry should the Immigration Restriction Act of 1901 ever become law, which it did. The region's leaders at the time of federation sought to leave the fledgling nation rather than have to recruit what was seen as less robust white labor to work in the enervating tropic climate. The strong industries located around this port city ensured that Townsville had a long political tradition associated with the union movement and was a long-term electoral stronghold of the Australian Labor Party (ALP) even in times when conservative governments were entrenched in power for long periods. However, the political culture of Queensland in the twentieth century was dominated by "agrarian socialism" (Stevens and Wanna, 1993).

The decentralized economy in this state, arising from its heavy dependence on primary industries, ensured that the conservative interests of landowners, farmers, and small businesses dominated the left/right political spectrum. Combined with this was a strong right-wing conservative tradition within the labor movement centered on the Australian Workers Union (AWU), one of Australia's oldest unions, whose members mostly worked in rural occupations. Agrarian socialism influenced both Australian Labor Party and the Country National Party administrations in the twentieth century, with a mix of neoconservative "god-fearing" social policies, strong regulatory economic frameworks, low levels of state taxation, and high levels of "pump priming" through government financing of large-scale development projects in regional Queensland. This policy mix has been termed "agrarian socialism" and under the control of an authoritarian populist has continued as the major policy mix until the late 1990s (Stevens and Wanna, 1993; Moore, 1995)

This policy mix also featured highly restrictive, racist laws governing the status, employment, and movement of Aborigines and Torres Strait Islanders, Australia's Indigenous peoples, that were rigidly enforced by a large police presence. Queensland governments were also typified by a cult of personality clustered around long-serving, strong, and influential state premiers such as T. J. Ryan, William Forgan-Smith, and Johannes Bjelke-Petersen (Steven and Wanna, 1993). These governments mobilized strong parochial interest groups based on partisan political loyalties that excluded those who were seen as opponents. A paternalistic network of patronage typified Queensland government in the Bjelke-Petersen era to ensure that political power was retained through a massive electoral malapportionment, a partisan public-sector, and a corrupted legal and police system. This government was also assisted in retaining power through strong associations with private sector entrepreneurs, who received favorable treatment in return for financial donations to the National Party. In the 1980s, this group of entrepreneurs was colorfully referred to as the "white shoe brigade" and enjoyed an open invitation by the government to engage in speculative real estate and tourist developments, many of which caused environmental damage and were of dubious economic value (Hede, Prasser, and Neylan, 1992).

The Queensland government often resorted to restrictive laws to crush opposition groups with legislation that banned gatherings of more than a handful of people. Most often these laws were directed at Aboriginal and anti-racist activists, as was the case at the time of the Springbok Rugby tours of 1971 and the Commonwealth games in 1982. Throughout the nineteen years of the Bjelke-Petersen era, Queensland was internationally recognized as having an undemocratic electoral structure, corrupt legal and administrative structures, repressive laws, and a civic culture that was reactionary, sexist, homophobic, racist, and anti-democratic.

The destruction of this long period of conservative government emerged from the findings of the Fitzgerald Royal Commission into the corrupt links among police, National Party government ministers, and organized crime. This landmark commission led to the jailing of a police commissioner and the charging of the premier himself. The exposure of gross impropriety in relation to public administration, widespread corruption, and links to crime gangs was a public relations disaster for what had been mythologized as a "god-fearing" government. The backlash was swift and enduring, with a Labor administration elected in December 1989 in an electoral landslide under the leadership of Wayne Goss. The urbane Goss arrived with great expectations concerning a platform based on democratic reform in government, a strong commitment to social justice, and a charter for inclusive forms of government involving women, Indigenous peoples, and environmentalists.

## Reform and Electoral Backlash: Resistance to Globalization in the Sunshine State

The Goss government was wedged between several contradictory trends associated with the gradual exposure of the Australian economy to globalization that had been accelerated by the federal Hawke government's unilateral deregulation of the economy. These included the floating of the dollar; drastically reducing tariff protections for industry, workers, and their communities; and removing restrictions that had limited foreign investment to productive enterprises rather than financial speculation on the stock market. The Goss administration then adopted key elements of the federal government's neoliberal agenda, arguing that Queensland required not only electoral and public administrative reforms but also structural adjustments and efficiencies in order to make the local Queensland economy more efficient and competitive in world markets. This reformist and neoliberal policy mix shifted Queensland from its regressive, parochial tradition toward a government that facilitated and serviced the global/local welfare needs of the market, stimulating growth and competition in the private sector. This approach of pursuing neoliberal politics by offering compensatory reformist concessions saw Labor administrations throughout Australia in the 1980s adopting and advocating corporate managerialism (Considine, 1990). This development was a further reflecion of the shift from the government's role of providing for the cultural formation and socioeconomic security of its citizens to the delivery of economic outcomes for the private sector.

Many aspects associated with this policy mix contradicted the role traditionally occupied by Labor governments and more particularly the promises of a reformist government claiming commitments to a more democratic and inclusive society. The tensions between the government's economic neoliberalism and its proclamations of a compensatory, reformist mission associated with social justice were evident in public education. Tension and struggle continued within the Goss government as it pursued public-sector reforms, claiming to be acting in response to, as much as giving expression to, pressures of globalization from above. This was the framework for the struggles over public education in Queensland and Townsville in the 1990s.

Reforms in public education under the Labor government conformed to the disruptive neoliberal trend, with moves toward the devolution of management for contracting financial resources and politically contentious curriculum issues (e.g., human relationships education) to schools (Caldwell and Spink, 1988; Lingard and Rizvi, 1992). In Queensland, the rationale was not strictly in terms of economic efficiency and effectiveness but was legitimated within a rhetoric that sought to win widespread consent through a strategy claiming to be "democratizing schools" and providing a more "inclusive public education." Thus, in tandem with reforms to public school administration was the development of a Social Justice Strategy in Queensland Education. The expectation for a more inclusive system was created partly through a round of government consultations with communities in 1990 that underpinned new policy developments. The report, *Focus on Schools* (Department of Education, 1990), called for a collaborative approach to planning through public school councils involving parents and the community in a strategic approach to education management centered on the school itself. Centralized controls such as the school Inspectorate and other manifestations of the National Party bureaucracy were to be dismantled. The expressed intentions of *Focus on Schools* were democratic and inclusive, and complemented the Social Justice Strategy, all of which appeared to deliver the participatory structures promised by the newly elected Labor government (Department of Education, 1993, 1994).

However, many of the government's other policies designed to put into effect local interpretations of the neoliberal agenda frustrated and confused teachers about the real intentions, flow-on effects, and consequences of *Focus on Schools*. Curriculum planning was linked to financial cycles, while the initial concerns about genuine educational qualities shifted to concerns about auditing school performance, thereby making the participation of community and teachers very difficult. The cycle of financially driven curriculum planning intensified teachers' work, proving to be onerous and time consuming and revealing the serious lack of adequate resources to meet the government's political and economic objectives (McGinty and Anderson, 1994). Further, teachers were not assisted by other government policies designed to restructure and destructure workplace entitlements and industrial relations by aligning these with the "international standards" framed by neoliberal globalism.

The government introduced a raft of industrial legislation to abolish the centralized wage-setting system by replacing it with an enterprise-based, industrywide collective bargaining system. These disruptive neoliberal policies were not well received in the public-sector and significantly eroded electoral support for the government among these workers (Burke, 1993). The trade-offs in working conditions and the lowered wage rises in this period of rapid change further undermined the credibility of the Labor government among its supporters (Kell and Carr, 1994a, 1994b). Anxieties about the government's strong neoliberal tendencies were exacerbated by the *Shaping the Future* curriculum review, which was used to introduce a battery of centralized state testing in primary schools, a move that contradicted the government's claims about devolution (State of Queensland, 1994). The curriculum review's recommendations were criticized as introducing a tool for the covert surveillance of teachers' performance. While the review had tried to move away from the corporate managerialist rhetoric by resituating the school principal as a "curriculum leader," this image management failed to resonate with teachers battling to cope with a demanding audit culture that now featured requirements for "international benchmarks" (Kell and Carr, 1994c).

The complacent Goss government did not detect the erosion of its support base until it went to the polls in 1995 in the mistaken belief that it would be returned easily to the government benches. In a major shock, the Goss government was first returned with a majority of one to see that majority disappear after the result in the Townsville seat was overturned on appeal. In the subsequent by-election in the electoral seat of Mundingburra, the destabilizing effects of destructuring public education and the neoliberal approach to industrial relations implemented by the Goss government led to its defeat. The Liberal candidate in the by-election used targeted teachers via postal mail in letters that promised the removal of state testing and better resourcing for public schools, particularly for special education. Curiously, opposition politicians, whose policies on economic matters were identical to those of Labor, were able to mobilize significant support against the government through combined critiques of its neoliberal economic agenda and appeals to the nostalgia of economic and monocultural protectionism. Aligned with this protectionism was a populist, neoconservative attack on Aborigines, unions, unemployed workers, and single mothers. The by-election in Townsville and the threat of the return of the National Party to the government benches revitalized public-sector workers, including those in public education. With Labor's power to attract support markedly diminished, it dumped an unpopular sitting member, replacing him with the local mayor as a candidate. However, many public-sector workers and teachers regarded him, a member of the conservative AWU faction, as an electoral liability. Not surprisingly, Labor lost the by-election, recording less than 35 percent primary votes, and subsequently lost the right to govern. In the long process of rebuilding, following both the defeat of the Labor government and its betrayal of workers, some features of new forms of education worker activism were evident. The dimensions of this education activism reflected the complexity of the contested terrain exhibited in North Queensland politics.

## Motivating Engagement: Grassroots Politics, Rorts, and Racism

The "grassroots" branch structures of Australian political parties have experienced a dramatic decline in membership as "democracy" has been reduced to a matter of economics: the market manipulation of consumer power. That branch participation in Australian political parties is in a moribund state can be attributed to the corporate managerialism of government, which has effectively circumvented the participatory democratic processes and organizations. The decline of party political membership in centers like Townsville also represents the distaste and lack of support by many for the neoliberal and neoconservative policy settings pursued by Labor governments, contradicting their social democratic mission by situating government as a key partner in effecting transitions to advantage transnational capital. The response to and expressions of neoliberal globalism by the Labor Party have undermined traditions of local branch activities, some good, some highly questionable.

The branch structure of the ALP in the region was characterized by neglect, corruption, and nonparticipation. At the time of the loss of government in 1995, Townsville branch membership was inactive, suffering from elected members who preferred passivity and inactivity. However, the branch's official records at the time gave a markedly different impression, one of a healthy and growing membership of over five hundred. However, this membership list reflected the unscrupulous practice of "branch stacking" conducted by the AWU union faction, whereby large numbers of "ghost" members were enrolled. The signing up of large numbers of passive and noninvolved "members" was a strategy used by this faction to achieve victory in party ballots and preselections for elected officials and other influential council representatives. On occasions, these passive "ghosts" were "parachuted" into electoral contests to enable AWU candidates to secure victory in vital ballots, often without even knowing they were members. A majority of public-sector workers, including teachers in the Labor Party who were aligned to the opposing "left" faction, found these electoral practices damaging and sought to make changes (Criminal Justice Commission, 2001).

The Queensland ALP found itself in a dilemma, being out of power despite the large membership rolls suggesting significant support. It was ripe for a takeover by public-sector workers, a move that accelerated after the defeat of the Keating Labor government in the federal elections of 1996. Three key phenomena spurred the involvement of nonaligned and new members to the "left" faction of the Labor party. Perhaps not surprising for a university city, the first issue was the 6 percent cut to the federal funding of universities announced by the newly elected, neoliberal, neoconservative Howard Liberal government. The second issue was continuing attacks by the National Party State government on workers' terms and conditions of employment. Queensland's Borbidge Government attacked the entitlements of public-sector workers to compensation for workplace injuries, rejected industrial representation by unions, initiated a regime of subcontracting, and privatized activities such as school ancillary services. This rolling back of state functions and workers' entitlements was justified with appeals to the neoliberal idea of making Queensland internationally competitive.

A third key feature was the resurrection of the White Nation movement under the leadership of Pauline Hanson, a former Liberal Party candidate. Hanson was elected as an independent in the 1996 federal election to represent a formerly safe Labor seat, after she was dropped by the Liberal part for her anti-Aboriginal, anti-Asian, and anti-Muslim campaign. This was significant in the struggles over white Australian politics. Hanson's movement symbolized a revival of the parochial and racist Queensland political culture and was in the long term influential in shifting the agenda of mainstream political parties toward an anti-globalization and xenophobic stance. Her populist rhetoric centered on a return to a protectionist era of government, a return to "real" Australian values, and a distrust for foreigners, politicians, academics, and elites.

These so-called authentic values centered around attacks on multiculturalism and immigration, arguing against Asian immigration on the basis that Australia was being "swamped" by Asians. Hanson also railed against the "special advantages" enjoyed by Aboriginal Australians in the "Aboriginal industry." She called for special payments and affirmative action programs for Aborigines to be abolished in order to provide a more equitable distribution of government transfer payments. Hanson's brand of xenophobia and nostalgia for an authentic nationalism based on racism emerged as a response from the ultra-right against the impact of globalization. Its appeal to disgruntled and marginalized white voters lay in its return to nationalism and traditional values, its identification of scapegoats, and the emergence of a regressive parochialism (Singh, Kell, and Pandian, 2002).

The mainstream media were uncritically fascinated by Hanson's emergence, and she was afforded saturation coverage, a tendency that helped boost support at around 18–20 percent of the electorate. Many voters, including public-sector workers, alarmed at the racist rhetoric of Pauline Hanson and the growth of her newly formed party (Pauline Hanson's One Nation Party), sought some formal involvement in opposing her growing influence on Australian politics. Many joined the Labor party and became recruits in a concerted campaign to revitalize and renew Labor's response to a cluster of economic and social policies associated with globalization and anxiety about the emergence of xenophobia.

This renewal process centered on a two-pronged approach of reforming the grassroots structure of the party to combat the populism of Hanson and generating the groundswell to dismantle the electoral stronghold of the AWU. The mobilization of this group was a leftist response to globalization that in many aspects had some commonality with Hanson in rallying against the dire consequences of globalization, most notably the erosion of the state provision of public services that accompanied the Australian response to globalization. In contrast to the right, this group rallied support for multiculturalism, reconciliation with Indigenous Australians, and support for immigration, as well as the "bread and butter" electoral issues associated with local politics.

At the next Queensland state elections in June 1998, eleven members of Pauline Hanson's One Nation Party were elected to the parliament of Queensland. The result shocked many observers, who were most surprised by the strong electoral performance of the new party in an Australian system that had been traditionally dominated by a two-party system involving a Liberal/National Party coalition and the Australian Labor Party.

In the days after the election, there was a sense of amazement and disillusionment that One Nation's new members, an odd assortment of populist right-wing political amateurs, might achieve government by going into coalition with the conservative Liberal/National Party members. The result was in the balance for almost a week, with the final results indicating a hung parliament, until Labor leader Peter Beattie was able to negotiate an agreement with an independent member to govern for the life of the parliament until 2001.

Almost unnoticed in the frenzy over One Nation's success and the return of a Labor government was the victory of two left-wing Labor members in the Townsville electorates of Mundingburra and Townsville. The new parliamentary members were education workers enjoying strong support from public-sector workers. The victory of two former teachers and academics Mike Reynolds and Lindy Nelson-Carr also represented the outcome of the major revitalizing of local grassroots politics in the Townsville region (Kell and Murphy, 1998). Their election probably preserved Australia from the embarrassment of a One Nation/National Party Coalition in government. For many Australians, the elevation of One Nation to Queensland's treasury benches and government would have been something like the Ku Klux Klan in the United States achieving state government.

## Redefining the Global and Renewing the Local

The victory against the tide, in an area that would have been traditionally seen as ripe for exploitation and victory by reactionary political movements, suggests some interesting trends emerging in the tensions around globalization. Contrary to the general impression that the strongest reaction to globalization will emerge from right-wing groups, there is a counter-tendency from a more diversified cluster of people whose sympathies lie with left-wing groups. Many of these groups are centered around unions, public-sector workers, and teachers who have the capacity to organize and collectivize on several different fronts. The resistance to globalization has several common features with the ultra-right, which at one level explains the shifts in Australian politics in the post-1996 period.

Both the left and the ultra-right exhibit a resistance to the erosion of the state and the deregulation of the economy, and they argue for the return of the capacity of the states to intervene on behalf of the citizen. In many ways the message of the right and the left, located in a strong Labor tradition, have similar themes around equity and equality in critiquing globalization for its capacity to polarize economic activity and create new forms of poverty and disenfranchisement. In a sense, this commonality is a reason why the One Nation/Hanson message has resonated with some Labor supporters and provides a powerful reason why policy themes associated with Aboriginal welfare and immigration have been embraced by mainstream parties after being initially derided as extreme.

The key differentiating factor associated with movements against globalization is the racialization of blame that has accompanied the right-wing thesis on economic collapse and crisis (Moore, 1995; Singh, Kell, and Pandian, 2002). This has been the identifying feature of radical right-wing groups emerging as a reaction to globalization, including the Hanson/One Nation party. As with other right-wing groups, it is reliant on wedge politics. This involves the identification and vilification of groups for the purposes of gaining electoral appeal. Incorporated in this wedge politics have been threats of punitive action against those who are perceived as working contrary to the collective good and who are generally represented as "battlers," a term that disguises the racialized nature of the conservative message to a self-perceived "aggrieved" white electorate. Wedge politics, used by conservative and established interests as a trigger for white anxiety, has made new claims at representing an embattled working class in direct contradiction to its adherence to orthodox economics that has directly impoverished a range of groups in the community.

On the contrary, the rallying points for teachers and educators were the themes of reconciliation, land rights, asylum seekers, and other issues centered on human rights. These new forms of citizenship and civic pluralism had a powerful effect in reconnecting supporters of Labor and left-wing politics, whose allegiances were tested during the period when Labor government's flirtation with hard-core economic deregulation and award restructuring. Many of the new recruits to the Labor movement in North Queensland were teachers, education workers, and public servants who had little experience or interest in political parties. They were generally clearly concerned about, and mobilized around, a concern over what are seen as "soft" issues rather than "hard" issues associated with economic reform. This is not to say that they were not concerned about these issues, but the principal reason for activism stemmed around their impact on the social conditions of the community.

The involvement of public-sector workers and teachers is often triggered around multiple issues, most of which have little or no direct relationship with either education or globalization. The rise of One Nation is a case in point, where activism is seen as an attempt to differentiate themselves and their communities from the more odious racial politics of the ultra-right and the compliance of mainstream politics to this message. Aligned with this is a new emerging class politics as Labor support, strongest in white-collar unions, become, the vehicle of the middle class to differentiate themselves from elements of radical white working-class racism. Ironically, left-wing unions colonized by middle-class workers like teachers are seeking to redefine the political landscape on "soft" issues and in doing so also profoundly alter the policy agenda as the balance of interest shifts within party membership. The effect of the renewal process in Townsville was to have a profound effect on the Labor party as the new membership shifted the balance of membership against the conservative right-wing AWU. The power of the left was also increased by the electoral rorts scandal in the period between 1999 and 2001, where investigations into electoral malpractices by AWU officials were conducted. The scandal ended in a major Royal commission that involved trials of AWU organizers and eventually the resignation of a number of senior ministers in the Beattie government associated with the AWU (Criminal

Justice Commission, 2001). Even the stench of electoral "rorting" that saw a Labor candidate jailed did not halt a landslide Labor victory in the 2001 state election, a win that was partly assisted by the unpopularity of a federal government in Canberra on tax policy and petrol prices.

The 2001 victory saw Labor in Townsville unseat former One Nation members, decimate the National Party political representation in the region, and institute a period of left-wing hegemony. This hegemony was built on local attempts to renew and redefine local political representation that had atrophied during the Labor governments in the 1980s and early 1990s where corporate managerialism replaced the local and peak councils as key policy making bodies. The branch structures were rebuilt and quickly colonized by the left to the extent that the left, a longtime junior partner to the AWU and right factions of the Labor party, became the dominant group in the region within a period of less than five years.

Contrary to the myth of apathy in political matters, Australians will become committed and involved if the political movement is flexible to their immediate needs, responsive to their ideas, and willing to give them important tasks and provide communal linkages beyond political meetings. Unlike the insular, passive, and compliant party structures favored by the right wing of the Labor party, the new branch structures started to become active and connected to the community. Most successful political movements are often bonded around a culture of celebration and festivity, and the left in North Queensland's politics embraced this strategy enthusiastically. In reaction to the wedge politics of their opponents, this collective style of rallying support involved Aboriginal and Torres Strait Islanders and members of non-Angloethnic communities who found themselves under threat from the shift to the right that Hanson and One Nation created. This festive and celebratory strategy was also accompanied by active policy forums at the branch level rather than the procedural and ritualized meetings that typified the Labor movement at the time. Moribund branch structures were revitalized through a broad community development role that sought to inform and educate members rather than use them as compliant "vote fodder."

While the traditional and ever-present raffle was a fund-raiser the cultural and political activities of the left occupied an important evangelizing feature of left politics that had the effect of occupying the grassroots space. These developments were largely unobserved by a complacent AWU and undocumented by a Murdoch-owned local press that was seen as a "voice piece" of that union and conservative interests. The electoral victories of the 1998–2001 period in this area were built on classic grassroots politics centered on voluntary groups, schools, mothers clubs, sports clubs, and other community groups. The emergence of the left hegemony in this region from the grass roots highlights an interesting case study where aspects of globalization embedded in generic policy structures of government have been challenged and to some extent modified by an emerging local response.

## 2001–2003: Race and Refugees Demolishes Labor

Many aspects of the victories in North Queensland were not present in the Australian Labor Party's 2001 federal election campaign. Even with an ambitious education program called *Knowledge Nation*, which enjoyed the support of key unions and also parent lobby groups in education, Labor was defeated on the so-called soft issues. In the wake of the anxiety and hysteria generated by the September 11 attacks, the arrival of refugees by flimsy boats in northern Australia triggered a new wave of racial xenophobia. The themes exploited by Hanson, who had by this time faded from public attention, rebounded during the election campaign, with the prime minister portraying the refugees as people with doubtful claims to be refugees, terrorists, and people who were bypassing the normal bureaucratic systems of approval. In the campaign launch, John Howard received deafening applause when he referred to the boat people, saying, "We will choose who comes to Australia."

This uncompromising position was largely supported in the last week of the election campaign by Leader of the Opposition Kim Beazley, whose party had not been able to develop a coherent alternative response to mandatory detention and the deportation of refugees to Pacific Islands such as Nauru. Indeed Labor had actually introduced this policy in the early 1990s; it was determined to maintain a small target policy on all issues throughout the last year of the electoral cycle and had failed to articulate an alternative position on these issues. The lack of morale authority on the issues of race and the failure to present a critique of globalization that incorporated a refugee policy told heavily as the disillusioned left supporters sought more active and engaged political allies. In the election, the left support that historically went to Labor leaked to the Greens, giving them a historically high vote and losing Labor an election it was predicted to win. By 2003, the One Nation phenomenon, like many other ultra-ring-wing movements, had momentarily collapsed. The One Nation party polled less than 1 percent of the vote, only two One Nation members held their seats in Queensland, and only one Queensland senator was elected. The party was characterized by infighting and scandals; Pauline Hanson was charged and convicted of electoral fraud in 2003 and jailed along with the party treasurer. Little comfort can be drawn form the fate of One Nation and its leader because the appeal to base racism had engulfed and overwhelmed the political culture of Australia. This mainstreaming of wedge politics and the regressive parochialism that now typifies Australian politics has also realigned the balance of the left in Australian politics, marginalizing the left, which includes many of those who rallied against Hanson in North Queensland, and facilitating their shifting their support to the emerging Greens party.

The contrast with the earlier Queensland state election experience illustrates the need for leftist parties to confront and articulate a position that encounters the manifestations of "wedge politics" based on race. Labor in 2003 remains uncertain how to handle issues of race and how to respond to the appeals for authentic localism and nationalism and with what groups to mobilize a response to these issues.

Teachers and educators have an important role in shaping and presenting these counter-positions, both in their work and in the communities in which they work. The success in the Queensland election and Labor's failure in the federal campaign highlight the importance of this group in linking with indigenous and refugee groups. Mostly profound, though, is the need for Labor to enlist this group to reenergize and revive its capacity to stake an alternative position to conservative populism based on racism and to argue it within both the party and in the community. In the period of the 1980 and 1990s, the reliance on corporatist politics in the Australian state has contributed to an atrophying of these capabilities to generate community-based politics, and at the beginning of 2001 many left-wing unions were ending their affiliations with the Labor party. The capacity to engage the community in a constructive and reflective dialogue about these issues is at the heart of revitalizing discussion on what the implications of globalization are on local democratic processes and structures. It requires a commitment to participatory forms of political organization and a determination to show leadership in the face of populism and argue the point within the community.

Clearly from the experience in Queensland, change is often prompted by a concern about the local reaction and responses to globalization. At the local level, this has been a concern about generic and orthodox economic policy designed to reinvent government as exclusively a managerial activity. There is also a reaction and response to the ultra-right's response that attributes blame on the basis of race and identity. While Labor has its own history of racism that it needs to confront, the experience of Townsville, a small part of the broader global picture, suggests that electoral success and reform cannot be assured unless Labor engages those Australians who are passionately interested in reflecting on and reshaping notions of race, community, and national identity in the context of globalization. This process is an absolute precondition if Labor is to return to and maintain long periods of government.

The North Queensland experience provides an interesting case study in the ongoing themes of race in Australian politics, the power and authority of education workers and teachers, and the need for activists to respond to the key local issues of identity, race, and equality in the context of the global politics of education.

## References

Burke, C. "Education, Promise, Policy and Performance." In *The Goss Government: Promise and Performance of Labor in Queensland*, edited by B. Steven and J. Wanna, 226–47. Melbourne: Center for Public-sector Management, Macmillan, 1993.

Caldwell, B., and J. Spink. *The Self Managing School*. London: Falmer Press, 1988.

Considine, M. "The Corporate Management Framework as Administrative Science: A Critique." *Australian Journal of Public Administration* 47, no. 1 (1990): 4–18.

Criminal Justice Commission. *The Shepherson Inquiry, an Investigation into Electoral Fraud*. Brisbane, Australia: Criminal Justice Commission, 2001.

Department of Education. *Focus on Schools: The Future Organisation of Educational Services in Queensland*. Brisbane, Australia: Department of Education, Queensland, 1990.

———. *Social Justice Strategy 1993–97*. Brisbane, Australia: Department of Education, Queensland, 1993.

———. *Corporate Plan 1994–1998*. Brisbane, Australia: Department of Education, Queensland, 1994.

Hede, A., S. Prasser, and M. Neylan, eds. *Keeping Them Honest: Democratic Reform in Queensland*. Brisbane,Australia: Australia: University of Queensland Press. 1992.

Kell, P., and J. Carr. "Change, Flexibility and Enterprise Bargaining in Queensland." *Education Australia*, no. 28 (1994a): 24.

———. "Industrial Strife in Queensland." *Education Australia*, no. 37 (1994b): 28.

———. "Shaping the Future." *Education Australia*, no. 27 (1994c): 25.

Kell, P., and L. Murphy. "Coming out from Under." *Education Australia* 39 (1998): 1.

La Nauze, J. *Alfred Deakin: A Biography*. Melbourne: University of Melbourne Press, 1965.

Lingard, B., and F. Rizvi. "A Reply to Barcan: Theorising Ambiguities." *Discourse: Studies in the Cultural Politics of Education* 31, no. 1 (1992): 111–23.

McGinty, S., and D. Anderson. "Does the Good Collaborative Review Have a Future?" *Education Australia*, no. 28 (1994): 14–17.

McMullan, R. *The Light on the Hill, the Australian Labor Party 1891–1991*. Oxford: Oxford Press, 1992.

Moore, A. *The Right Road? The History of Right Wing Politics in Australia*. Oxford: Oxford University Press, 1995.

Robertson, S., and H. Smaller. *Teacher Activism in the 1990s*. Toronto: Lorimer and Co., 1996.

Singh, M., P. Kell, and A. Pandian. *Appropriating English: Innovation the English Language Teaching Business*. New York: Peter Lang, 2002.

State of Queensland. *Review of Queensland School Curriculum: Shaping the Future* Vols. 1-4. Brisbane, Australia: Authors, 1994.

Steven, B., and J. Wanna, eds. *The Goss Government: Promise and Performance of Labor in Queensland*. Melbourne: Center for Public-sector Management, Macmillan, 1993.

Wiseman, J. *Global Nation? Australia and the Politics of Globalisation*. Cambridge, UK: Cambridge Press, 1998.

# Chapter 15

# Making Progressive Educational Politics in the Current Globalization Crisis

Suzanne Franzway

## Introduction

"We want a world where inequality based on class, gender and race is absent from every country and from the relationships among countries....We want a world where the massive resources now used in the production of the means of destruction will be diverted to areas where they will help to relieve oppression both inside and outside the home....We want a world where all institutions are open to participatory democratic processes, where women share in determining priorities and making decisions. (Sen and Grown, 1987: 80)

What can education policy actors and practitioners of new pedagogies do in a world where the pressures of political and economic forces have reached a global scale? What are the possibilities for progressive action when capital and the state grasp at the flows of globalization, while communities, individuals, and social institutions flounder in pessimism and passivity?

This is the crisis: the sense that in the face of overwhelming forces of globalization from above, little can be done. Hope and confidence in the potential of progressive pedagogies and social movements have been severely shaken by the successes of the ideological, political, and economic projects of neoliberal globalism. It has shaped the ways nation-states respond to, mediate, and engage with economic, cultural, and political globalization, producing enormous obstacles to any progressive education, community, and workplace politics. The power and purposes of the state, public bureaucracies, governance, citizens, and education have all been subjected to "structural adjustments" that limit and oppress rather than liberate. Progressive social (justice) movements that seek to engage with these changes are themselves suffering from the effects of globalization from above, brought about through continuing attacks by neoliberal states. The possibilities for political activism are thus being challenged and transformed to the extent that a major consequence of the current transitions in globalization and "its discontents" is that progressive and effective collective action appears increasingly difficult or futile.

This is how it appears. But I want to argue that this appearance is part of the problem. Opportunities for progressive political activism may be found; indeed, education policy actors and political movements already engage in creative and effective global/local politics. The point is to recognize, understand, and incorporate these into our analyses and practices. It is also being recognized that sexual politics is integral to this political activism. This is not the time to claim, once again, that sexual politics is "all too hard," an irrelevant distraction (Wichterich, 2000). Rather, feminist theorizing and practices provide useful and inclusive perspectives on political activism in relation to globalization from above. In turn, the pressures of neoliberal globalism are changing the terms of feminism and sexual politics in formal, nonformal, and informal education.

## Globalization from Above

Meanings of "globalization" are many and varied, depending on what elements are emphasized. They include the compression of world space and time, the permeability of state borders, and the accelerated integration of capital through the internationalization of trade, labor, finance, cultures, and communities. Whether a truly global economy currently exists is still being debated, but there is general agreement that processes of economic globalization are intensifying (Castells, 1996). For some commentators the "globalist project" is already under threat with a prolonged economic crisis, the spread of global resistance, the reappearance of the balance of power among center states, and the reemergence of acute interimperialist contradictions (Bello, 2003). For others, globalization is construed as constituted by anonymous forces, which no one controls. It therefore seems untameable and unstoppable. Against these forces, "the local" is posed as the site of everyday experience that produces diverse knowledges and practices of named, known actors who are both the victims and the opponents of globalization from above. Political strategies associated with the local involve development of networks and alliances premised on place-based politics. For feminists, this theoretical and political strategy connects with an analysis that understands the local as feminine and women as suffering from globalizing economies and cultures.

However, the problem with the global/local conceived in this way is that the local is the weaker force. As Gibson-Graham (1996: 145) points out, globalization from above inevitably overwhelms the local; there is no room for any reversal of this process: "Localization, it seems, is not so much 'other' to globalization as contained within it, brought into being by it, indeed part of globalization itself." Rather than accepting a discourse of globalization from above in which capitalism and the multinational corporation are hegemonically represented as superior and ultimately invincible, Gibson-Graham (1996: 147) proposes that alternative discourses might see globalization (from below) as "capable of inscribing a proliferation of differences." Challenges to a monolithic discourse of the globalization from above of an invincible capitalism provide more useful ground for progressive activism than simply the righteous resistance of its victims. This does not deny the damage and discrimination caused by the globalization of invincible capitalism, but it does suggest ways to discover progressive activism.

We might begin this search for new kinds of political (and policy) activism in education, broadly understood, with Claus Offe's (1996: vii) interrelated questions: What political agency has the capacity to make collectively binding choices and to carry them out? I suggest the trade union movement, a traditional institution of political activism, can have just such a capacity. The political possibilities of trade unions are seen as worn out, inadequate to the task of taking on globalized capital. While progressive movements are not free of racist logics that confound their efforts at internationalization, the trade union movement has a history of internationalism and some claims to a practical unity that extends across national boundaries. The trade union movement is therefore useful on two counts. One, it has the capacity, by virtue of its essential characteristics, solidarity and universality, to challenge a key element of the political and cultural economy of globalization, given the effects of globalization on work, particularly women's work; two, trade unions are a potentially important resource for feminist politics, since women have made some gains within the trade union movement.

This chapter proposes that the political and cultural economy of globalization presents both opportunities and obstacles for progressive activism and new pedagogies. While globalization, with its attendant issues and dilemmas, is sometimes represented as responsive only to the new, and to rely on tradition is represented as hopelessly inadequate, making politics requires starting with what we have. What can be done may be discovered through a search for political possibilities, in this instance examining the potential of the trade union movement. This search focuses on political activism that aims at reconfiguring the dominating power of globalization from above into something far more permeable and potentially liberating.

The argument draws on ethnographic relational studies by the author of Australian and Canadian women union officials and activists over the last decade. The women occupy formal positions (either elected or appointed) in labor organizations with coverage of workers across a wide range of industries and occupations, as well as women who work in related nongovernment organizations, such as Working Women's Centers and union training organizations. Australia and Canada are among those countries that have enduring patterns of gendered power relations in common, but the circumstances in each country differ, partly due to the differences between their centralized and decentralized industrial relations systems and partly due to the historical distinctions between their labor movements. Nevertheless, the women are confronted with similar and serious challenges from dominant processes of globalization from above, with increasing attacks by the state that are destabilizing labor markets, eroding the state's commitment to underwriting public socioeconomic security, and recasting the relations between public and private spheres in favor of the latter.

## Gender and Globalization

Processes of globalization from above are affecting gender relations. Global restructuring has increased gender divisions with the feminization of the international workforce and of poverty. Both the World Bank and the International Labor Organization acknowledge that unequal gender relations lead to women making up 70 percent of the world's poor. The construction of women workers, in the international division of labor, as cheap labor, or as Jan Jindy Pettman (1996: 590) puts it, "labor made cheap," is worsening. Poorly paid women workers are gathered together to subsidize the operation of "free" trade zones created in deregulated labor markets; women domestic workers flow from poorer states to wealthier states, while sex workers are caught up in the international sex tourist industry, both within and across nation-states. Traffic in women is a significant aspect of the expanding worldwide migration of labor. Although some men on the bottom rungs of the global economy suffer from these oppressive effects as their labor is exploited or made expendable, and their bodies may be sexually degraded, overwhelmingly the beneficiaries of globalization from above are men on the top rungs of the global economy and in senior positions in corporate and corporatized institutions.

Gender differences cannot be isolated within or from historically specific gender regimes, but gender relations are no longer matters of "local" conditions and cultures. Gender relations now require analysis and a politics of global dimensions. If we define enduring patterns of gender relations as gender orders, then a global gender order is constituted by gender practices that are reshaped by global processes. Such practices may be local but they "carry the impress of forces that make a global society" (Connell, 2002: 111). It's this global/local gender order to which transnational feminist politics and women's movements are both response and expression. Both loose and more formal organizations, such as the Women's Edge Coalition, DAWN (Development Alternatives with Women for a New Era), and the Sisterhood Is Global Institute, build alliances and campaigns within proximal and extended communities and organizations that extend across borders and boundaries.

Such a politics and analysis suggest a complex notion of power that is not limited to hierarchical control. Power may be understood as a productive network, which reaches into every part of the social field and is woven into the fabric of everyday life. Social conflict and resistance therefore cannot be centralized. Political resistance must be heterogeneous as well as specific to the social logic of its particular sociopolitical field, for example, schools and sexuality. Resistance continues to be possible if power is understood as potentially constructive rather than necessarily repressive. This understanding of power conceives of globalization as involving transnational networks and flows of power. These transnational flows may give those on the periphery access to new technological, cultural, and economic resources that are open to adaptation and that connect local groups to transnational networks. Thus power may be located in the production of global/local networks of activists.

Trade unions are overtly hierarchical institutions. Making feminist politics within the trade union movement involves contesting these explicit but nevertheless complex structures of power. Further, as I discuss below, women union activists use networks across and beyond trade unions. Their political strategies take diverse understandings of power into account to create a politics that confronts and resists, challenges and transforms. These likewise incorporate more fluid notions of gender that allow for the heterogeneity and diversity of women's experiences.

## Trade Unions and Borders

The trade union movement claims a history of over a century of international alliances and political activism, and it is this internationalism that now may be a valuable political resource. However, the international labor movement is not only riven with national barriers within states, but unions are also separated by borders of their own creation. A trade union that recruits members from areas outside its traditional coverage is seen as "poaching" and as hostile to other unions. This continues to be the case in countries like Australia in spite of the compression of hundreds of unions into a couple of dozen through amalgamations in the early 1990s—a process that was a calculated response to neoliberal hostility to unionization. In addition, the historically specific divisions created by industries, occupational hierarchies (managers, skilled, unskilled workers), gender, race, public and private sectors, and blue-collar and white-collar differences and boundaries are difficult to bridge, let alone blur. As a result, the potential effectiveness of united groups of unions, such as peak national and international trades and labor councils, can be limited.

One such limitation too often arises from the obstacles created by sexual politics. Vital to trade unions as much as to schools and other social organizations, sexual politics typically works through practices of invisibility (see also Shore in this volume regarding invisibility and whiteness). As with so many fields of politics and research, women are absent from, or insignificant to, the central concerns of the history, culture, politics, and economy of (paid) work, industrial relations, and organizational studies. Judy Wajcman's substantive review of industrial relations shows that attention continues to be limited to a narrow band of "women's issues" (Wajcman, 2000). This is partly because only women are imagined as gendered; gender is detached from men. Since subjects are male, gender is not considered a relevant factor of analysis. Where women are inescapably present, as they are in female-dominated unions, such as teacher unions, "gender" is still regarded by many in these fields as an insufficient analytical tool. This, in turn is connected to the narrow conceptualization of "woman" and "gender," which fails to explain how men achieve and maintain their dominance of union leadership, even where women constitute significant proportions of the membership.

Overall, women make up 40 percent of trade union members in Australia with similar proportions in Canada, but according to surveys carried out during the 1990s, women are underrepresented at almost all levels of union activity, especially at the more powerful levels of full-time and paid secretary and president positions (Mezinec, 1999). Women have gained some leadership positions and made inroads into union agendas and resources. However, these remain quite disproportionate to women's participation rates and, on any measure, inequalities continue. As one woman official in my research observed, "When I go to the national office I look around their walls and their photographs over years and years, and there is not one woman in sight, not one." Difficult to achieve as it may be, feminist politics aims for much more than winning leadership positions for women. It seeks to gain women's rights and social justice comprehensively and in all their necessary diverse manifestations.

In spite of the obstacles, women's workplace and political commitment, activism, and militancy are not insignificant. The minority positions of union women activists together with feminist politics give them strong incentives to work across the state and union borders to make creative alliances. The next section deals with examples of political strategies that seize opportunities in the pedagogic possibilities available in trade unions.

## Making Politics: Activism and Alliances

What is being done depends on the capacity to seize opportunities for progressive political activism, but putting resistance into effect is no simple task. The impact of global/local forces can be daunting. Attention is given to specific cases addressing two kinds of strategies; first, what I call parallel strategies, which are responses in different locations to similar conditions and are based on comparable or shared knowledges and practices; and, second, transnational networks that utilize international mobility, resources, and communications.

## Parallel Strategies

A widely used feminist strategy for change is based on winning hierarchical positions of public power. Targeting the top is, in some senses, an individualist strategy, although creating and winning positions for women depends very much on a viable political movement. It is a risky business for those in such positions since they must negotiate dominant structures of cultural power while championing feminist interests. In trade unions, some formal positions, with their associated resources, have been won, but these victories have come to seem quite tenuous. In Australia, trade union restructuring and union amalgamations took place in the late 1980s as a defense against neoliberal globalism and its assaults on workers' organizations and their industrial conditions. It was surely a consequence that the numbers of formal union positions were markedly reduced with serious impacts on designated "women's" positions and on those that served the needs for industrial training. Jennie George, the first woman president of the Australian Council of Trades Unions (ACTU) was noted as commenting:

> Women were starting to come through the ranks when [union] amalgamations took place, and by the time all the important positions were sorted out, the young women were pushed further back. (quoted in Cooper, 2000: 163)

Canadian trade unions were also forced to respond to these global pressures, including the demands for so-called "free trade," with internal conflicts over strategic priorities consuming union attention. Unlike most trade union movements in the West, the Canadian movement has managed to maintain a high rate of unionization, close to 32 percent in 2002, but the effects on the sexual politics have been similar:

> The boys [male union officials] have really succeeded in retaining their positions inside organized labor...and they're in a position now where they can just trade with each other. [Canadian union official]

Such defeats are disheartening for political and policy activists. They demonstrate very clearly the limits of a politics aimed at getting women into formal, paid, and influential positions. This has led many women union activists, as well as women outside the labor movement, to conclude that intervening in hierarchical structures of power in this way is not sufficient to produce successful progressive politics. Both Canadian and Australian union women are moving to this view:

> I think it's hard for any woman in a difficult position in a male culture. There was a time when we considered that to get a woman in the position would change the culture of the organization. ...we have changed dramatically from getting individuals into positions to trying to look at cultural change. ...I would say we've got to do both. [Australian union official]

Women have therefore looked for ways to change that "male culture." As a consequence of the male dominance of trade unions and power networks, very few union women accrue appropriate experience and knowledge. Such circumstances have suggested that pedagogic projects have political utility and feasibility, a strategy that union women have derived from other social movements as well as from trade union traditions. Or as the ILO declares, "Educate, educate, educate" (International Labour Organization [ILO], 2003, booklet 5: 3; see also Burke, Geronimo, Martin, Thomas, and Wall, 2002). Trade unions have a long history of providing educational programs for their members, while the women's movement has produced its own knowledges and pedagogic methodologies. Although the meaning of "pedagogy" is problematic, it can be a valuable site of challenge and transformation. Women union activists, including those in Canada and Australia, have had some political success with pedagogic projects. They have devised creative and useful "training" initiatives such as the two following examples of parallel strategies. One is an annual summer school held in British Columbia, while the other is a program of training support for union members in Australia, known as the Anna Stewart Memorial Project.

The aims of the Anna Stewart Memorial Project are to increase women's active union involvement and to increase the union movement's acceptance and understanding of women members. The Anna Stewart Project was created in 1984 to honor a well-known and inspirational woman union official and to provide an exemplar and practical experience of support for union women. This was at a time when women's feminist activism in the labor movement and around workplace issues was particularly vibrant. The Working Women's Charter was developed then along with networks, and organizations such as Working Women's Centers were established. However, few women had formal, paid union positions. In 1981, women held only 41 out of a total of 281 full-time positions in 25 ACTU-affiliated unions (Kleimaker, 1999: 6).

The "Anna Stewart," as it is popularly known, is organized by state-based committees of union women. Each year, nominated union women invest two weeks in a union office, not necessarily their own, interspersed with time in workshops and group discussion opportunities. By 1998, almost three-quarters (73 percent) of South Australian unions were participating in the project (Mezinec, 1999: 18). A report of the approximately 400 women who had participated in the Victorian Project until 1999 found that most thought it was inspirational, although some were left feeling "let down" by the problems union officials faced. Others were satisfied that they had discovered "you can make a difference" (Kleimaker, 1999: 24). Many current women officials began their careers with Anna Stewart. It is not particularly innovative as a pedagogic project, but the point is that it is being endorsed by the union movement as a way to meet union women's needs, which in turn are being accepted by the movement as different from men unionists' needs. Peak union bodies of the Trades and Labor Councils and individual unions are being persuaded to fund and support participation by their own members. This requires a significant change in union political discourses and practices.

The British Columbia Summer Institute for Union Women has similar goals and motivation to the Anna Stewart. It was set up as an alternative for women unionists since the residential programs organized by the broader labor movement were often hostile to them. Referring to such programs, one participant reported that "It wasn't a good experience. I just felt kind of dumb." Structured as an intensive summer school, the Institute provides a mix of workshops, panel discussions, and open-ended plenaries for labor educators, and community activists as well as union members. By contrast, the Anna Stewart is available to union members only. I was a participant observer at the Summer Institute in Vancouver in 1998, where I found that many of the several hundred participants traveled long distances to attend and included Aboriginal women, migrant women of color, lesbian workers, and women with disabilities. The approach adopted by the organizers, who were union officials, sought to create union commitment and to celebrate solidarity, as well as to engage in theoretical discussions and political skills development. This program combines influences from university short summer and winter schools, labor education and trade union training, and feminist community self-care workshops.

Similar programs are sponsored by peak union bodies at national and international levels. Others are sponsored by individual unions. The International Labor Organization, the International Congress of Free Trade Unions, and the worldwide trade union organization of education personnel, Education International, endorse, develop, and provide varieties of educational programs aimed at social change for equality. None of these would have occurred without the considerable efforts by women themselves, who came to feel that ways needed to be found to sustain themselves and their activism and to confront what they saw as the hostility of men unionists and the union movement's blindness to women's interests (Franzway, 2001).

These parallel strategies of programs for women unionists/workers have considerable significance for feminist politics and union activism. Their political purposes resemble Freirean pedagogic models that link learning with action through which transformation can and does occur. In Paulo Freire's (1972) view of education, learning to take control and achieving power are not separate or individualistic objectives. Here the aims of education are to strengthen the power and purpose of the many around a common vision and to make real historical and material gains through these particular and collective forms of political and policy interventions.

## Transnational Networks

Feminist politics and the trade union movement have used resources of globalization to create transnational networks of political activism. Women's nongovernment organizations, international conferences, and projects struggle with differences among women while they simultaneously campaign for justice and equality for all women. Transnational networks connect women across areas of concern as well as across national borders. For example, the World March of Women 2000, born out of the experience of a Women's March against Poverty held in Canada in 1996, brought women together from peace organizations, community groups, and trade unions in an explicitly global campaign for peace and equality. The international network created by this action has developed into an international organization, under the same name, which connects with other feminist global networks such as the World Social Forum.

A less visible but equally significant example of progressive political activism by community and education policy actors has developed in response to the alarming rates of homophobic discrimination and prejudice in many workplaces, including schools (Ferfolja, 1998). A recent study of Australian workplace experiences of lesbians, gay men, and transgender people, "The Pink Ceiling is Too Low," reports that over half of the respondents suffered from homophobic behavior or harassment, and eleven percent experienced verbal abuse, including threats of physical and sexual abuse (Irwin, 1999). The report was launched under the auspices of the Australian Council of Trade Unions (ACTU), demonstrating that the trade union movement can become a useful resource for challenging and transforming oppressive practices of sexuality. This might seem unlikely, since trade unions have a well-known reputation for defending patriarchy expressed through their domination by an overwhelmingly masculine heterosexuality. In this sense, the trade union movement is little different from other public organizations in most societies in the ways it contests challenges to patriarchy through widely held repressive meanings of sexuality, including homosexuality and homosexual desire among men.

Nevertheless, inroads into the politics of sexualities in trade union movements have been made through the efforts and impact of transnational gay and lesbian movements, along with feminist activism that connects unionists with advocates for sexual rights. Ostenfeld (1998) argues that the trade union movement has a relatively sound history of responding to the needs of gay and lesbian workers, particularly through the efforts of white-collar and "left"-wing unions, despite the resistance of some "right"-wing union officials. In my research, the Canadian and Australian women officials recognize the political significance of patriarchal expressions through hegemonic sexuality. Together with other activists they pushed peak union councils to develop relevant policies and organize national conferences for gay and lesbian unionists. The Canadian peak union body, the Canadian Labor Council (CLC), held its first national conference for lesbian, gay, and bisexual union activists in 1997, described as "a bit late in the day coming, but it's a major victory" by a Canadian union activist. Groups of lesbian and gay unionists have campaigned on explicit issues such as protection from homophobia in workplaces and in trade unions since the early 1970s in the face of much opposition. In 1980, the May Day parade of the labor movement in Sydney (Australia) had a gay section organized by the Sisters of Perpetual Indulgence, which was not well received by some in union hierarchies. More recently, networks of lesbians and gay men have established support committees such as the Gay and Lesbian Australian Services Union Members, which won the award for best recruitment campaign at the ACTU Congress 2000, with their slogan "Job security never goes out of style." The Canadian Union of Public Employees (CUPE) has a national Pink Triangle Committee that tackles homophobia and challenges the attitudes that isolate and demean people who aren't "straight." Some unions participate in the annual Sydney Gay and Lesbian Mardi Gras in spite of internal conflicts and threats of resignation by union officials and members.

The impact of events like the Sydney Mardi Gras derives from the development of networks, organization, debates, and material support that are necessary for such participation. Provocatively, Fortescue (2000: 64) suggests that Mardi Gras has become "the biggest labor festival of the year." Similarly, the world conferences of lesbian and gay trade unionists grew out of, and extend, global/local networks of gay, lesbian, and transgender workers. The second conference held in Sydney in 2002 was endorsed by the ACTU, along with nine out of the ten global union federations. Its organizers stress the political value of such networks, but also the political necessity of global campaigns to tackle the appalling working conditions of those who "live in countries that still execute their homosexual citizens" (*Workers Online*, 2002: 139). Such transnational networks have the capacity to be effective when they are able to draw on union resources, to create forums and spaces for lesbian, gay, and transsexual workers in and around the trade union movement.

## Possibilities for Political Activism

Globalization from above causes problems for progressive politics because it appears impervious to human agency, and, at some levels, the anonymous forces of the political and global economy are destructive of communities that imagine themselves as tied exclusively to some geographic or political locality.

And yet, opportunities for political interventions are available as differences proliferate and as those on the periphery gain access to new resources from the flows of transnational processes. The trade union movement is a useful example. Under pressure from neoliberal global capital, it has modified its traditional politics to include the needs and interests of the great variety of potential members. The foundational concept of the universal worker—that is, the full-time male industrial worker—has had to change in recognition of the complexities of others. In the same vein, it may be said that feminism has been enlivened by the requirement to include the diversities of global gender relations. In recognizing these shifts and changes, our search discovers that there is no lack of possibilities for progressive action. Such possibilities are exemplified in the constructive strategies that are shaping feminist and union politics in the examples discussed here. They depend critically on perspectives that can identify creative political practices, for discursive adaptations and modifications articulated by political activists.

In the contemporary era of intensified globalization from above, there are not only obstacles to political movements. There are also new options emerging from the interconnections of networks and communities, which can reveal common needs and concerns and produce new forms of alliances. But alliances are always difficult to sustain, particularly when groups are under the pressure of competing interests and demands. It is the case, whether alliances are being forged at local or at transnational levels, that they are always at risk of breaking down over questions of strategy. Painful conflicts may occur over whether to focus on what can be done or on achieving consensus about the value of the principles at stake. One such danger is that sexual politics is modified to make some gains; issues around sexuality may be sanitized in exchange for human rights. Queer organizing gives way to calls for same-sex pension rights. Here is the perennial dilemma for activists: "Focus on what we can organize," as one union woman said, or stay anchored by political principle?

As always, progressive political activism demands mutual respect, recognition, and representation of diverse interests and needs. What is being done is that "progressive politics" is being made within, through, and across contemporary practices of "globalization from above and below."

## Conclusion

This chapter has posed the question: What might workplace educators do in the face of the seemingly overwhelming forces of globalization from above? It argued that these processes of globalization are far from impermeable and present opportunities as well as obstacles for progressive political activism by policy actors. Although it is a traditional institution, and thus not usually regarded as relevant to these times, the trade union movement is identified as having the capacity to challenge a significant effect of globalization from above, namely work, particularly women's work. Feminist politics is central to this argument since gender, understood in terms of gendered power relations, is no longer a matter of local conditions and cultures. Through discussion of two general approaches to making politics based on parallel strategies and transnational networks, the problem of the oppressive impact of neoliberal and neoconservative globalism on the world may be challenged.

## References

Bello, W. *The Crisis of the Globalist Project and the New Economics of George W. Bush, Focus on the Global South* 2003 [cited August 3 2003]. Available from http://www.focusweb.org/index.

Burke, B., J. Geronimo, D. Martin, B. Thomas, and C. Wall. *Education for Changing Unions*. Toronto: Between the Lines, 2002.

Castells, M. *The Rise of the Network Society*. Cambridge, MA: Blackwell, 1996.

Connell, R. *Gender*. Cambridge. MA: Polity Press, 2002.

Cooper, R. "Fighting on the Inside: Jennie George in the Women's Corner." In *Party Girls*, Edited by K. Deverall, R. Huntley, P. Sharpe, and J. Huntley. Sydney: Pluto Press Australia, 2000.

Ferfolja, T. "Australian Lesbian Teachers: A Reflection of Homophobic Harassment of High School Teachers in New South Wales Government Schools." *Gender and Education* 10, no. 4 (1998): 401–15.

Fortescue, R. "Mardi Gras: The Biggest Labour Festival of the Year." *Hecate* 26, no. 2 (2000): 62–65.

Franzway, S. *Sexual Politics and Greedy Institutions: Union Women, Commitments and Conflicts in Public and in Private*. Sydney: Pluto Press Australia, 2001.

Freire, P. *Pedagogy of the Oppressed*. Harmondsworth, UK: Penguin, 1972.

Gibson-Graham, J. *The End of Capitalism (as We Knew It): A Feminist Critique of Political Economy*. Cambridge, MA: Blackwell, 1996.

International Labour Organization (ILO). *Promoting Gender Equality: A Resource Kit for Trade Unions, Booklet 5—Organizing in Diversity* 2003 [cited October 2 2003]. Available from http://www.ilo.org/public/english/employment/gems/eeo/.

Irwin, J. *The Pink Ceiling Is Too Low: Workplace Experiences of Lesbians, Gay Men and Transgender People*. Sydney: Australian Center for Lesbian and Gay Research, 1999.

Kleimaker, E. *Report, Anna Stewart Memorial Project, October 1999 Program*. Melbourne: Victoria Trades Hall Council, 1999.

Mezinec, S. *Gender Representation in Australian Unions 1998,* Research Paper Series No. 11. Adelaide, Australia: Center for Labour Research and the United Trades and Labor Council of South Australia, 1999.

Offe, C. *Modernity and the State: East, West*. Cambridge, UK: Polity Press, 1996.

Ostenfeld, S. "Identity Politics and Trade Unions: The Case of Sexual Minorities in Australia." Paper presented at the Conference of the Association of Industrial Relations Academics of Australia and New Zealand, Waikato, New Zealand, 1998.

Pettman, J. *Worlding Women. A Feminist Internationalist Politics*. Sydney: Allen and Unwin, 1996.

Sen, G., and C. Grown. *Development, Crises, and Alternative Visions*. New York: Monthly Review Press, 1987.

Wajcman, J. "Feminism Facing Industrial Relations in Britain." *British Journal of Industrial Relations* 38, no. 2 (2000): 183–201.

Wichterich, C. *The Globalized Woman. Reports from a Future of Inequality*. Melbourne: Spinifex, 2000.

*Workers Online*. 2002 [cited June 7 2002]. Available from http://www.workers.labor.net.au/ 139/.

# Chapter 16

# Rethinking the Democratic Purposes of Public Schooling in a Globalizing World

Alan Reid

## Introduction

For the first two-thirds of the twentieth century, public schools—that is, fully government provided and supported—were the only schools to receive government funds in many countries throughout the world. Private schools operated solely on private income and were seen largely as an option for the wealthy or for ethno-religious groups like the Irish, Italians, and Polish Catholics. However, since Commonwealth and state governments began funding private schools in the 1960s in Australia, there has been a significant expansion in their number and a concomitant drift of students from public systems. For instance, in 2002, 31 percent of school-age children and young people in Australia attend publicly subsidized private schools and the number is growing steadily.

The movement to private schools was consolidated in Australia after the Liberal/National Party coalition was elected to office in 1996. Building on the previous Labor government, it overtly embraced neoliberal economic and neoconservative cultural ideologies to drive changes in public education. Its central strategy has been to establish a "quasi-market" in education (Whitty, 1997), a central aspect of which is consumer choice and competition within and between public and private schools. This is producing paradigmatic change in public education, one aspect of which is a blurring of the historical division between public and private systems of education (see Apple in this volume for examples in the United States).

Accompanying these policy trends has been a dramatic increase in government funding for private schools (Reid, 1998), consequently rekindling and renewing a bitter debate over "state aid" or public welfare subsidizes to support private interests. This debate, although motivated by contemporary circumstances, has tended to be a rerun of historically established positions that fail to take into account the changing role of education inside a nation-state in a globalizing world. As a result the debate, and its reference points, are eerily redolent of times past and also indicate the long revolution waged by neoliberal and neoconservative interests. If the debate is to progress, there is an urgent need for a renewed consideration of the nature, role, and purposes of public education.

One key aspect of such reconsideration is the connection between public education and the structures and practices of democracy, and it is this aspect that is the focus of this chapter. In particular, I argue that there is a need to move beyond traditional assertions about the "nation-building" role of public education by retheorizing the contribution of public education to democracy in a globalizing world. I will argue that this retheorization demonstrates the dangers of neoliberal education policy and suggests some social democratic policy alternatives. First, though, I turn to an examination of the outcomes, effects, and consequences of the contemporary neoliberal policy regime on the democratic role of public schools.

## Neoliberal Education Policy and the Democratic Purposes of Public Education

Ever since the establishment of mass public schooling systems in the nineteenth century in the various countries throughout the Minority World, there has been an important connection between public schools and democracy. This connection has often been based on constrained views of democracy. The structures, practices, and outcomes of public schooling have not always been "democratic" in the sense that they have been implicated in helping to reproduce an unequal status quo (Miller, 1986). Despite this fact, public schools have been understood in public policy discourse as key sites for the production of the nation-state and its citizens. Over the course of the past two centuries much of the contestation about the structure and form of public schools has been focused on how this production might occur.

Public schools have multiple purposes, including, for example, being an avenue for social mobility for working-class children. They also have other important public purposes, being spaces that play an important role in constructing some of the key characteristics needed for living together in diverse communities. That is, from the nineteenth century onwards public schools have been seen as doing more than only enhancing the life opportunities of their students. They have public purposes, and in this sense they are a public good. By contrast, private schools have primary allegiances to particular religious, cultural, or ethnic groups rather than to the public as a whole; for some this may be because of their cultural marginalization, while others seek to reproduce their power and privilege.

Despite the persistence of unequal educational outcomes (Teese, 2000; 2003), the idea of *public* schools is as places where young people from a range of varied backgrounds and experiences can mix. Here they learn to appreciate and respect difference, and such learning is fundamental to democracy. In the absence of other public spaces where this social learning can occur systematically, the challenge is to pursue public policies that work toward achieving this ideal in practice, not to abandon the ideal because it has not yet been fully realized. And yet the opposite is occurring as the concept of public education as a public good is being rapidly eroded by the contemporary neoliberal policies committed to privileging the personal rather than collective benefits of education.

Policies of choice encourage differentiation, and invariably this differentiation is organized around socioeconomic status, ethnicity, religion, and race (Thomson, 2001; Whitty, Power, and Halpin, 1997). These divisions have social and material effects that are damaging public schools. Examples of the goals and outcomes of neoliberal policies for restructuring and destructuring public education include:

- public education becoming a "residualized" system for those who can't afford private schooling, with a consequent loss of diversity of student population.
- the public education system itself becoming more stratified and individualized as individual schools fight for a share of the education market.
- the curriculum becoming more differentiated and hierarchical as schools seek to identify market niches.

- a significant growth in disparity of resources between schools.

Connors (2000: 72) argues that neoliberal policies are "demutualizing" schooling. By this she means the loss of that sense of reciprocity, altruism, and "love of strangers" that characterizes an education system governed by a commitment to the common good. In a commodified education system organized around the concept of consumerism, the dominant ethos is that of individual self-interest. As Cuban and Shipps (2000: 7) argue, "when individual purposes trump public purposes, when private interest overcomes public interest, both children and adults in a democracy lose."

Here then is a fundamental issue now facing many societies around the globe. Neoliberal educational policy responses to and expressions of neoliberal (and neoconservative) globalism are threatening the contribution public schools can make to the sense of community, mutuality, and reciprocity that has been so important to building and sustaining democratic societies. Is this an inevitable product of neoliberal globalism? Is pursuing public education as a public good still a worthwhile goal, or is it simply a modernist throwback irrelevant to changing circumstances? These questions can be answered by retheorizing the connection between public schools and democracy, a task that can begin with a review of the changes to democracy in a globalizing world (see Apple, this volume).

## Globalization and Democracy

The contemporary social world is a complex mix of local/global restructurings and destructurings born of structural adjustment schemes. Technological changes, the interruption of the taken-for-granted time-space connections created for the industrial era, and the rapid growth of the global market economy coexist with the reemergence of regressive parochialism such as chauvinistic ethno-nationalism, manifest most clearly in White Nation politics. Falk (1999) describes as "new" the political contest between the neoliberal political economy of market-driven "globalization from above," and "globalization from below" that arises with grassroots social (justice) movements created by feminists, environmentalists, and human rights advocates pushing the agenda required to nurture and sustain a global civic society and its mechanisms of democratic government. Not surprisingly, the complexity of these disruptions is exerting pressure on many of the institutional structures, practices, and conceptualizations of nation-states, including those of citizenship and democracy. In this chapter, I focus on the political economy of "globalization from above." I describe the government responses to and their efforts to give expression to "market-driven" globalization and examine the effects of these on the structures, practices, and conceptualization of democracy. I commence this analysis by identifying the challenges to democracy posed by three contemporary aspects of economic globalization.

## Shifts in the Relations Between Nation and State

The first disruption relates to shifts in the relations between nation and state, between citizens and government, as a result of, and as a manifestation of, contemporary transitions in the historical, ideological, and localizing practices of globalization. The claims about the death of the nation-state may have been exaggerated, as most national governments in the Minority World still have a degree of economic policy-making discretion, although it is constrained (Held, 1999). To enable transnational companies to expand and create international mesh-works of coordinated production, nation-states have been invited to or coerced into opening—or have willfully opened—their financial borders. The inciting of fear about "capital flight" has been used to limit the autonomy of national governments that now must attend to the needs of this unelected and unrepresentative economic power.

International governance, in various forms and guises, also influences the conduct of nations in a range of ways through a patchwork of treaties and conventions. Increasingly, governmental decisions are being made by international bodies such as the World Bank and the International Monetary Fund, as well as various United Nations—sponsored organizations (e.g., Food and Agricultural Organization), regional institutions (e.g., the European Union, Asia-Pacific Economic Cooperation, and North American Free Trade Association), and Minority World organizations (e.g., the Organization for Economic Cooperation and Development). These developments in international governance mean that many decisions affecting nation-states and their citizens are being made beyond the control of electors. While elected representatives are ambivalently positioned in terms of whose interests they now serve, it is parliamentarians who continue to vote to put into effect locally a selection of these international initiatives.

Held (1999) argues that the present foundations of the international political order constituted around nation-states are increasingly limited as a basis for dealing with the world's political, economic, and social problems. The political decisions affecting citizens' lives, work, and education that are made in the international arena do not necessarily emanate from public discussion and civic debate, although they often evoke such debates. Governmental decision making has now been captured by and reflects the interests of the world's powerful elites, who are not directly accountable for these decisions, and yet they have real effects on people's everyday lives. What does this mean for Australian democracy? Kerr (2001: 118) maintains that, when "real power has shifted from the local and national level to the international sphere, then the attention of those who value democracy must also shift to that arena." Working to democratize the international sphere has become a matter of urgency.

## Decline of the Public Sphere

Another related disruption created by the nation-state's mediation and mitigation of neoliberal economic globalization is the decline in the role of the public sphere. Hand-in-hand with promulgating the ideology of neoliberal globalism and the politics of the unfettered market, many nation-states have been busy winding back the mechanisms that were designed to ensure people's social and economic security in the face of a dangerous and endangered world, in particular to protect people against the risks and whims of markets. The regressive dismantling of the state's mechanism for underwriting its citizens' socioeconomic security has been advanced in language dealing with costs and efficiencies, on the grounds of these being obstacles to the growth of private capital. Public money is now deployed to provide for the welfare of transnational businesses. This neoliberal policy trajectory has weakened the foundation of social protection by individualizing notions of success and failure as well as undermining the spirit of cooperation and practices of collective social support.

By representing the state's mechanism for underwriting its citizens' socioeconomic security as a threat and an impediment to private entrepreneurial interests, the advocates of neoliberal globalism have been able to advocate the sale of the common wealth (as represented in public agencies) to the private sector. "Privatization" became the catch cry late last century, as community infrastructure, social welfare, and education were destructured so that they could be sold to the private sector. The public-sector has been regressively constructed as a safety net for those who cannot look after themselves and must rely on the state for sustenance.

To legitimize private-sector activities in this way, public-sector programs and institutions have been constructed as less worthy, not least because they do not generate financial profits for shareholders. More than this, civil society has become saturated with commercialism: It is difficult to escape the ubiquitous presence of corporate sponsorship in many areas of community activity. Many societies are fast becoming a "paradise divided" (Kelly, 2000), with an affluent section of the population being privileged to take advantage of opportunities offered by the market and consuming hard (see Nixon, this volume), while another larger section of the world's population is condemned to the margins, picking up begrudgingly provided welfare support and being blamed for the many social ills that have been spawned by the government structuring of these very inequalities.

What are the effects of these disruptions on democracy? Perhaps the most telling effect is the way in which societies in the Minority World are becoming more individualistic. They are turning away from the concept and practice of collectively provided and owned community facilities and infrastructures that exist for the benefit of all. The ideology of neoliberal globalism and its politics of individualism diminish the public spaces where people can meet to share common dreams and hopes, to understand and respect differences, and to look out for the interests of others. Commenting on the postsecurity, postdemocratic state, Kerr (2001: 78–79) argues:

> If the public domain shrinks to nothing, the idea of commonality disappears with it. Without any shared public domain, there is no area of life in which all citizens meet and interact as equals....[A] cowed and residual public sphere is not able to fulfil its traditional role in a democratic society as a unifying force of common ownership, common interests and common good....The reduction of the public sphere to a residual role inherently creates an excluded underclass—an echo of Disraeli's "Two Nations." The minimalist post-welfare state is thus in deadly danger of also becoming a post-democratic state.

Clearly there is a need to reclaim the public sphere. Places are needed where people can share and understand differences and where they can demonstrate a collective concern for all members of the global/local society. Without such places, nation-states are in danger of becoming societies of isolated individuals exclusively concerned about the self, with people being marked off by differences in power relations rather than enriched through community advancement. A search for ways to promote commonality and cohesion is an urgent priority. Strategies are being developed that allow these goals to be achieved across, as well as within, national boundaries.

## The Growth of New (Counter)Publics

Another disruption that has significant consequences for democracy is the fragmentation of what remains of the spaces for public discussion. The explosion in the number of commercial media that target niche audiences (the Internet, multiple pay TV channels) suggests that it is no longer possible to talk of or use this media in forming a single national public. These voices, talking past one another, are hardly conducive to the sort of consensus on which civic and political life should be based. This fragmentation divides rather than unites. Rather, there are many publics, some intersecting, some overlapping, some self-contained. What does this mean for democracy?

Catherine Lumby (1999) argues that the existence of fragmented interests and audiences is evidence of democracy at work. The diversity of voices that can be identified by race, ethnicity, gender, sexuality, and allegiance to various political groups can be seen as giving life to democracy. The public explorations of the difficulties of living with difference stands at the heart of a healthy democracy. Nancy Fraser (cited in Lumby, 1999: 246) describes these community groups as "counter publics" that have a dual character: "On the one hand, they function as spaces of withdrawal and re-groupment; on the other hand, they also function as bases and training grounds for agitational activities directed towards wider publics."

The insistence on "consensus" too often runs the danger of imposing the views and identities of society's dominating groups. But to spurn consensus as merely a weapon of conformity is not to totally reject the idea and practice of negotiating (and renegotiating) a common ground, preserving a common wealth. A community needs to share some common ground where individuals and groups can talk to one another. This is not incompatible with diversity; rather, it is central to it. Regressive parochialism is not a healthy or productive stance in today's world; being inward-looking and being restricted to a single perspective on the world are serious concerns. The isolation of international decision-making elites breeds suspicion and conflict. Democratic societies need forums for thinking about and negotiating differences, not with a view to reaching agreement but with a commitment to recognizing that there are ways other than our own to view the world. As Kalantzis (2001: 13) puts it, negotiating the difficulties of living with diversity in global/local societies through promoting inter-ethnic dialogues is a new way forward for nation-building:

Negotiating diversity is now the only way to produce social cohesion. Pluralistic citizenship is the most effective way of holding things together; and an outward looking internationalist approach to the world is now the only way to maintain the national interest. This requires a paradoxical new universal in which negotiating differences becomes the national essence. And the state needs to assume a dual task: to develop community whilst securing diversity; and to create pathways for all while respecting differences. This… is something that needs to be imagined as a possibility, an ideal for which we can strive.

## Responding to the Challenges of Rethinking Democracy

For those committed to a social democratic project in a globalizing world, the three disruptions described above suggest the need to rethink the democratic structures of nation-states. Those working to find new ways forward are seeking to:

- increase citizen involvement in decision making at the global level as well as at the level of the nation-state, by working to establish structures and processes that advance the democratic project
- reclaim the public sphere by advocating notions of mutuality and community above those of selfish individual interest
- establish processes of negotiating ecological and multicultural diversity within a commitment to cohesion in our civic and political life

How can these ends be achieved at a time when the neoliberal expressions of and responses by governments to economic globalization are moving us in the opposite direction? First, alternative policy responses to globalization need to be developed. Neoliberalism and the constrained view of democracy it sustains are not "inevitable" in a globalizing world. There are social democratic alternatives to the dominant paradigm of market democracy that privileges the self-regarding individual, fee-paying consumer. These alternatives emerge from a paradigm that is based on social justice and the collective public good in association with a commitment to multicultural and ecological diversity. Kymlicka (1998) describes this as a "cosmopolitan moral democracy." Those arguing for a social democratic agenda of this kind have tended to congregate around two major camps: a cosmopolitan-globalist view of citizenship and democracy, and a liberal communitarian argument based on the nation-state as the foundation of citizenship and democracy (Orchard, 2001). These views of democracy have been treated as though they were dichotomous.

In many respects, however, they are complementary, and constructing them as such provides new ways to consider the relationship between democracy and public education.

The cosmopolitan-globalist view of democracy (Nussbaum, 1996; Held, 1999) has a commitment to a universal moral outlook based on respect for universal human rights and obligations. While nation-states continue to be important, in an increasingly integrated world, the challenge is to create institutions and processes at the global level, in ways that are consistent with this moral framework and that will deal with those ecological, economic, and social problems that cross national boundaries.

In contrast, the liberal-communitarian view of democracy and the nation-state starts from the premise that human interests, far from being universal, are defined locally, historically, and contextually. While there is recognition that a cosmopolitan outlook is important in thinking through the many social, economic, and environmental issues that cross national boundaries and in resisting regressive parochialism, communitarians believe that these issues are best confronted in the context of a strong sense of belonging, tradition, institutional coherence, and citizenship. Thus nation-states must extend and deepen their democratic processes, tending to the identities, interests, and needs of their citizens while seeking to participate with other states in addressing global issues. Kymlicka (cited in Orchard, 2001: 277) calls this a "democracy of states" rather than of individuals, an "international" rather than "cosmopolitan" democracy.

It is not inconsistent to argue for a progressive nationalism and a progressive cosmopolitanism at the same time. The two orientations can be complementary, supporting progressive aims from the bottom up as well as from the top down. It is possible to have a "positive nationalism" that eschews myopic localism and is based on deep knowledge and respect of cultural differences. It is possible that they work in harmony with the structures and processes that look beyond the borders of nation-states to address global issues. To this point on *cosmopolitan nationalism* Orchard (2001: 267) argues that:

> an adequate response to the problems we face will require the building and renewal of democratic political institutions at all levels—global, national, local. The new global capitalism tears the social, environmental, cultural and political fabric alarmingly. Responding to worsening inequality, continuing environmental degradation, and growing political and social disengagement will require both the renewal of social democratic "nation-building" government and the building of new democratic capacity at the global, international level.

It is clear that if we want to build from the classical democratic tradition, there is much work to be done on democratic structures and practices in the context of a globalizing world. Public schools are still key institutions in developing these capacities. So, I now return to the question of the connection between public education and Australian democracy.

## Retheorizing the Democratic Role of Public Education: Forming the Cosmopolitan Nation-State

The scale and urgency of the challenges to democracy point to an enlarged role for public schools in a globalizing world. Public schools represent the only spaces in our society where young people from a wide range of cultures, experiences, and backgrounds can learn with and from one another on a systematic basis, developing the understanding, respect, and tolerance that is the lifeblood of a cosmopolitan democracy. If it was important in the twentieth century for public schools to produce "national publics," it is even more so in the twenty-first century to contribute to the formation of cosmopolitan citizens in each nation-state. In this sense, education in public schools should not be constructed primarily as a private and positional good. The importance of public education to the development of democratic national/global communities means that it also has important public purposes. Contemporary neoliberal policies driving education narrowly focus on the individual economic benefits of education and force public schools to compete in quasi-education markets. The privileging of private education is promoting the development of stand-alone schools with homogenous student communities, serving the needs of particular subgroups based on class, wealth, ethnicity, culture, or religion.

Education policy actors continue to struggle to assert and to reassert the specific contribution that public schools can make to our democratic life. But as I have pointed out, the changes to democracy and the challenges to it in a globalizing world suggest that the relationship between education and democracy that existed in the past cannot be assumed in the twenty-first century. There is no point in returning to twentieth-century concepts of public education that have little practical or theoretical purchase in contemporary times. A new discourse for public education is needed, one that moves beyond the language of "nation building" by addressing the connections between public education and the changing role of the nation-state in a globalizing world. In short, a pressing task for education policy actors is to retheorize the role of public schools in building and sustaining a cosmopolitan moral democracy and a cosmopolitan nation. How might this occur? In the remainder of the chapter, I draw on my earlier analysis to make a number of suggestions. These are organized around possible processes and strategies for the work of education policy actors.

## Processes

Given that public education is central to the construction of a cosmopolitan moral democracy, the processes of educational policy making must be consistent with the values on which this model of democracy is based. This means that the public/private debate must go beyond its emphasis on the technical detail, such as funding formulae, and locate this debate within a broader framework. Carr and Hartnett (1996) provide a lead here by arguing that education policy actions can be usefully informed by a democratic theory of education. Such a theory would not describe a fixed image of the kind of education that would produce a "good society" but rather would describe the ways in which education can enable all future citizens "to participate in the process of contestation through which their society—including its system of education—is reproduced and transformed" (Carr and Hartnett, 1996: 187). There are some important implications of this view; I will deal with two of them.

First, if a democratic theory of education assumes deep democratic engagement as a characteristic of a democratic society, it follows that education policy actors might pursue a vision that could reasonably advance that aim and itself be developed democratically. This requires attention to the way that policy is constructed to ensure that all voices are heard, especially those that have traditionally been excluded from educational policy making.

Second, proponents of public education can enable consistency in the discourses used to defend and justify it by drawing on contemporary theorizations of the democratic, cosmopolitan nation-state in a globalizing world. This means reconsidering some of the iconic concepts of public education, such as "nation building" and "public good." Thus, while the "nation-building" role of public education is still an important concept, the term elides the contribution of public education to the building of global democratic, cosmopolitan perspectives. Established understandings of the "public good" are being problematized in the light of the importance of diversity to a cosmopolitan moral democracy. There is a danger that the concept of the "public good" can function as a totalizing and normalizing construct where the "community" is understood as a unified whole that speaks with one consensual voice and represents one set of interests, and where all conduct is judged against some predetermined standard (Carlson, 1996). A new discourse is needed for public education for contemporary times.

## Strategies

The analysis of the role of public education in promoting and sustaining a cosmopolitan moral democracy in a globalizing world suggests a number of possible ways to move the public/private debate beyond its current impasse. One of these might be to redefine the concept of public education from one based on administrative definitions to one based on a set of publicly agreed principles for (public) education. These principles would be the foundation of all public education systems and would form benchmarks for the funding of private schools. That is, instead of all private schools receiving government funds automatically, with only minimal accountability in terms of a commitment to building democracy, funding would be dependent on operating in ways that are consistent with the following sorts of public principles:

- *That the school offers a curriculum that develops a number of publicly agreed capabilities.* These capabilities would include developing the understandings, skills, and dispositions needed to become informed and active citizens of a cosmopolitan nation-state and a global/local community: transnational citizens who can "perform the state" (Albrow, 1997), creating practices required for the successful functioning of a cosmopolitan moral democracy in a globalizing world. This would go well beyond what has been needed to participate in national politics. If citizens are genuinely to engage in such an agenda, they will need a range of political and social capacities, not the least of which are *deep cosmopolitan understandings*, skills of critical thinking, a commitment to the collective good and to social justice, and well-developed political skills.
- *That the pedagogies, structures, and processes of the school reflect and give expression to democratic principles.* This principle would involve demonstrating that the school is itself a model of democratic practices, through its organization, work, and language. That is, the school would need to demonstrate that it is always in the proc-

ess of becoming a community characterized by systematic democratic enquiry and democratic curriculum. Once again, this requirement would extend and deepen the capabilities for being an informed and active citizen in/for a nation-state with a cosmopolitan democracy.

- *That the school operates in ways that value diversity through building community.* This principle might include requirements to demonstrate that school structures and strategies are in place to promote inclusiveness, so that students are not cosseted in homogenous communities but are exposed to young people from a range of cultures and backgrounds. It would eschew assimilationist notions of diversity in favor of negotiating diversity while developing a sense of shared community. This might mean making formal and substantial connections beyond the school with a breadth of local, national, and international communities and their knowledges.
- *That no student is excluded from participating in the life of the school for reasons of difference.* This principle focusing on nondiscrimination would ensure that no school could receive government monies if it refused to accept students on the basis of some predetermined norm.

Tying funding to a set of public principles in this way could mean that public monies are spent to advance a publicly and democratically agreed educational agenda for a globalizing world. Private schools that did not meet these public requirements would not receive public monies. There would need to be agreed public processes for developing these principles and for subjecting them to ongoing critical review. Beyond these principles there might be funding differentials for particular private schools, based on wealth and resources and using public education as the benchmark for funding.

But the point is that discussion about funding formulae would not take place in a values vacuum. Such an approach would serve to shift the public/private debate from one based on past traditions and technical detail to one that encourages community debate about changing democracy and the role of fully funded public education, and publicly subsidized private education, in meeting the new challenges.

## Conclusion

I have argued that there is a crucial role for public education in contributing to the development of a cosmopolitan moral democracy in a globalizing world. This is not a pipe dream. The struggle for democratic education is a continuing project that is being attacked currently by a neoliberal market-based agenda. However, there is a deeply ingrained commitment to democracy and to the democratic role of public education in many communities worldwide. This commitment may be drawn upon to advance a rejuvenated democratic agenda. But given the contemporary globalizing context, this project cannot assume an unchanging role for public education. In particular there should be a rethinking of established understandings about the relationship between public education and democracy. The challenge is to shift the focus of education policy from the individual right of (some) individuals to choose between schools to the collective responsibility of society to develop the sorts of citizens who can play an informed, active, and committed role in a cosmopolitan moral democracy. Such a shift will reaffirm public schools as institutions that lie at the heart of democracy in a globalizing world.

## References

Albrow, M. *The Global Age: State and Society beyond Modernity*. Stanford: Stanford University Press, 1997.

Apple, M. *Official Knowledge*. New York: Routledge, 2000.

———. *The State and the Politics of Knowledge*. New York: Routledge, 2003.

Carlson, D. "Economic Metaphors and the Remaking of Public Education." *Review of Education/Pedagogy/Cultural Studies* 18, no. 1 (1996): 39–49.

Carr, W., and A. Hartnett. *Education and the Struggle for Democracy*. Buckingham, UK: Open University Press, 1996.

Connors, L. "Schools in Australia: A Hard Act to Follow'." In *School Resourcing: Models and Practices in Changing Times*, edited by P. Karmel. Canberra, Australia: Australian College of Education, 2000.

Cuban, L., and D. Shipps, eds. *Reconstructing the Common Good in Education. Coping with Intractable American Dilemmas*. Stanford: Stanford University Press., 2000.

Dahl, R. "Can International Organisations Be Democratic? A Skeptics View." In *Democracy's Edges*, edited by I. Shapiro and C. Hacker-Gordon, 19–36. Cambridge, UK: Cambridge University Press, 1999.

Falk, R. *Predatory Globalization: A Critique*. Cambridge, UK: Polity Press, 1999.

Held, D. "The Transformation of Political Community: Rethinking Democracy in the Context of Globalisation." In *Democracy's Edges*, edited by I. Shapiro and C. Hacker-Gordon, 84–111. Cambridge, UK: Cambridge University Press, 1999.

Kalantzis, M. "Recognising Diversity. The Barton Lectures Part 3." In *Sunday Special. Radio National*. Melbourne, Australia: Australian Broadcasting Commission, 2001.

Kelly, P. *Paradise Divided*. St. Leonards NSW: Allen and Unwin, 2000.

Kerr, D. *Elect the Ambassador: Building Democracy in a Globalised World*. Annandale, Australia: Pluto Press, 2001.

Kymlicka, W. *Finding Our Way: Rethinking Ethnocultural Relations in Canada*. Toronto: Oxford University Press, 1998.

Lumby, C. *Gotcha: Life in a Tabloid World*. St. Leonards Australia: Allen and Unwin, 1999.

Miller, P. *Long Division: State Schooling in South Australian Society*. Netley, Australia: Wakefield Press, 1986.

Nussbaum, M. "Patriotism and Cosmopolitanism." In *For Love of Country; Debating the Limits of Patriotism*, edited by J. Cohen, 2–17. Boston: Beacon Press, 1996.

Orchard, l. "It Never Has Been Easy: Democacy." In *Globalisation: Australian Impacts*, edited by C. Sheil. Sydney, Australia: University of New South Wales Press, 2001.

Reid, A., ed. *Going Public: Education Policy and Public Education in Australia*. Canberra, Australia: Australian Curriculum Studies Association and the Center for the Study of Public Education, 1998.

Teese, R. *Academic Success and Social Power: Examinations and Inequality*. Melbourne: Melbourne University Press, 2000.

———. *Undemocratic Schooling: Equity and Quality in Mass Secondary Education in Australia*. Melbourne: Melbourne University Press, 2003.

Thomson, P. "The Sound of One Hand Grasping at Straws? The Struggle for Equity and Quality in Public Education." In *Left Directions: Is There a Third Way on Australian Politics?*, edited by C. Bacchi and P. Nursey-Bray. Perth, Australia: University of Western Australia Press, 2001.

Whitty, G. "Creating Quasi-Markets in Education: A Review of Recent Research on Parental Choice and School Autonomy in Three Countries." *Review of Research in Education,* (1997): 3–47.

Whitty, G., S. Power, and D. Halpin. *Devolution and Choice in Education: The School, the State and the Market*. Buckingham, UK: Open University Press, 1997.

# Contributors

**Michael W. Apple** is the John Bascom Professor of Curriculum and Instruction and Educational Policy Studies at the University of Wisconsin, Madison. He has written extensively on the relationship among culture, power, and education. Among his recent books are *Educating the "Right" Way: Markets, Standards, God, and Inequality* (Routledge, 2001) and *The State and the Politics of Knowledge* (Routledge, 2003). C/o: University of Wisconsin, Curriculum and Instruction, 225 North Mills Street, Madison, WI 53706, USA. E-mail: apple@education.wisc.edu; Phone: 608 263 4592, Fax: 608 263 9992.

**Lynton Brown** has been an ethnographer, educational program evaluator, self-evaluation facilitator, policy analyst, research center manager, and university lecturer. After teaching in Victorian technical schools in the seventies, heworked in curriculum research and development before joining a Deakin University research team evaluating government programs of reform. He went on to work as an in-house evaluator and became responsible for co-ordinating a process of organizational learning, linking, action-research, publication, and professional development in the Commonwealth's Participation and Equity Program (PEP). He subsequently published "Group Self-Evaluation," a manual for practitioner-conducted evaluation and was appointed as a senior policy analyst in the School Councils and Participation Unit of the Victorian Ministry of Education. In 1992, Lynton was appointed manager of the Monash Center for Research in International Education. He is now a lecturer at RMIT in the International Studies Program with interests including action research and learning communities, the social consequences of technology, and media and the cultural processes associated with globalization.

**Elizabeth Bullen** is a research associate in the Center for Studies in Literacy, Policy, and Learning Cultures, University of South Australia. She was awarded her PhD in Australian Literature by Flinders University, South Australia. She has published on various aspects of popular culture, gender, and education. *Consuming Children: Education–Entertainment–Advertising* (Open University Press, 2001) with Jane Kenway is one such publication. She is a co-editor of *Innovation and Tradition: The Arts, Humanities and the Knowledge Economy* (Peter Lang, 2004).

**Suzanne Franzway** is associate professor in gender studies and sociology at the University of South Australia, and she is director of the Research Center for Gender Studies. Her research interests include labor movements, sexual politics and activism, workplace cultures, caring labor in aged care and childcare, and casualization in universities. She recently published *Sexual Politics and Greedy Institutions: Union Women, Commitment and Conflict in Public and in Private* (Pluto Press Australia, 2001). C/o: University of South Australia, Magill Campus, St Bernards Road, Magill SA 5072. E-mail: Suzanne.Franzway@unisa.edu.au; Phone: 61 8 83024626; Fax: 61 8 8302 4393.

**Sue Grieshaber** is an associate professor in the School of Early Childhood, Queensland University of Technology, Brisbane, Australia. Her research interests include early childhood curriculum and policy, technologies and early childhood curriculum, families, and gender. She has recently published *Rethinking Parent and Child Conflict* (RoutledgeFalmer, 2004) and *Embracing Identities in Early Childhood Education: Diversity and Possibilities* (New York: Teachers College Press, 2001) with Cannella. Contact Information: c/o: School of Early Childhood, Kelvin Grove Campus, Queensland University of Technology, Victoria Park Road, Kelvin Grove Queensland, Australia. 4059; E-mail: s.grieshaber@qut.edu.au; Phone 61 7 3864 3176; Fax 61 7 3864 3989.

**Peter Kell** is associate professor of adult and further education at the University of Wollongong. He was previously associate dean (research) in the Faculty of Education Language and Community Services and head of Department of Industry, Professional and Adult Education and associate at RMIT University. From 1993 to 1997, Peter Kell worked at James Cook University in North Queensland and was state reporter for Education Australia, where he observed and reported the events described in this chapter.

**Jane Kenway** is professor of education at Monash University, Australia. Prior to this she was at the University of South Australia as dean of research in the Division of Arts, Education, and Social Sciences. Her research expertise is in educational policy sociology with reference to education systems in the context of the wider social and cultural changes associated with globalization. Her latest co-written book is *Consuming Children: Education—Advertising—Entertainment*(Open University

Press). She is currently working on two new co-written books *Masculinity beyond the Metropolis* and *Haunting the Knowledge Economy.*

**Gayle Morris** is a lecturer at the University of Melbourne, having worked in adult, industry, and professional education, she is currently researching the relationships between identity and language learning.

**Helen Nixon** is senior lecturer in the School of Education at the University of South Australia and a key researcher in the Center for Studies in Literacy, Policy, and Learning Cultures. Her research interests include multiliteracies in the new media age, children and adolescents and popular media cultures, and English/literacy education and ICTs. C/o: University of South Australia, Underdale Campus, Holbrooks Rd, Underdale. South Australia. 5032. E-mail: helen.nixon@unisa.edu.au; Phone: 618 8302 6592; Fax: 618 8302 6315.

**Scott K. Phillips** is associate professor (Youth Affairs) at RMIT University, Melbourne, Australia. He has extensive experience in social policy development (having worked in the Australian Public Service for twelve years in the areas of youth affairs, international development, multiculturalism, and education and training). In the Office of Multicultural Affairs in the Department of the Prime Minister and Cabinet, he was director of the Access, Equity, and Legal Section and played a leading role in developing the government's *Charter of Public Service in a Culturally Diverse Society.* His research interests cover public policy, with special interest in new forms of participatory governance; inter-religious relations post S 11; and cultural diversity and multiculturalism.

He has undertaken consultancies for the Victorian and New South Wales Departments of Education (1999 and 2002, respectively) to research and develop multicultural drug education programs, the Victorian Office of Youth Affairs (2000) to research and draft a youth strategy for the Victorian government; RMIT University (2001) to research values associated with volunteering in community sport; and the Timber Towns Victoria Group within the Municipal Association of Victoria (2003) to produce a socioeconomic impact assessment of the bushfires in northeast Victoria.

**Helen Raduntz** is an adjunct research fellow with the Center for Research in Education, Equity, and Work and the School of Education within the University of South Australia. Her career has spanned working in industry and secondary education, education union activism, and academic teaching and research. She has published several journal articles, edited a book of critical essays on issues in Australian Catholic schooling, and researched and devised a study guide on issues and methods of social research for the University of South Australia's Aboriginal Studies master's degree program. Currently, she is a member of the Editorial Advisory Board of *Journal for Critical Education Policy Studies* published in the UK. Her research interests center on the dynamics of the relationship among educators' work, the marketization of education, and the globalzsing capitalist market economy, on the implications of intellectual property ownership for freedom of inquiry and public access to information, and on the development of a dialectical critique drawing on the Hegelian-Marxian classical tradition specifically for the study of these issues. C/o: Email: Helen.Raduntz@unisa.edu.au.

**Alan Reid** is professor of education at the University of South Australia. In 2004 he has been seconded from the University into the South Australia Department of Education and Childrens' Services to lead the development of a culture of inquiry and research across the public education system and to review the senior secondary provision in South Australia. He was the 2002–3 Department of Education, Science and Training (DEST) national research fellow based in Canberra. Prior to that he was dean of education at the University of South Australia. Professor Reid's research interests include educational policy, the history and politics of public education, and curriculum change and he has published widely in these areas. C/o Underdale Campus, University of South Australia, Holbrooks Road, Underdale, S.A. 5034. E-mail: alan.reid@unisa.edu.au; Phone: 616 83026431.

**Sue Shore** works at the University South Australia and is a key researcher in the Center for Studies in Literacy, Policy and Learning Cultures. She has edited special editions of journals focusing on feminism and women in adult education and recently completed a six year funded term of sponsored research in Australian adult literacy and numeracy in collaboration with a consortium of six Australian universities. Her research expertise includes mapping the effects of whiteness in educational theory building and devising a number of pilot projects to explore these effects in settings such as educational management, research degree training, higher education pedagogy, and policy making. She recently co-edited *Adult Education @ 21st Century* (Peter Lang) with Peter Kell and Michael Singh. C/o: sue.shore@unisa.edu.au

**Michael Singh** is professor of education at the School of Education and Early Childhood Studies, University of Western Sydney and convenor of *Green Wired Safe Australia*, an educational research, leadership and policy action forum. Singh was responsible for conceptualizing, designing, and initiating a bachelor's degree in International Studies and founding Director of the Globalism Institute at RMIT Unviersity. His current research focuses on urban development, employment, and education; schools and youth crime prevention; a relational study of educational reform in Australia and China; knowledge producing pedagogies and new technologies; international student mobility and curriculum innovation; and the motivation and engagement of boys in achieving successful academic outcomes. He is the author of *Appropriating English: Innovations in the Global Business of English Language Teaching* (Peter Lang) with Peter Kell and Amby Pandian, and editor of *Adult Education@21$^{st}$ Century* (Peter Lang) with Peter Kell and Sue Shore

**Pat Thomson** is professor in education at the University of Nottingham (UK) and an adjunct professor in the Center for Studies in Literacy, Policy, and Learning Cultures at the University of South Australia. Her current research focusses on family interactions with schools; pedagogies, writing, places, and identities; the work and lives of school principals; and student participation in school decision making and community regeneration. She recently published *Schooling the Rustbelt Kids: Making the Difference in Changing Times* (Allen and Unwin, Sydney, 2002) and co-edited with Alan Reid *Rethinking Public Education: Towards a Public Curriculum* (Australian Curriculum Studies Association, Brisbane, 2003). Forthcoming books include *Romancing the Principal: Popular Pedagogies of School Administration* (Peter Lang) and with Barbara Kamler, *Text Work.,Identity Work: Pedagogies for Doctoral Supervisors* (Routledge-Falmer). C/o: University of Nottingham, Dearing Building, Jubilee Campus, Wollaton Road, Nottingham. NG8 2BB, United Kingdom. Email: Patricia.Thomson@nottingham.ac.uk; Phone: 44 (0) 115 846 7248; Fax: 44 (0) 115 846 6600.

**Nicola Yelland** has researched over the last decade the ways in which children learn with new information technologies in school an out of school. She is the author of *Early Mathematical Explorations with* Carmel Diezmann and Deborah Butler and has edited four books, *Gender in Early Childhood* (Routledge), *Innovations in Practice* (NAEYC), *Ghosts in the Machine: Women's Voices in Research with Technology* (Peter Lang), and *Critical Issues in Early Childhood* (Open University Press). Yelland works with teachers exploring the ways in which ICT can be incorporated into learning contexts to make them more interesting and motivating for children, so that outcomes are improved. She has worked on numerous

Australian Research Council projects related to the use of ICT in educational contexts and has written numerous articles about her research that have been published in national and international journals.

**Christopher Ziguras** is deputy director of the Globalism Institute at the Royal Melbourne Institute of Technology and is currently acting head of RMIT's School of International and Community Studies. His research interests include international education policy, transnational higher education, commercialization of education, international trade in services, trade policy, and the individualization of health care. He recently published *Self-Care: Embodiment, Personal Autonomy and the Shaping of Health Consciousness* (Routledge, 2004) and co-edited *The International Publishing Services Market* (Common Ground, 2002). C/o: School of International and Community Studies, RMIT University, GPO Box 2476V, Melbourne. 3001, Australia. E-mail: christopher.ziguras@rmit.edu.au; Phone: +613 9925 2501.

# Index

**A**

abstinence, 160, 167
accountability, 14, 72, 210, 223, 293
   concerns, 69, 191, 219
   measures, 68, 195, 204
   public, 177, 220
   regimes, 247
   teacher, 196, 201
accountancy criteria, 15
agrarian socialism, 249–250
alienation, 16, 23, 116, 118, 133, 154
alliances, 10, 148, 161, 177, 185, 213,
   222, 225, 227, 249, 267, 269–271,
   278
ambiguity, 66, 69
anthropocentrism, 115, 122, 125
anti-immigrant, 222
anti-market mechanism, 130
apartheid, 157
artificial microcosm, 39
assimilationist, 72, 294
Australian Labor Party, 250, 257, 261,
   264
authoritarian populist, 11, 211, 214, 250

**B**

backlash politics, 116
bilingual communities, 125
biotechnology, 242
bobbysoxers, 160
bodgies, 160
body counts, 15
boundaries, 178, 217, 269
   blurring, 38–39, 45, 182
   class, 132, 270
   formal, 73, 182
   global, 52

   national, 93, 128, 267, 287, 290
   permeable, 5, 33, 118, 131, 141
   program, 179, 205
   religious, 146
bourgeois project, 65
brain drain, 94, 101

**C**

capital
   global, 4, 277
   accumulation, 41, 236, 240, 243
   flight, 215, 285
carnivalesque, 36
centralized control, 175, 241
child care centers, 191, 196
citizens
   -consumers, 81
   global/local, 172, 247
   multicultural, 138
   national/global, 11, 14, 17, 20–23,
      25–26, 114, 118–119, 127, 132
   sovereign, 131
   student-as-, 127
co-dependent, 11
colonial structuring, 66
colonialism, 3, 7, 65, 73–75, 122
colonization, 24, 40, 182
colonizers, 65
commercial
   media, 288
   television, 39
commercialism, 287
commercialization, 16, 192, 302
commodification, 16, 38, 102, 110,
   175–176, 181, 185, 235
commonsense, 209, 211
communication

technologies, 9, 14, 34, 96, 191, 204, 241–242
communications
media, 47
community
infrastructure, 286
productivity, 65
complex connectivity, 4, 8–9, 33
compliance
institutional, 15
techniques, 11
conservative
evangelicals, 211
modernization, 11–12, 209, 212–214, 221, 228
policies, 209, 216
conspicuous consumption, 87
consumer choice, 215
consumer-driven response, 99
consumerism, 14, 38, 81, 115, 121, 175, 234, 284
contrapuntal readings, 64, 75
corporate
curriculum, 18, 31, 36–37, 40, 42
managerialist, 187, 253
pedagogues, 36, 41
corporations
transnational, 6, 234
corporatization, 14, 177, 183, 247
cosmopolitan
moral democracy, 289, 292–293, 295
nationalists, 120
nation-state, 292
cosmopolitanism, 121, 156, 290
cosmopolitical trajectory, 120
crisis intervention, 87
cross-border delivery, 95
cross-cultural settings, 107
cultural
capital, 27, 55, 58, 223
dominance, 64
economies, 5
fixity, 137
marginalization, 283
mediators, 47
policy, 45, 48, 55

culturalist, 8
culturally homogeneous, 132
culture
global/local, 168
culture
Anglo-ethnic, 137
audit, 32, 254
consumer, 37–38, 41–42, 192
consumer-media, 18, 31, 34, 36–39, 41
dimensions, 41, 159, 197
global/local, 160, 164
market-oriented, 10–11
media-consumer, 42
mono, 16, 25, 117
of philanthropy, 67
production, 47, 184
promotional, 32
sub-, 163
youth, 32, 160, 162–164, 168
curricula
globalized, 109
curriculum
democratic, 294
early childhood, 196
globalized, 108
-in-practice, 192
narratives, 119–123, 125
nationalized, 175
online, 51, 55
standardized, 186
transformative, 21
cyberspace, 171, 182
cyborgs, 185

**D**

deconstruction, 84, 144
de-differentiation, 35
delinquents, 160
demobilization, 226
democratic
anti-, 251
governance, 20
impulse, 249
procedures, 11
project, 244, 289

transformation, 10
democratizing schools, 252
deregulation, 15, 251, 258–259
destructure, 18
    connections, 10, 45, 115
    economy, 20, 117
    global, 119, 129, 133
    power, 114
    programs, 182, 254
    workplace, 253
destructuring, 32, 85, 89, 176, 178, 219,
    283
determinist logic, 7
deterritorialization, 3, 5, 7, 8
detraditionalization, 4
diaspora, 136
diasporic
    families, 152
    spaces, 149
digital technology, 4, 131
disaffection, 16, 23, 116, 118, 133, 154,
    199
discrimination, 40, 97, 104, 106, 267,
    275
disenfranchisement, 16, 258
disorganized capitalism, 4
Distributed Learning System, 181–182,
    186
diverse communities, 155, 283
diversity, 72, 125, 135, 156, 161, 220,
    234, 288, 292, 294
    cultural, 23, 107, 161, 162, 270, 299
    cultural and linguistic, 22, 151, 155,
        157
    ethnocultural, 157, 159, 167
    multicultural, 128–129, 156–157,
        289
    multilingual, 158
    negotiating, 136, 145, 289
    productive, 158–159
    youth, 24, 159, 163–165, 283
dysconsciousness, 72, 75

**E**

eco-cultural codes, 119
ecocultural sustainability, 179

ecological, 6, 11, 20, 118–121, 125,
    128–129, 132–133, 289–290
economic
    (quasi-) models, 10
    entities, 66
    orthodox, 259
    productivity, 64, 68, 71, 212
    rationalism, 248
    reductionism, 128
    reductionism, 26, 85
economic rationality, 214
economy
    cultural, 9, 33, 45, 46, 48–49, 52, 54,
        58, 127, 267–268
    global cultural, 46, 56, 58
    global information, 48
    global/local, 195
    libidinal, 34
    post-industrial, 174
    restructured global, 48, 83
education
    adult community, 63, 67, 75
    competition, 242
    drug, 151–152, 155–159, 163–165,
        167, 299
    early childhood, 42, 191–192, 195,
        206, 298, 300–301
    exporters of, 99
    fundamentalism, 32
    future of, 242
    governance, 17, 18, 25–26, 199
    higher, 49, 58, 95–103, 105, 108–
        109, 171–178, 185–186, 193, 237,
        300, 302
    inclusive public, 252
    industrial, 10, 26, 57, 142, 174, 175,
        184, 194, 203, 205
    international, 17, 94, 95, 99, 103,
        107–108, 110, 302
    international trade in, 93–94, 109
    market-driven, 14
    marketplace, 50
    multicultural, 117, 178
    offshore, 95
    online, 49–52, 95, 108, 186
    policies, 17–18, 23, 74, 212, 225

policy actors, 265–266, 275, 291–292
postindustrial, 57, 184, 205
private, 100, 104–105, 109, 291, 294
privatization of, 102
products, 19
public, 46, 49, 86, 88–89, 92, 99, 100, 102–104, 110, 175–177, 193, 195, 197, 218, 227, 247–249, 252, 254, 281–284, 290, 291–295, 300
quasi-, 291
quasi-markets in, 216
racialized construction of, 62
rationalization of, 102
responsive, vi, 10, 13, 20–21, 23, 113–115, 116, 118–119, 121–122, 127, 130–131, 133
software, 50
trade, 100, 107
transnational, 95
values, 51, 172
work-creating, 22
work-related, 216
educational policies, 1, 7, 9
effective citizenship, 74
egalitarian norms, 212
egalitarianism, 27, 212
elites
    cosmopolitan, 5
    nation's, 54
    non-, 7
    socio-political, 186
embodied subjects, 138
emotional valence, 210
enfleshed subjectivity, 144
English-only politics, 115, 117, 120–121, 157
entrepreneurialism, 16, 177
entrepreneurs, 46, 58, 109, 250
entrpreneurialism, 25
essentialism, 138
ethnic minority, 140
ethno-nationalism, 117–118, 120, 123, 284
ethnonationalists, 7, 11
ethnoscape, 131, 159

exclusionary politics, 17, 20, 131

**F**

feminist
    activism, 273, 276
    cultural, 46
    global networks, 275
    movements, 23
    policy, 23
    politics, 275, 278
feminization
    of the international workforce, 268
fixed origin, 140
flexibility, 5, 66, 183–184, 195, 237, 241, 243
flow-on effects, 18, 37, 89, 102, 104, 173, 181, 253
flows
    energy, 130
    global/local, 5, 128, 152, 154, 159
    images, 9, 65
    knowledge, 63, 107
    linguistic, 130
    linguistic, 123
    market-driven, 187
    media, 132
    organic, 131
    workers, 269
fragmentation, 4, 8, 35, 288

**G**

geographies of centrality, 8
global
    orientation, 23
    tycoon, 55
    village, 173
    flows, 130
global/local
    connections, 4, 21, 24, 126, 173, 249, 271
    culture, 269
    diversity, 165
    economy, 83, 159, 172, 252
    education, 110, 151, 158, 172–173, 187

market forces, 16, 19, 117
markets, 153, 176
nexus, 136, 269, 277
politics, 266
practices, 84
restructuring, 129
societies, 192, 287–288, 293
villages, 116
globalism
neoconservative, 1
neoliberal, 3, 7–10, 15–16, 20, 22–23,
     25–26, 79, 89, 103, 116–119, 128,
     132–133, 147, 175–176, 178, 182,
     195, 215, 233
globalization
archaic, 123
crisis, 12–13
cultural, 31, 33, 132, 178
from above, 1–3, 5–6, 8–11, 16, 20,
     23–24, 91, 115, 117, 129, 133,
     176, 247–248, 252, 265–269,
     277–278, 284
from below, 2, 7, 8, 10, 120, 128,
     284
neoliberal economic, 3
post-colonial, 123
proto-, 123
governance, 9, 12–13, 15–20, 23, 25,
     128, 172, 179, 199, 266, 285, 299
governmental coalition, 19
grassroots politics, 254
green biopolitical agencies, 128

**H**

harm minimization, 154, 158, 163, 167
harmonization, 105
hegemonic, 13, 32, 74, 174, 187, 215,
     228, 276
counter-, 25
homogenization, 33
human capital, 88, 109, 176, 214
humanistic enterprise, 74
hybridization, 35, 42, 140
hyperreality, 38–39

**I**

identity
construction, 139, 144
cultural, 33, 64, 108, 140
eco-cultural, 133
embodied, 145
fixing, 139
material, 144
national, 54, 263
pedagogical, 201
regional, 249
service, 81
transnational, 13
white, 63
ideological
commitments, 11
counter-hegemonic, 13
critiques, 14, 25–26
ideoscapes, 130
illegal money, 153
illiteracy, 65, 139
immaterial understandings, 144
immigrant, 140, 150
imperatives, 4, 9, 13–14, 32, 49, 52,
     113–114, 116, 118, 120, 122–123,
     127, 130, 132–133, 196, 217
imperialism, 7, 10, 22, 115–116, 173
information
age, 45, 50, 53, 173, 198, 203
production, 197
society, 53
superhighway, 54, 171
infrastructures, 49, 80, 287
institutional reflexivity, 33
instrumental efficiencies, 11
interactive
exclusion, 39
package, 204
interconnectedness, 5, 173
intergenerational
dynamics, 36
production, 19
international mobility, 95, 107, 271
internationalization, 3, 266, 267

**J**

*jouissance*, 36, 38

**K**

kill ratios, 15
knowledge
    changing base, 21, 22
    community, 118, 143, 148, 159
    computer-based, 205
    cosmopolitan, 179
    creation, 21, 197
    economies, 61, 115, 121, 129, 130
    experiential, 10
    gap, 68
    international, 107
    legitimate, 10
    marginalized, 62
    production, 13, 21, 62, 130

**L**

Labor administration, 248, 251
labor movement, 23, 250, 270, 272–274,
    276
language extinction, 129–130
learners
    adult literacy, 148
learning
    lifelong, 22, 64, 67, 71, 75, 96
    packages, 188
    reusable objects, 21, 178, 180–181,
        204
    work-related, 22
lighthouse schools, 89
literate
    computer-, 46
    media-, 46
local/global, 128–129, 248, 284
    connections, 4
long-day-care, 195

**M**

majoritarian, 12

Majority World, 8, 24, 40, 98, 100, 107,
    109, 114, 120–121, 124, 126, 140,
    153, 196
managerialism, 18, 21, 26, 171, 184,
    252, 255, 260
marginality, 8
marginalized, 8, 20, 25, 69–72, 114, 117,
    149, 225, 242, 256
market
    access, 97, 99, 106
    motif, 34
    socialism, 114
    unfettered, 12, 81, 211, 219, 286
market-driven choice, 62
marketization, 3, 13, 16, 45, 50, 86, 103,
    109–110, 175, 211, 213, 217, 226,
    231–232, 234–239, 242–244, 247,
    300
    international, 18
market-oriented, 10–11, 26
mass public schooling, 282
mean-stream, 118
mediascapes, 47, 132
mesh-works, 4, 8–9, 21, 129, 285
micromanagement, 14–15
migrant, 140, 274
militarism, 32
Minority World, 6, 9, 24, 31, 98–99,
    107–109, 114, 118, 120–121, 124,
    126, 129, 131, 140, 146, 151, 153,
    191, 193, 195–196, 282, 285, 287
mobilization, 7, 228, 257
modernity, 3, 64, 137, 173
modulate material, 9
monopolization, 41
monopoly enterprise, 241
multicultural
    code, 128, 133
    commodities, 130
    consumerism, 114
    industry, 116
multiculturalism, 24, 115, 131, 157–158,
    256–257, 299
    corporate, 121
multidimensional adults, 148

multilingual, 61, 96, 115, 121, 129, 131–132, 158, 167
   media, 166
multiliteracies, 196, 299
multimedia software, 45
multiracial immigration, 84
myopic localism, 290

**N**

nationalized curriculum, 14
nationalized literacy, 195
nation-building, 106, 109, 282, 288, 290, 292
   role, 93, 108
nation-state, 9, 10, 14, 20, 33, 58, 65, 70, 82, 102–103, 105, 117, 122, 128, 132, 247–248, 282, 285, 286, 289–291, 293, 294
naturalization, 16
neoconservative, 1, 14, 16, 18, 49, 80–81, 86, 118, 186, 222, 224–225, 227, 248, 250, 255, 278, 281–282, 284
   alliance, 19
neoliberal
   agenda, 3, 17, 220
   globalism, 11, 15, 17, 19–20, 25, 79, 141, 195, 204
   governance, 14, 16
   ideological project, 11
   policies, 18–19, 85, 195, 215, 217, 219, 223
   post-modernization, 11
   struggles, 54
networked villages, 116
networks, 5–6, 48, 49, 51, 81, 88, 120, 159, 267, 269, 270–271, 273, 275–278
nondiscrimination, 294
non-human actors, 124
numeracy, 69, 88, 195, 197, 203–205, 300

**O**

Othered languages, 137
overconsumption, 128, 173

overdeveloped World, 174

**P**

parochialism, 17, 116, 249, 256, 262, 284, 288, 290
patriarchial relations, 23
patriarchy, 115, 117, 122, 125–126, 275
pedagogical politics, 187
pedagogy
   cultural, v, 45, 46, 52, 58
   interactive, 155
   knowledge producing, 114, 179, 182, 186, 301
   of everyday life, 46, 47
   orientation, 151
   postindustrial, 22, 199
   responses, 139
   technologization of, 187
   work-related, 22
performance
   administration, 15, 18
   administrators, 15
peripheral spaces, 7
polarization, 79
policy
   activism, 63
   activists, 63, 74, 272
   agenda, 33, 81, 175, 259
   makers, 6, 22, 31–33, 35, 41, 83, 86, 89–90, 209
   making, 62–66, 71–72, 74–75, 260, 292, 300
political activism, 266–268, 270–271, 275, 278
popularization, 12, 49
positive nationalism, 290
post
   colonialism, 4
   modernization, 4
   industrialization, 4, 178, 192, 194, 195, 198, 203
postindustrial,
   era, 27, 45
   knowledge, 130
   markets, 130, 132
   societies, 53, 171, 194, 197

postmodern theories, 235
postmodernism, 144, 234
postmodernity, 35, 38, 144
power, 3, 5, 6, 8, 14–15, 19–20, 34, 269,
    272, 286, 297
    blocs, 10
    engagement with, 23, 36, 41, 74, 123,
        157, 185, 213, 263, 271, 275
    generative, 25, 70, 126, 181, 225
    global, 120, 127, 128, 268
    institutional, 102, 125, 130, 132, 186,
        218, 223, 265, 283
    interplay, 23, 35, 172, 177, 213–214,
        255, 266, 270, 273
    political, 33, 106, 217, 233, 235–237,
        239–240, 250, 254–255, 259
    relations, 24, 34, 35, 114, 116, 119,
        137, 148, 173, 185–186, 210, 217,
        224, 249, 268, 278, 285, 287
    social, 46, 54, 73, 144, 225
    technologies of, 174
privatization, 26, 102, 109, 224, 226,
    235, 237, 286
programmatic ambitions, 17
proliferation of differences, 267
protection, 82, 117, 163, 242, 276, 286
protectionism, 115, 121, 254
public-sector, 32, 85–86, 92, 100, 102,
    104, 247, 249–250, 252–259, 286

Q

quality assurance, 68, 71, 96, 98, 105,
    177
quasi-market solutions, 216

R

racial
    other, 222
    segregation, 222
racialized
    construction, 62, 72
    discourses, 75
    fears, 213
    landscape, 63–64
    systems, 62

racism, 65, 75, 117, 125, 249, 256, 259,
    262–263
racist logics, 222, 267
reductionism, 20
re-engineering society, 48
refugee, 139–140, 146, 261–262
regimes, 13–14, 16, 21, 25–26, 73, 81,
    86, 153, 247, 269
regressive parochialism, 130, 248
religious fundamentalists, 211
re-regulation, 6
residualization, 247–248
responsive
    approach, 71
    policy actors, 23
restructuring, 10, 13, 18, 32, 45, 68, 85,
    89, 114–115, 117, 119, 129, 133, 176,
    219, 231, 234, 237, 240–241, 253,
    259, 268, 272, 283
retrogressive forms, 222
rightist policies, 209
risk management, 6
rustbelt, ix, 79–81, 84, 86–90
rustbowl, 80

S

sado-masochistic logic, 39
sameness, 140
secularization, 222
self-
    reflection, 26, 27
    regulating, 20, 215
semiotics, 55
sexuality, 39, 62, 65, 126, 156, 269,
    275–276, 278, 288
simulation, 38
skunk weed, 162
Social Darwinist, 12
social justice, 49, 67, 85, 91, 175, 193,
    196, 227–228, 251–252, 271, 289,
    293
social movements, 8, 117, 119, 128, 210,
    226–227, 265, 273
social trajectories, 53
social welfare, 213, 286

sociocultural, 11, 114, 118, 133, 136, 147, 179, 196
socioeconomic
    security, 19, 117
socioeconomic
    gap, 79
    league table, 79
socio-political movements, 23
sovereignty, 11, 14, 20, 27, 103, 109–120, 123, 132, 233
spaces of enclosure, 142
standardization, 14, 33, 185, 191, 204
structure/agency, 4
structures of attitude, 65, 72
subjectivities, 24, 63, 192
subjectivity, 37, 47, 70–71, 74–75, 144, 152
sunbelt, 80
supranational organizations, 14, 121, 128
surveillance technologies, 11

**T**

teaching
    Anglo-ethnic, 24
technologies
    digital, 21, 173
    self-disciplinary, 15
techno
    -power, 34
    scape, 130
    -tycoons, 46
the 5D
    generation, 42
    relationship, 31
the global now, 4, 151

the lucky country, 125
Third World, 126
time/space reorganization, 9
trade union traditions, 273
transformative, 1, 8–9, 13, 15, 23, 25, 27, 114, 116, 118, 127, 132, 235, 243
transgender, 275, 277
transnational
    movements, 23, 121
    order, 21, 128
    politics, 159
tribalization, 35

**U**

universalization, 3
utopianism, 39

**V**

vulnerabilities, 127

**W**

wedge politics, 258, 260, 262
western civilization, 124
Western Marxism, 234
Westernization, 3
White
    empowerment, 66
    privilege, 73
White-nation, 115, 117, 120–121, 126
Whiteness, 62, 64–66, 71–73, 75, 212, 270, 300
women domestic workers, 269
women's movement, 273
workfare, 86

# Studies in the Postmodern Theory of Education

*General Editors*
*Joe L. Kincheloe & Shirley R. Steinberg*

Counterpoints publishes the most compelling and imaginative books being written in education today. Grounded on the theoretical advances in criticalism, feminism, and postmodernism in the last two decades of the twentieth century, Counterpoints engages the meaning of these innovations in various forms of educational expression. Committed to the proposition that theoretical literature should be accessible to a variety of audiences, the series insists that its authors avoid esoteric and jargonistic languages that transform educational scholarship into an elite discourse for the initiated. Scholarly work matters only to the degree it affects consciousness and practice at multiple sites. Counterpoints' editorial policy is based on these principles and the ability of scholars to break new ground, to open new conversations, to go where educators have never gone before.

For additional information about this series or for the submission of manuscripts, please contact:

Joe L. Kincheloe & Shirley R. Steinberg
c/o Peter Lang Publishing, Inc.
275 Seventh Avenue, 28th floor
New York, New York 10001

To order other books in this series, please contact our Customer Service Department:

(800) 770-LANG (within the U.S.)
(212) 647-7706 (outside the U.S.)
(212) 647-7707 FAX

Or browse online by series:
www.peterlangusa.com